Calvin
and the
Reformation

Calvin
and the
Reformation

Edited by William Park Armstrong

Four Studies by
Emile Doumergue,
August Lang, Herman Bavinck,
and Benjamin B. Warfield

BAKER BOOK HOUSE
Grand Rapids, Michigan

Reprinted 1980 by
Baker Book House Company
from the 1909 edition issued by
The Princeton Theological Review Association
ISBN: 0-8010-2901-5

PHOTOLITHOPRINTED BY CUSHING - MALLOY, INC.
ANN ARBOR, MICHIGAN, UNITED STATES OF AMERICA
1980

PREFACE

The Four Studies which make up this book were prepared for "The Princeton Theological Review" and published during the current year. The editors of the Review in reissuing them in book-form hope that they may thus become more readily accessible and more widely circulated, and that in this way they may continue to serve their original purpose of contributing in some measure to the celebration of the four hundredth anniversary of the birth of John Calvin. The Study on "Calvin: Epigone or Creator?" was translated by Joseph Heatly Dulles, A.M., Librarian of Princeton Theological Seminary. That on "The Reformation and Natural Law" was translated by J. Gresham Machen, A.M., B.D., Instructor of New Testament Literature and Exegesis in Princeton Theological Seminary. This Study will appear also in German in the "Beiträge zur Förderung christlicher Theologie" edited by Schlatter and Lütgert. The Study on "Calvin and Common Grace" was translated by Geerhardus Vos, Ph.D., D.D., Charles T. Haley Professor of Biblical Theology in Princeton Theological Seminary. The Four Studies have been edited by William Park Armstrong, A.M., Professor of New Testament Literature and Exegesis in Princeton Theological Seminary, on behalf of the Faculty of the Seminary, the editors of "The Princeton Theological Review".

Princeton, N. J., May 4th, 1909.

TABLE OF CONTENTS

CALVIN: EPIGONE OR CREATOR?

By Émile Doumergue

Was Calvin a Reformer? This is a question under discussion to-day. Was Calvin a Protestant or was he a Catholic? Is the Reformation a part of modern times? This is discussed to-day.

We might be surprised that these questions should be discussed, that they could be discussed. Yet is it not to-day a matter of debate whether St. Paul was a Christian or not? In reality these amazing questions are logical and natural. We shall show this, while confining ourselves to the sphere within which the discussion is now carried on, the social sphere.

I. RITSCHL.

1. Are there beginnings in history that are altogether new? It may be doubted. Yet we may, with sufficient exactness, regard Ritschl as the originator of a chauvinism, at once theological and Germanic, and of a kind of Lutheran nationalism, the methods and views of which are no less obnoxious than the methods and tendencies of the most vexatious political chauvinism and nationalism.

It is Ritschl who has given to Lutheran theology this anti-Calvinistic watchword: "So far as the ideal of Calvinism is anti-Catholic, this is due to the instigation of Luther; so far as it departs from Luther, it goes back to the ideal of the Franciscans—of the Franciscans and Anabaptists."[1]

Every one who knows the exegetical and historical violence by which Ritschl deduces his theological system from the Bible, can surmise how he treats the texts of Luther and Calvin. As to Luther, he himself confesses that he interprets him, not as he has formally expressed himself, but according to what his words seem to him to suggest.[2] And as to Calvin—we have mere fiction, mere romance. In our opinion Ritschl makes him say exactly the opposite of that which he thought.

To Ritschl the distinguishing thing in Calvinism is its tendency to monastic asceticism,—"a near approach to monastic flight from the world that is easily recognizable."

In order to prove this, Ritschl goes back to Egypt and Gaul: "I recall that the ancient monachism, developed in Egypt, was first accepted in Gaul." It is easy to pass from Gaul to France, to the great reforms of monachism: those of Cluny, Chartreux, Citeaux. This shows the French temperament. Then, France was the country of the Crusades. After that the University of Paris furnished "a striking example of the subjection of many persons to discipline" (*Disciplinirung*).[3] In the 17th century there were the Trappists, Jansenism, Quietism. Quietism, it is true, was not born in France. But that matters little, since it found there an important representation. And the French Reformers were Frenchmen. Then Calvin resembles a Catholic monk. He had no need of recreation (we shall see the contrary). He set himself against many things that pertained to free living, to the delights of art, as did the Franciscans (we shall see the contrary).

On the other hand, over against Calvin, with his French temperament and its defects, stands Luther, with his German temperament and its traits. On the one side, the instinct of severity; on the other, the instinct of liberty. "Along with the coarseness, reproved by Luther, and the independence of the Germans, their sense of individual and moral liberty is the true reason for their resistance to a general law of ecclesiastical discipline. While, on the other hand, the Frenchman (Calvin, for instance), who thought it natural to put into universal practice the rules of discipline found in the New Testament, relied upon the instinct of equality and upon the inclination to permit all sorts of discipline, in which his French fellow citizens are distinguished from the Germans."[4]

We must pass by the development, not less suggestive, that Ritschl gives to this fundamental thesis, and confine ourselves to mentioning the method of treating texts and facts, which reduces Calvinism to the rank of a mere Prussian corporal, relieved through German Lutheranism of the creation of the Huguenots, the Beggars and the Puritans.

2. This Ritschlian and pan-Germanic method of writing history has had an enormous success, and many German theologians have regarded as the word of the Gospel the affirmations of the theologian, who, after all, adjusts the Gospel to his fancy. We cite only two theologians, otherwise moderate and remarkable for their scientific attainment.

F. Kattenbusch[5] is willing to grant a place of honor to Calvin alongside of the two great German Reformers, because he was "the most gifted organizer" of churches. But he has made "the idea of Protestantism" submit to a "certain mutilation" (*eine gewisse Verkümmerung*). He has given it a form that cannot be regarded as entirely authentic.[6] Without doubt he belongs "to the epoch of the epigones". This epoch did not have the "energy", the "vivacity" of the preceding. Calvin had a "mechanical conception" of the examples left by the theocracy of the Old Testament and by the Apostolic communities. "In what measure was he in-

fluenced by the ideas of certain reformers of the Middle
Ages?" This question must be left open for the present.
In any event, he did not have the "spiritual liberty" of
Luther and Zwingli.[7]

3. That we find these ideas entertained by scholars as
distinguished and as moderate as Professor Loofs of Halle,
shows to what extent they are disseminated and in what
degree they are fixed in stereotyped formulas. "It is certain that Calvin, because of his practical activity, should be
regarded as a Reformer, but as a theologian he is an
epigone of the Reformation."[8]   All that may be conceded
is that in the first edition of the *Institutes* he seems to be a
Lutheran of Upper Germany (*oberdeutscher Lutheraner*).[9]
But Catholic influence came.   "As with Zwingli, the Aug-
ustinian-Catholic leaven must be recognized here (*à propos*
of the sacraments)."[10]

4. This Ritschlian conception of Calvinism has taken a
new start with two treatises published by Martin Schulze.[11]
The honorable theologian believes that he has made
a discovery; for according to him only two authors have
suggested his idea: the aged de Wette, who limits himself
to a brief reflexion, and Pierson, the Dutch writer. The
latter is well known to all historians of Calvin for his para-
doxical theses, based on critical and exegetical exaggerations
and on a blind opposition to Calvinism. Why does Schulze
not cite Ritschl? Is it on account of the "variations" that he
introduces in his thesis? Schulze adds a Platonic to the
Catholic influence, but the result is always the same: Lutheran superiority, Calvinistic inferiority, because of the ascetic and monastic tendency.

"Calvin differed from Luther in this, that with him—
Calvin—salvation is essentially a matter of hope, and so
relations with this world take an ascetic form."[12] "After all,

it must be said that Calvin did not, in principle, rise above the Monastic ideal of life, although life had for him a more profound meaning, and although the effort to realize it was far purer with him than in monachism.[13] Moreover, "Calvin's conception of life resembles exactly that sketched here, essentially after the Phædo. The agreement extends, as I have shown, even to the detail of exposition and expression."[14]

5. The views of Schulze have been outlined by Th. Shoell in the *Bulletin de la Société de l'histoire du protestantisme français* in the following terms: "Calvin, in principle, at least, did not rise above the monastic ideal of life. . . . These ideas went back to the Bible only in a measure, and proceeded rather from Plato. . . . The theologian remained humanist. But Calvin was not conscious of this fusion of Christian and Platonic elements. . . . Erasmus and Calvin preached the monachism of sentiment."

And after having been so indicated these opinions are approved: "We conclude. The first impression of the reader is that Schulze defends a preconceived thesis, inasmuch as every one of his chapters issues inexorably in the same result. However, after a close study of his numerous citations and his synoptic tables, one is persuaded that these conclusions agree, on the whole, with the reality, which (he makes us aware of this from the beginning) lessens the originality of Calvin only in an insignificant degree."[15]

We make this citation without asking how the fact that he did not, in principle, transcend the monastic ideal of life, could not at all lessen the originality of a Protestant Reformer!

6. A recent author has united and, as it were, condensed and popularized the ideas of Ritschl and Schulze, namely, Bernhard Bess in *Unsere religiösen Erzieher*.[16] Between

Luther and Calvin there is the difference of the two nations which they represent, Germany and France. In France we have monachism, the organization of asceticism, the discipline of the masses; in Germany, we have an almost morbid bent to individual liberty. With Zwingli, also, there is "a German feeling for liberty" (*ein germanisches Freiheitsgefühl*). "For Calvin's nature, sanguine to the point of fanaticism, servile submission to the letter was contentment."[17] At first Calvin showed himself to be Lutheran, and it is only in 1539 that his fall occurred. Bess takes from Calvin what his predecessors still allowed him, for example, the preëminence of his ecclesiastical conceptions. Just the reverse of this is true, according to our author: "On no other point is it seen so clearly that Calvin was not a theologian of original significance (*kein Theolog von originaler Bedeutung*), and that the penetration (*die Schärfe*) of his understanding deserted him, when opposing interests struggled within him. In the chapter on the 'Church' he has reproduced partly Luther, partly Zwingli."[18] Alongside of recollections of Luther there is also the doctrine of the Middle Ages, that the State is only the body, but the Church is the soul . . . On one side, an attempt to keep to the words and ideas of Luther; but under the surface a profound contrary current, in which the ideas of the Middle Ages, pure and simple, are seen. "And it is this current that, in fact, bore him away." What happens as to the Church, happens as to morals: the Middle Ages again! All that has been said by Ritschl and by Kattenbusch recurs: "his very contemporaries saw a new monachism (*Möncherei*) in his regulations of morals."[19]

7. Finally, this movement has produced an article which we shall not discuss. But, for the just punishment of those who have posited so many false principles, we shall point

out the conclusions which the Rev. Thomas C. Hall, Professor of Christian Ethics in Union Theological Seminary of New York, draws from them. They may be found in an article which bears the title: "Was John Calvin a Reformer or a Reactionary?"[20]

Here is the truth ("as a simple matter of fact"), which has escaped Schweitzer, Lobstein, Kuyper, Stähelin, de Wette, Gass, Ziegler. One asks why Dr. Hall does not cite those, whom this truth has not escaped, and who have pushed these principles to the extreme,—Ritschl, Schulze, and others. We read: "As a simple matter of fact, the ethical system of Calvin is profoundly reactionary, scholastic and Roman Catholic in both method and aim."[21] "The whole conception of the Christian life, as Calvin draws it, is Roman Catholic rather than Protestant."[22] "In the relation of the authoritative Church to the authoritative State, Calvin adopts, substantially, the traditional Roman Catholic point of view, save only that it must be a true Biblical Church to be authoritative."[23] "In point of fact, Calvin's State is a theocracy after the type of Gregory the Great, with the 'divine ministry' in the place of the pope."[24] "On such a basis no Protestant ethics can be built up. Calvinism has, in point of fact, been singularly barren in ethical work. Even her casuistry has been poor and feeble."[25] "Hence it is quite comprehensible how barren Calvinistic theology has been on its ethical side."[26] "Hence on ethical grounds we may say that Calvin was one of the last, though not one of the greatest, of the schoolmen. Thomas Aquinas is really greatly his superior in almost every particular as an ethical thinker." It is not enough, even, to speak of Thomas Aquinas. The ethics of Calvin calls to mind the ethics of Loyola. "Holiness plays a large part in Calvin's thought, just as it does in that of Thomas Aquinas and Ignatius

Loyola, whose ethical system is most nearly akin to that of Calvin."[27]

We shall take good care not to discuss this rare, this unique series of oddities .We should be afraid of weakening the convincing force of this *reductio ad absurdum* of the Ritschlian theories.   Only, at the risk of being accused of real cruelty, after having inflicted on the Ritschlian school the reading of the criticism with which it has inspired Dr. Hall against Calvin, we shall afflict it with the reading of his praise of Luther.   Calvin has all the faults and Luther all the virtues.   Dr. Hall is an admirer of Luther.   And truly we are sorry for Luther, who is as much above these eulogiums as Calvin is above this criticism.   "On the intellectual and philosophical reconstruction of ethics Calvinism has left no such mark as that made by one single work of Luther's, *Die Freiheit des Christenmenschen.*"[28]

In order to prove this it suffices to declare anti-Lutheran the doctrines of Luther on the sacraments and on the subject-will,—precisely the doctrines which the Reformer held most tenaciously.   And then, to lend Calvin Luther's ideas!

We read: "In Luther's system sacramentalism was an unfortunate and illogical intrusion upon his fundamental thought."[29]   "In spite of Luther's most unfortunate realism in his interpretation of *hoc est corpus meum,* he remains substantially (though not wholly) unaffected in his ethics by the element of sacramental magic."   And it is not Luther, it is Calvin, who attached too great importance to the sacraments.   "In Calvin the sacraments are essential to the Christian ethical life."[30] And the same is true of the subject-will: "Thus, again, Luther's unfortunate incursion into the realm of metaphysical speculation on the freedom of the will had a genuine ethical interest and can be resolved into a relatively harmless though unfortunate psychological determinism. This is not the case with Calvin's doctrine of decrees."[31]

The only conclusion that can be drawn from this is that there are theologians who are not afraid to be ridiculous.

II. TROELTSCH.

1. Unhappily, before the Ritschlian system had fallen under the assaults of such a *reductio ad absurdum,* it was caught up by Prof. Troeltsch, whom one of his critics calls "the very learned, penetrating, able and spiritual representative of systematic theology of Heidelberg."[32]

The address which he gave on the 21st of April, 1906, at Stuttgart, in the Ninth Congress of German Historians, was much talked of. Its echoes still reverberate. The subject was: "The Importance of Protestantism for the Rise of the Modern World."[33]

The discourse is noteworthy. With very great ability the author discusses the Church, the State, science, art, sociology, political economy, and in all these subjects compares the Catholic, the Lutheran, the Calvinistic and the modern ideas. It is a whole religious encyclopædia condensed into sixty-six pages.

It is not the least remarkable that Troeltsch divests himself of all chauvinistic, nationalistic passion; he speaks as a historian; and if he receives his idea from his master Ritschl, he presents it with true impartiality and real knowledge.

Thus, all at once, the idea is entirely changed. What Ritschl had said against Calvin Troeltsch maintains must be applied equally to Luther. Calvin, an epigone? Yes, but Luther also an epigone; two epigones of the Middle Ages. Calvin an ascetic? Yes, but Luther also an ascetic; two monastic ascetics, etc.

And then it is truly amusing to observe the attitude of certain Lutheran theologians. What they found quite correct when said of Calvin, they have found out of place and injurious when said, texts and facts in hand, with equal justice, of Luther. They are like children, who, after having played with dangerous weapons, are terrified when they perceive that they themselves are wounded. We have a conspicuous refutation of Troeltsch by Loofs.

As for us, we congratulate the Heidelberg Professor on his serenity, his scientific impartiality. When one speaks of the Reformers—not of this or that detail of their work, but of the work itself—they may not be separated. They stand or fall together. And there is no need of changing our point of view, as we look at men and facts. The thesis which we found false, when directed against Calvin alone, appears no more true when directed against the entire Reformation. Only we add, that under this new form, the old idea of Ritschl has become what it was not, specious,—at times seductive. It appears supported by many arguments. Hence it is worth while to examine it and to discuss it carefully.

2. According to Troeltsch the influence of Protestantism should neither be denied nor exaggerated (*einseitig übertrieben*).[34] We have to do with three terms and their reciprocal relations: Catholicism—identified with the Middle Ages,—Protestantism, and Modern Times. Let us define them, according to Troeltsch.

Catholic or mediæval culture is characterized by two elements: authority and asceticism; a divine authority exercised by the Church, in virtue of which everything is related to God; and asceticism, that is to say, the concentration of every activity of life in God.

Modern culture is the reverse of mediaeval culture. To authority it opposes autonomy, with its resultant individualism; to asceticism it opposes the enjoyment of this world's goods. No more hereditary corruption, and no more extra-mundane deliverance from this corruption! Life finds its aim and its ideal more and more here below. And what of Protestantism? Naturally, it is not a question of modern and modernized Protestantism, but of the old, primitive, only authentic Protestantism.[35] This latter wished to produce and did produce a culture of authority and asceticism. "The old, true Protestantism, in its Lutheran and Calvinistic form, is altogether an ecclesiastical culture, in the mediæval sense. It would regulate the State and society, civilization and science, political economy and law, according to the supernatural rules of Revelation."[36]

Hence the modern world begins, in reality, not at the opening, but at the close of the century of the Reformation, with the second half of the 17th century, in such sort that Protestantism still belongs to the culture of the Middle Ages. Indeed, more often it has reinforced the mediaeval spirit of this culture. "It endeavors to cause the conception of ecclesiastical civilization, etc., to triumph with its own methods, and to make it triumph more sternly, more profoundly, more personally, than the hierarchial institution of the Middle Ages could do. The authority and the saving power (*Heilskraft*) of the Bible alone effect that which bishops and popes could not do with their external means and the vast secularisation of their Institution."[37]

Troeltsch concludes that the influences of Protestantism upon the modern world are above all indirect, unconscious, accidental (*zufällig*),[38] involuntary. As to the "direct, immediate" influences,—these are due, not to Protestantism, properly so-called, but to two intimate adversaries of the old Protestantism, so vigorously repulsed and attacked by it, the rationalism of the Renaissance (incarnated in Arminianism and Socinianism) and the spiritualism of the Anabaptists."[39]

3. Certainly, all this looks very simple. Troeltsch, however, has simplified his study by overlooking a fourth term. And what is that? Christianity. Neither more nor less! The Middle Ages present a culture in which Christianity (which does not come from the Middle Ages) and Catholicism are mingled. Protestantism received Christianity, which it tried to lead back to its primitive purity: it rejected Catholicism. As to the modern world, it includes Christian and anti-Christian elements. It is the boast of Protestantism that it has transmitted the Christian elements; it is useless to prove that Protestantism has not transmitted the anti-Christian elements; it boasts of this also! Such is the thesis of the true Protestants, who think themselves the legitimate successors of the Reformers. As Troeltsch refutes another, altogether different thesis, they might well content themselves with meeting Troeltsch's argument with a simple dismissal. Far from having transfixed them by his brilliant assault, Troeltsch has not even touched them. He has been fencing with a phantom. But this is precisely what we have to explain.

4. Let us begin with the more general principles. According to Troeltsch, Protestantism is limited to stating the old question of salvation: "This (he tells us repeatedly), is only the old question" (*durch und durch nur die alte Frage*).[40] Now this question, — What must I do to be saved? is not at all a specifically Catholic and mediæval question; it is, on the contrary, the specifically Christian question,—that of the Apostles, that of the Gospels, that which Christ came to answer. What is Catholic is the answer which the Middle Ages gave to this question. But Troeltsch declares that "Protestantism came only to bring

a new answer."[41] It answers, not by sending man to the saving institution of the hierachy, the Church of the priests, to the *opus operatum* of the sacraments, but by speaking to him "of a personal decision of faith" (*einen persönlichen Glaubensentschluss*).[42] Yet Protestantism is a different form of religion from Catholicism; it gives men another attitude toward the Church, toward God. Man (believing) in the view of Protestantism is different from man (believing) in the view of Catholicism. So over against the old man of the Middle Ages there is a modern man that the Reformation sets up. And, once more, the scaffolding erected by Troeltsch crumbles at its base.

5. Let us urge a particular example which is supplied by Loofs. This theologian presents, *à propos* of justification by faith, some observations which might be presented *à propos* of a mass of resemblances between the Middle Ages and the Reformation. Too often the old proverb is forgotten : When two say the same thing, they do not say the same thing. "Troeltsch emphasizes the tie that unites Luther's doctrine of justification with the Augustinian tradition of the Middle Ages. . . . There is nothing new in this for a dogmatician. Luther did not simply exhume the Pauline conceptions; the age-long development of ideas before him did not pass without exercising some influence upon him . . . But, verily, where is there in history anything new for which there has not been some preparation? The ideas of Luther on justification are new with respect to the Middle Ages, although their genesis can only be understood in their relation to the Middle Ages. For Dilthey is mistaken, when he thinks that St. Augustine, St. Bernard, Tauler and the so-called *Theologia Germanica,* had already taught the doctrine of justification that Luther taught. No doubt, the thesis according to which man be-

comes just before God only by faith is not unknown in the
Catholic Church, as has been shown since the affirmations
of Dilthey. Not in the works of St. Augustine, but
throughout the West in his time and up to the middle of
Scholasticism it was widely current. But what was understood by this doctrine was only that God demanded
faith alone, that is to say, the acceptance of ecclesiastical
beliefs, in the man who presented himself for baptism and
who in baptism received the pardon of all his sins committed
up to that time. For Luther this doctrine had a totally
different meaning. With him it was a question of the foundation upon which the long-since baptised believer could
build his assurance that he could stand before God: Not
upon any act whatsoever, but solely upon the grace of God,
confidently received by faith. Here is what was new over
against the Middle Ages: Religion was, in principle, separated from age-long ethical, mystical and metaphysical
perversions. . . . With Luther the idea is entirely clear.
. . . To be justified is to enter into the right relation to
God upon the basis of an experience of His grace. In this
idea the fulcrum of Archimedes was found, by which the
whole papal Church could be overthrown."[43]

6. But, returning to the more general ideas, we must
notice the asceticism with which Ritschl and his school have
so much reproached Calvin, and which Troeltsch discovers
equally in the entire Reformation.[44] As to this equalization
he is not wrong. Far from having put an end to ascetism,
Protestantism, says Troeltsch, has preserved heaven and
hell, while it has suppressed purgatory, which made the
other world a little less terrifying.[45] Now in the Gospel,
of which Troeltsch does not speak, heaven and hell are
mentioned, but purgatory is not. Must it be inferred from

this that the primitive Gospel is reinforced mediaeval Catholicism?

Further, says Troeltsch, the central question of Protestantism is always the certainty of salvation, deliverance from the deserved condemnation of original sin. And Protestantism has, on this point, strengthened the Augustinian dogma.[46] But once more, the question of salvation is, preeminently, the evangelical question. And St. Paul is more strict than Pelagius. Must we conclude from this that the primitive Gospel is reinforced mediæval Catholicism?

Troeltsch admits that in Protestantism the ascetic idea has changed its form and meaning. He adds, "only" (*nur die Form und den Sinn gewechselt*).[47] But one has the right to ask what is an idea, which has changed its form and meaning? And what can two ideas, which have neither the same form nor the same meaning, have in common?

We proceed: "Protestantism", says Troeltsch, "has rejected monachism and the monastic life of the clergy. But it has not done this because it regarded the values and possessions of this world as ends in themselves (*Selbstzwecke*) . . . The world . . . is the natural soil, the condition of the Christian life. This natural condition must not be artificially avoided . . . This would only encourage the illusion of merits, of the coöperation of man with grace, and conceal the real difficulty, which is to possess the world as if one possessed it not."[48] All this is true, but all this is authentic Christianity, and no less authentic anti-Catholicism. How shall we conclude from the fact that Protestantism has broken from the Middle Ages in order to return to the Gospel, that it has continued the Middle Ages in an aggravated form?

Indeed, Troeltsch becomes embarrassed, confused; he flounders about with facts and words. "Without doubt", says he, "there is here a higher instinctive estimation of the order of creation than in Catholicism; . . . there is here a more intimate union of the natural order and the redemptive order, than in Catholicism . . . We must live in the world, and overcome it while remaining in the midst of it, resting our salvation, our happiness, solely in our justification and in the expiatory death of Christ. We ought never to trust in the world, never to forget the penalty of sin . . . There is an asceticism which is not less ascetic, because it does not show itself in the form of monachism, because it denies the world inwardly and from within, instead of fleeing from it outwardly. It might be designated asceticism in the world (*innerweltliche Askese*) in contrast with Catholic asceticism, which is characterized by a life without and alongside of the world."[49] Here then is the Protestant asceticism which is contrary to Catholic asceticism. How can it be said that the one is a continuation of the other? Do not these two asceticisms presuppose a contradictory conception of the religious life and of the world? Why keep the same name to designate two contrary things,—and does not the adjective here devour the substantive? What is this intra-mundane, one might say this almost mundane, asceticism, this asceticism that permits the use of the world? It is true that this is not the conception of the Renaissance or of modern poetry. Assuredly not, any more than Christianity is paganism.

Troeltsch ends by distinguishing Lutheran asceticism, which is "essentially an accommodation (*Sichfügen*) and surrender (*Ergeben*), a transference of all hope to the happy beyond, and a martyr's joy in the world", from Calvinistic asceticism, which had an altogether different character. "It is, like all Calvinism, active, aggressive; it would transform the world, to the honor of God. . . . In order to this

end, it rationalizes and disciplines all life by its ethical theories and by its ecclesiastical discipline. . . . In mere feeling
(*Gefühligkeit und Stimmung*) it sees only inertness and
lack of seriousness; it is filled with a fundamental sentiment: labor for God, for the honor of the Church! Thus
the spirit of Calvinistic ethics produces a lively activity, a
severe discipline, a complete plan, a social-Christian aim".[50]
Is it not, truly, an abuse of words to speak thus of asceticism?

In reality, when one thus sees that Protestantism, and
(note it well) particularly Calvinism, inspires souls with
this anti-Catholic conception of life, of activity in society,
one can but be surprised at Troeltsch's conclusion: "In these
conditions it is evident that Protestantism was not able immediately to prepare the modern world. On the contrary,
it appeared at first as a renovation and a recrudescence
of the ideal of civilization by compulsion from the Church,
as the complete reaction of the thought of the Middle
Ages, which suppresses (*verschlingt*) the first efforts of
a free and secular civilization . . . Whoever studies
the history of religion and science cannot escape the impression that it is the great struggle for freedom of the
close of the 17th and of the 18th centuries, which marks
the end of the Middle Ages."[51] This conclusion is diametrically opposed to what may be deduced from the facts and
ideas presented by Troeltsch himself.

7. If Troeltsch has such a confused conception of the
religious principles of the Reformation, it is not surprising
that he presents the application of these principles to society in a manner no less confused. Let us consider the relation of the Church and State.

As to the Church, Troeltsch contends that Protestantism
holds to the idea of an "institute of salvation, purely divine

and founded upon authority". Of the Catholic conception
Protestantism rejects only (*nur*) the divine right of the
hierarchy, superiority of the hierarchy over the State, the
sacraments as means of grace in the possession of the
Church alone and bestowing something other than what
faith gives, and finally tradition. *Nur!* Only! Everything
is brought back to the Bible, everything is replaced by the
Bible. We do not dispute it; we accept it (*concesso, non
dato*). Are the two churches the same Church? Are they
not contradictory?

Troeltsch contends that, with Protestantism, the problem
of the relation between the State and the Church has no
place, for it does not see in State and Church two distinct
organizations, but two different functions of a single social
body, the *corpus christianum*. "Only (*nur,* always the
same formula!) Protestantism organizes the relation between these two functions in a new way: no more supremacy of the hierarchy over the civil power! The State, like
the Church, is subject to the Bible directly." Once more,
we do not dispute it; we accept it. Can it be said that this
is still (*toujours*) the "ecclesiastical civilization" of the
Middle Ages, and even reinforced? Is a Christian society
identical with an ecclesiastical society? Why call this
Christian society a "theocracy", when one is immediately
obliged to change the accepted meaning of the word "theocracy"? "It is the theocratic idea, only the exercise of
theocracy is different. It is no longer the hierarchy that
commands the magistrate, it is the Bibliocracy."[52] Is there
not an abyss between the theocracy of the Middle Ages and
the Bibliocracy of the 16th century?

Finally as to the State. Protestantism has not created an
independent political ethic (*eine selbständige Ethik der Politik*).[53] It has, however, freed the State from legal submis-

sion to the hierarchy; it has affirmed the "definitive, formal, fundamental autonomy" (*Verselbständigung*) of the State. And yet Protestantism did not have the modern idea of the State, since in it the State remains a religious institution, concerned with morality, with Christian duties.[54] Does not the word ecclesiastical seem to become, little by little, synonomous with religious, and the word modern with non-religious? In such sort that Protestantism belongs to the Middle Ages simply because it was religious, and that it did not found modern times simply because these are non-religious?

8. We are reminded that the conception of the State depends upon the conception of natural rights and that there are three forms (*Gestaltung*) of natural rights, that of the Middle Ages,—in which Stoicism, Aristotle and the Bible are mingled,—that of Lutheranism, and that of Calvinism. We do not ask what are these three forms of natural rights, which produce three entirely different States, and we pass over without consideration the natural rights of Lutheranism, which is conservative, which aims at territorial absolutism and pushes this absolutism to the extreme.[55]

The natural rights of Calvinism are sufficiently "conservative". When it is entirely free, it favors a "moderate aristocracy". But "in the great conflicts with the Catholic powers,—persecutors of the word of God among the Huguenots, in the Netherlands, in Scotland, and in England,—Calvinism has developed its natural rights in a much more radical sense". Troeltsch speaks of the right of resistance, granted by Calvinism to lower magistrates (which is correct), even to the individual (which is less correct), and extending inclusively even to tyrannicide (which is more incorrect). And here there appears "an ideal of the State specifically Reformed". A little while ago there was no specific political

ethic.   Now there is a specific ideal of the State, at least for
the Reformed, and so specific that this ideal comes from the
new ideal of the Calvinistic constitution of the Church.
"The primitive cell,—this is the Presbyterio-Synodal constitution of the Church, with its representative system."[56]   In
the Church, elections and colleges of elders; in the State, elections and colleges of chosen men. . . . Finally, an entirely
logical conclusion, the Calvinistic natural rights accept the
idea of governmental contract.   The Covenants appeared.

Here, then, is not only the foundation of the modern State,
its autonomy, but its whole constitution, governmental contract, representation, college of representatives. . . . And is
not this the modern State?   No, for all this is of religious
origin; all this remains religious, according to the Calvinistic
idea.   Then, once more, whatever is religious comes from
the Middle Ages.   Yes?   No?

What confusion there is in such explanations as these:
"The trend of the modern world to democratic government
ought not to be referred solely (certainly, no one maintains
this) and directly to Calvinism.   The mere natural right of
Rationalism, devoid of religious conception, [why is mere
natural right devoid of religious conception, if religion is
natural? and by what authority is it denied that religion is
natural?] is a more powerful factor in this, although Calvinism has a very great part (*hervorragenden Anteil*) in the
production of a disposition favorable to the democratic
spirit."[57]

9.   We have at length reached the subject of natural
rights.   Troeltsch says: "Here we find ourselves, according
to Jellinek, in the presence of an extremely important influence of Protestantism, which realized a fundamental law,
a fundamental ideal of the modern world."   And yet
Troeltsch here again denies this honor to Protestantism.

"In a general way, the exposition of Jellinek constitutes a truly luminous discovery." But if the discovery is to the honor of M. Jellinek, it is not to the honor of Protestant-ism. Indeed, after having stated a fact, Jellinek is mistaken in the attribution which he has made of it. For "the Puri-tanism, which, according to his view, was the father of this idea and the creator of these formulas of right, is not Cal-vinistic,—it is Anabaptist." What is there to say?

Troeltsch changes the historical formula: "The rights of man", to this: "The rights of man and of liberty of con-science", and concerns himself only with the second part of the formula, which he has added. He observes that this lib-erty of conscience was proclaimed in Rhode Island by Roger Williams, who went over to the Baptists, and in Pennsylva-nia by Penn, who was a Quaker. He concludes: "The fa-ther of the rights of man is then not Protestantism, properly speaking, but the hated Baptists, expelled by it."[58]

However, he hastens to correct himself in part: "The Anabaptism which proclaimed the rights of man, is not Ana-baptism properly speaking, but a modified Anabaptism, which has abandoned its *apolitie* [that is, the absence of the idea of government, anarchism], and which is mixed with Calvinism in many respects (*in mancherlei Verschmelzung-en*), an Anabaptism revivified (*neubelebt*) and merged with a radical Calvinism."[59] It has thus created a civiliza-tion by which "the State and the religious community are completely separated", in which, however, "the State keeps strict watch over the fundamental Christian principles of morality and purity of life."[60] "This, precisely, is the design of the idea of the civilization of the Middle Ages."[61]

It is, indeed, a pity that it cannot be known definitely what belongs to Anabaptism and what to Calvinism; a pity, truly, that it should be a question of an Anabaptism, which is not

Anabaptism, but an Anabaptism transformed by Calvinism; and finally, it is truly a pity that these inextricable confusions should have as their result the doing honor to an Anabaptism which is not Anabaptism; a conception of the State, which, according to all the preceding definitions, is altogether mediaeval, and which affected the rupture with the Middle Ages!

10. There remains the paradox of Troeltsch to which this conception leads up, and according to which Puritanism did not come from Calvinism.   Upon what does Troeltsch base this paradox?   His discourse does not say.

We may be permitted to oppose Troeltsch with an authority which he will find it hard to refute, that of his own master, Ritschl.   Ritschl not only says, but expounds what follows: "For Protestant theologians, it is certain that the Reformation of Luther and of Zwingli [Ritschl does not say: and of Calvin], in principle at least, transcended the form of Christianity which was constituted at the end of the second century, and which is especially designated as the Catholic form.   On the contrary, it is evident that the motives and aims, the means and the special regulations of Anabaptism, all continue in line with the Middle Age and find their most immediate analogies in that epoch.   As proof of this assertion I go back to the suggestions of Bullinger.   Whilst the Anabaptists announce that they are the only true commonwealth, agreeable to God, they put the accent on activity, on 'the manifest amelioration' of life among them, which was as little pursued (*erstrebt*) in the evangelical Church as in the papal Church.   Hence, they reject the evangelical doctrine of the satisfaction of Christ, and of justification by faith, to wit, that man becomes righteous before God by faith and not by works.   They reject, consequently, the doctrine of a law that cannot be kept, since all Scripture commands the keeping of the law. In these two fundamental principles the Anabaptists are in agreement with Catholicism. Furthermore, they deduce from the obligation to love the conclusion that the Christian should possess neither property nor wealth, since love has everything in common with the brethren. This principle is only the generalization of a law which has always been regarded by monachism as a condition of Christian perfection."[62]

Moreover, the statements of Ritschl are confirmed by a historian as little Ritschlian as Lang, who has made the study of the relation between Anabaptism and the Reformation a specialty. The Anabaptists, says he, did not accept justification by faith; they made a new law of Christianity: "in this respect they are incontestably on the platform of the Catholicism of the Middle Ages". Only—and this is the original part of Lang's studies—the valuable, the serious elements of Anabaptism (there were such), instead of making their appearance in the 17th century, in opposition to Calvinism and by virtue of an incomprehensible transformation, were absorbed, from the beginning of the 16th century, by Calvinism itself. It cannot be denied that the Reformed, without sacrificing the Palladium of the Reformation,—justification by faith,—allied themselves with Anabaptism through their idea of the Church. "The ecclesiastical idea of Calvin had its historic cradle not so much in Geneva as in Strassburg,—the citadel of Anabaptism on the upper Rhine. To what extent the efforts of these men influenced the ecclesiastical organization of Calvin, by means of the Church of Strassburg, is a question which has not yet been sufficiently explored, and as to which perfect clearness has not been reached."[63] We do not here try to lift this veil. But even if Lang may have exaggerated his discovery a little, still it is evident in what direction the truth must be sought.

We add, for good measure, the conclusion of Loofs: "Does not Troeltsch work with an idealized conception of the Renaissance and of Anabaptism? Certainly the Anabaptism of the 16th century would scarcely have been capable of creating a modern world, if it had attained to hegemony! Not only the events of Münster prove this. The attitude of Anabaptism, as a whole, with respect to asceticism and the State, is, originally, much more mediæval than is that of primitive Protestantism. . . . It is a monstrosity that no amount of sympathy for Anabaptism can excuse, when Troeltsch, in unreflecting forgetfulness of the forms of Anabaptism of the 17th century, represents Anabaptism as having abandoned its *apolitie* (*i. e.,* its anti-political character or what to-day is known as its anarchy), and when, nevertheless, he accords to the Anabaptism, despised by the Reformers and cherished by modern spiritualism, the honor of having been one of the two principal factors of the modern world. He who attributes this to Anabaptism,—that is to say, to certain ideas derived from Anabaptists and elsewhere, formed under the influence of long persecutions, the progress of civilization in England, and by the admixture of Calvinistic tradition—has certainly lost all right to oppose the new Protestantism to the old as a child raised in a strange family, which betrays its family traits only to the eyes of the nearest relatives."[64]

11. We might stop here. This then is the thesis of Ritschl in its latest evolution, the thesis of Ritschl in all its force and all its consequences. It not only strikes at Calvinism, it strikes at the entire Reformation; and Calvinism is even found to be less touched by it than Lutheranism itself; a just recoil and a merited punishment for so

many chauvinistic assaults. The evil weapons have pierced the hand of those who forged them.

Happily for Luther, even more than for Calvin, and happily for the Reformation, the thesis of Ritschl set forth logically, brilliantly, acclaimed by an entire congress of German theologians, is found buried in its very triumph.

Presented in its most scientific form, it offers no resistance to scientific study. Under an exact analysis, this dazzling thesis, supported by wonderful erudition, becomes hesitating, obscure, full of confusions and distinctions, all alike unjustified. The continual concessions, which it is obliged to make, suffice for its refutation, and after all it remains an immense ambiguity; in such sort that, after having refuted Troeltsch, step by step, we might say that in the end we are in accord with him. Finally, with Troeltsch, true Christianity is not the Christianity of the Middle Ages (as to which he is certainly right); but no more is it apostolic and evangelical Christianity that the Middle Ages have more or less affirmed or contradicted.

What is not said in the lecture that we have analyzed, but is implied in it, is explained in the other works of Troeltsch. We let Loofs, who is less under suspicion in this matter than we, speak. "Luther, says Troeltsch, stops in the Middle Ages because he did not go back to Jesus but to Paul, who changed the teaching of Jesus to a Gospel of supernatural salvation; and the root of the Middle Ages was in this Gospel."[65] Here it is, the Middle Ages, that is Paul! Loofs goes on with his resumé of Troeltsch: "Erasmus appears as the ideal type of this humanistic theology. With him Christ was the incarnation of religion that is the same everywhere. It is he who began the retreat from Paulinism toward the Sermon on the Mount, toward the simple religion of the faith of Jesus. In

the presence of Luther he was not only the moralist before
the religious genius, but also the representative of the modern conception, of the anti-supernatural and universal religion."[66]

After this all is clear.   From the moment when St. Paul
is the Middle Ages, and Erasmus is the modern world, it is
evident that the Reformation, which fought Erasmus (and
who fought him more than Luther?), and which preached
St. Paul (and who preached him more than Calvin?), was
against the modern world and for the Middle Ages.   But
there was no reason for proving this in a great number of
learned pages.   It would suffice to say it: we should have
agreed at once, *a priori.*

What is perhaps more curious, is that we find ourselves
also almost in accord as to the two reflections with which
Troeltsch resumes his study.   Protestantism, says he, was
above all a religion; it wished to indicate "a new means",
faith *(sola fides)*, for attaining the old end, salvation: "the
end was the same, the path was radically new".[67]   And
once again, this is evident.   Who could contradict this?
Not we.   Religions, indeed, could scarcely be differen-
tiated by their aim.   All, even fetish religions, seek to assure their adherents of salvation.   To say that two religions
seek salvation by "radically different" means, is to say that
they are "radically different".   And two radically different
religions give birth to two radically different civilizations.
There is then an abyss between Catholicism (as Catholicism) and Protestantism; between the culture of the Middle
Ages and Protestant culture.

Troeltsch afterwards admits that modern times have
made the means the end.   They announced that they had
the end when they had the means, according to Lessing's saying, the search for truth is of more value than the

truth. The idea of faith has everywhere triumphed over the content of faith.[68] In this sense it is very evident that the modern times do not come from the Reformation; that they come from Semler, from Lessing, from Rationalism, mystical or not mystical, from the Renaissance and from Anabaptism, in so far as these are contrary to the Reformation and evangelical Christianity. But once more, who denies this? In any event, not we,—above all, not we. This is our favorite thesis.

Hence nothing of all this is the true question. This is the true question: Does what is best in the modern times come from this mystical Rationalism or from the Reformation? And above all, the true question is this: Has modern culture in itself, apart from the principles of the Reformation, the future, the certainty of its continuance, of its perpetual triumph? Troeltsch doubts this. And he has written these very significant words: "Modern culture is in every instance characterized by a prodigious diffusion and intensity of the idea of liberty and personality. This is the best thing about this culture. The idea is spontaneously (?) developed in all the domains of life, thanks to a particular conjunction of circumstances, and has received from Protestantism only *(nur)* a metaphysico-religious basis, very strong, but in itself independent. The point is to know if this conjunction of circumstances, if this fecundity which it has obtained for the idea of liberty will be maintained. It is hard to think so—yet I think I can conclude—at least this is my particular conclusion: let us keep the metaphysico-religious principle of liberty. Otherwise there might be an end of liberty and of personality at the moment when we vaunted ourselves most of their progress".[69] Truly, what should we add?

III. MAX WEBER.

Our readers must pardon us: in putting Troeltsch after
Ritschl, we have neglected a link of the chain, and certainly
not the least remarkable one: Max Weber, and his study on
"Protestant Ethics and the Spirit of Capitalism", a study
which appeared in 1904 and 1905.[70] This study has been
much less spoken of than Troeltsch's address. And yet,
it seems to us almost more worthy of attention. We have
rarely met with pages richer and more suggestive than these
two articles of 164 pages, cram full of erudition and of
ideas. Taking them up after the preceding section, we can
be brief and yet, we hope, show their true worth.

Troeltsch and Weber are Professors in Heidelberg and
appear almost as collaborators. Troeltsch cites with praise
the works of Weber once. Weber cites many times the
works of Troeltsch that have appeared, and that are to appear. One might then almost speak of a Heidelberg
school. At least, Troeltsch would not dispute the authority
of Weber.

Weber and Troeltsch treat of the same subject in the
same general spirit. Only Weber has a more special, a
more central point of view. He embraces a little less; he
grasps much more. Now, there are singular differences between these Heidelberg colleagues, in the midst of a mass
of analogies; and if the principles and the facts seem the
same with both, the conclusions are entirely different.

Weber like Troeltsch makes a distinction in Protestantism between Lutheranism and Calvinism, and accords to
Calvinism a much higher social influence than to Lutheranism. On this point, the thesis of Ritschl and of Lutheran chauvinism may be considered definitely overthrown.
Troeltsch borrowed from Weber his conception of intra-

mundane *(inner-weltlich)* asceticism, of Protestant asceticism. And indeed this is Weber's central idea.

But there is in Troeltsch an idea that is not found in Weber, the idea that Protestantism continues the culture of the Middle Ages, is a part of the Middle Ages, and neither opens nor begins modern times, is not a part of modern times. Now it is precisely this idea that attracted the attention of the general public to Troeltsch's lecture, and gave it its vogue; yet not only is it absent from Weber's article,—his article in reality refutes it. This is the extremely interesting and important fact that should be stated.

Weber sums up modern culture in the word, "capitalism". "The spirit of capitalism" is the modern spirit. Then, he sums up the moral, practical and social tendency of Protestantism in the word, "asceticism"; but a very special asceticism, which must always be accompanied by two epithets: Protestant and intra-mundane. And finally Weber's special thesis is that this Protestant asceticism of the 16th century has been one of the great factors of the capitalistic or modern spirit.

This is how he expresses himself: "The spirit of labor", of "progress", or whatever you wish to call it, to which one is inclined to attribute the awakening of Protestantism, must not, as it is the habit nowadays to do, be taken in a Rationalistic sense *(aufklärerisch)*. The old Protestantism of Luther, Calvin, Knox, Voet, concerned itself little with what to-day is called "progress". If, then, there is an intimate kinship between the old Protestant spirit and modern capitalistic culture, we must try to find this relationship, rightly or wrongly, not in a pretended "delight in the world" *(joie du monde)*, more or less materialistic, or at least anti-ascetic, but rather in purely religious principles. Montsquieu *(Esprit des Lois,* xx, 7) says of the English: "They are the

people of the world who have best known how to excel at
the same time in three great things: religion, commerce
and liberty". Did their superiority in the domain of industry and their capacity for appropriating liberal political institutions, of which we shall speak elsewhere, depend on
the religious ideas which are a matter of record, according
to Montesquieu? Such is the question to which Weber
answers Yes, with a knowledge that can be called positive,
avoiding equally Rationalism (*Aufklärung*) on the one hand,
and the Middle Ages on the other. "The modern conception, indicated by the expression, 'spirit of capitalism',
would have been proscribed in antiquity as well as in the
Middle Ages, as sordid avarice and mentality without dignity".[71] In the Middle Ages it was the general opinion
that the merchant could not please God *(Deo placere non
potest)*; that there was something shameful *(pudendum)*
in a mercantile condition. And it was necessary to break
away from this "tradition" of antiquity and of the Middle
Ages in order to make way for modern times.

Who broke with this tradition? The Protestantism of
the 16th century; the Protestantism and not the Rationalism.
Those who are tempted to believe that the "capitalistic
spirit" is a product of Rationalism, and that Protestantism
intervenes only so far as it is a forerunner of Rationalism,
Weber confronts simply with the facts.[72]

Protestantism has worked through its religious conceptions, properly so-called, in the list of which Weber puts
the great idea of vocation. The Latin-Catholic peoples
have no word, any more than has classical antiquity, to express this idea of vocation (*Beruf*), in the sense of social
condition, life in a determined sphere. On the other hand
this word exists among all Protestant peoples.[73] "And as
the significance of the word is new, so also is the idea; it is

a product of the Reformation. No doubt, already in the Middle Ages certain attempts at appraising daily toil in this way are found. But what is entirely new is this: the esteeming the accomplishment of duty, in the earthly vocation, as the ideal of personal morality. This it is that has logically produced the view of the religious importance of the daily task in this world and which has given birth to the idea of vocation. Thus, that which finds its expression in this idea of vocation is the central dogma of all the old Protestant denominations, which rejects the distinction between the precepts and the counsels in Christian ethics, and indicates, as the only way of leading a life agreeable to God, not the excelling of worldly morality by monastic asceticism, but the being content merely with the fulfilment of one's duties in the world, as the situation of each requires, that is to say, fulfilling his vocation."[74]

"That this moral character of 'vocation' is one of the merits of the Reformation, the consequences of which have been most important, and that it is specially due to Luther, is incontestable and of common notoriety."[75] However, if Luther began, he did not continue. Luther became more and more a traditionalist.[76] "He did not discover the new theoretical basis on which the relation between vocation and religious principles rests."[77] "So the simple idea of vocation, in a Lutheran sense, remained (in the domain in which we are), of problematical importance."[78]

But Calvinism came. "Calvinism, historically, is one of the incontestible factors of the 'capitalistic spirit'."[79] And it is Calvinism that has been the most opposed to the Middle Ages. "It is with reason that Catholicism has regarded Calvinism, from its origin until to-day, as its real enemy."[80] Luther created Protestantism; Calvin saved it.

It is seen how the article of Weber excludes the thesis

of Troeltsch, and how it proves that the Reformation broke with the Middle Ages, and inaugurated modern times. Undoubtedly, in Weber's work, aside from the fundamental thesis, there are points upon which we are not in agreement with the author. But that matters little here. We confine ourselves to formulating two regrets. The first is that Weber has called the "spirit" with which the Reformation has inspired modern culture, "the capitalistic spirit." Of course, I know Weber's reservations. I know that he is not concerned with capitalism, but with its "spirit", with that which has been its quality, to wit, a power of incessant toil systematically disciplined. This spirit, which does not urge on to pleasure, but to production, is so contrary to human nature that it could only arise through the influence of an extremely efficacious spiritual power. . . . However, there are two ideas in the word "capitalism", as in all the words in *ism,* one good and another evil, the exaggeration of the good, which, by its exaggeration, makes a false and dangerous idea out of the good idea. But I know also how dangerous it is to designate by the same word two things so different. The words in *ism* have two senses: still, it is generally the contemptuous sense that is intended, when the word is spoken. And we can see this in the abuse which the adversaries of Protestantism could make of this word "capitalism". They could say: Protestantism is the father of capitalism, of that capitalism which is so horrible, so nefarious, so anti-Christian, so hateful, etc. Further, all the precautions that Calvin took against the evil capitalism, the idea of which is wholly contrary to Calvinism, should be noted. It is not sufficient, in our opinion, to have reiterated that Calvinism itself is shown many times to be in disagreement with Calvin.[81]

Not less regrettable is the use of the word "asceticism".

All the abuse that Ritschl has made of it was known, as well as that which Troeltsch was going to make. Here, again, I am aware that with Weber Protestant "asceticism" is contrary to Catholic "asceticism". If there are points of resemblance, Weber gives the following excellent reason for this: "All asceticism that arises out of Biblical soil ought to have, necessarily, certain common traits".[82] Just so. So much the more since, if Weber, like Troeltsch, does not broach the question, essential nevertheless, of the evangelical teaching on pretended asceticism, he allows his theological idea, which is the idea of the modern school of theology and of Troeltsch, to emerge, namely, that the Middle Ages have their origin in St. Paul and in the New Testament. "The apostolical epoch, which speaks in the New Testament, and especially in Paul, because of the eschatological expectations, has either an indifferent or an essentially traditionalistic attitude with respect to this life as a vocation."[83] In this way we might say, on the one hand, that what Protestant asceticism has in common with the asceticism of the Middle Ages comes from St. Paul and the Gospels: and on the other hand, that what does not come from St. Paul and the Gospels is contrary to the asceticism of the Middle Ages.

Indeed, instead of being external, this asceticism is internal; instead of fleeing from the world, it seeks it out. Further, according to Weber, Protestant asceticism impels to the acquisition of this world's goods, makes this acquisition lawful,—shall we say, the will of God? It only combats the temptations attached to riches . . . not mortification (*nicht Kasteiung*), but the use of possessions for necessary and practically useful purposes, is its ideal. The idea to which this asceticism tends, logically and in fact, is that of "comfort".[84]

Then we ask: why take a single word to designate con-

trary things? Why take the word asceticism in a sense
opposed to that which ecclesiastical history and ordinary
usage give it? Is there not risk of provoking misunder-
standings and equivocations?

To sum up, the prodigious and admirable work of Max
Weber results in the anticipated correction of Troeltsch's
paradox, and we should accept willingly Weber's conclusion,
were it not for two words that are in danger of being taken
in a sense in which Weber does not take them.

IV.   CALVIN.

We now come to our Reformer.   If we had to do only
with Ritschl and his three faithful disciples, we could say:
since Calvin is of all the Reformers the one whom you regard as the least a Reformer, the most mediæval, by showing
how far Calvin broke with the Middle Ages, we have proved
a fortiori how the whole Reformation was reformative.
But, with respect to Troeltsch, we cannot use this language.
Troeltsch, in fact, with his knowledge independent of Lutheran chauvinism, has made it apparent that the accusations of Ritschl hit Luther even harder than Calvin.   In
this, Troeltsch has come back to the unanimous opinion of
the Catholics (and in this they may be believed), who have
recognized in Calvin their most dangerous adversary, because he was the most logical Reformer.

But, in reality, the disagreement between Ritschl and
Troeltsch little concerns us.   To our mind there is no contradiction between Luther and Calvin.   Coming after Luther, Calvin has profited by this, and has carried on the
Protestant results of all Protestantism.   It suffices us to
concern ourselves with Calvin; by justifying Calvin we shall
justify Luther and the entire Reformation.   I add that we
shall treat only of a single point of the Calvinistic concep-

tion, the pretended asceticism of Calvin. Nothing but his asceticism; because it is upon this that Ritschl and the whole Ritschlian school build their theories. And we confine ourselves to this point, because even with this restriction, the subject in its entirety is still too large for full treatment here.

1. "Self-denial" is the means of attaining the end of human life. The difference between paganism and Christianity is shown in this. Paganism preaches the autonomy and pride of men. Christianity preaches heteronomy,[85] and humility. "Christian philosophy bids reason withdraw itself in order that it may give place to the Holy Spirit and be subject to His guidance, so that the man no longer lives of himself, but has Christ living and reigning in him."[86] Saint Paul said: "It is not I that live, it is Christ that liveth in me"; and in a highly rhetorical unfolding of this theme Calvin repeats: "We are not our own . . . we are not our own . . . we are the Lord's . . . we are the Lord's . . . "[87]

And yet it is said: this self-denial is asceticism,—the beginning, the root of asceticism. But he is certainly mistaken who holds to appearances and sees in Calvinistic renunciation only a negative meaning. On the contrary, it is positive, essentially and doubly positive; denying oneself means the giving oneself to men and to God. Calvin says this in so many words: "This self-denial,[88] which Christ requires so carefully of all His disciples, has respect partly to men and partly to God".[89]

Men. The particularly difficult thing is to seek the good of our neighbor; and only self-denial removes this difficulty: "All that we have received of the Lord has been granted us on this condition, that we use it for the common welfare of the Church . . . The lawful use of this grace is a loving and liberal sharing of it with our neighbors . . . no member has his powers for himself, and he does not apply them to his own particular use, but for the profit of others . . . the common benefit of the Church."[90] Thus this "self-denial" is the basis of solidarity (but we must forego here to indicate the very beautiful development given by Calvin to this idea).

God.   Self-denial for the sake of God will be in its turn the basis of integrity and tranquillity of spirit.   "Whoever rests in the divine blessing, will not by wicked and crafty means seek any of those things that men seek with mad desire.   And he will have a solace in which he can better satisfy himself than in all the riches of the world . . ., he will account all things to be ordered of God, as is expedient for his salvation."[91]   Thus self-denial is the great means of Christian activity in the world, for men.   We see how far words must be distrusted.

2.   It is true that with Calvin self-denial is a manner of "bearing his cross", and that this cross is frequently mentioned.   But here again it is not at all a matter of suffering for the sake of suffering, and of a seeking after suffering. Calvin writes the very opposite of this in one of the numerous passages in which he has branded the ascetic folly of Stoics, fakirs and monks.   "To bear the cross patiently is not to be altogether stolid, and to feel no grief, like the Stoic philosophers . . . There are even among Christians fellow creatures who think that it is vicious not only to groan and weep but also to be sad and anxious.   These wild opinions proceed from idle natures . . . For our part we will have nothing to do with this hard and rigorous philosophy."[92] And again: "If we were like a block of wood or a stone, there would be no virtue in us . . . the brute beasts sometimes have no feeling, but this does not make them virtu-

ous."[93] And yet again: "No one need be astonished if we esteem the tears and groans of David more than the hardness and stolidity of many, a hardness and stolidity which many praise as the highest virtue."[94]

3. In addition to self-denial, another means of attaining the end of the Christian life is meditation on the life to come. And here, in his great fervor, Calvin makes use of some of those strong expressions, to which he is addicted. He is speaking of contemning the present life. For his anti-aesthetic temperament is concerned only with the "two extremes", "either the earth must be despised by us, or else it enslaves us by an intemperate love of it."[95]

But, once again, we must not forget the vehement forms of speech affected by Calvin. And the proof is that if he says here: there is no mean between the two extremes; elsewhere he declares that "there is as much danger of falling into one extreme as the other".[96] We should, then, avoid both. And after having given the reasons for despising this earth and this life, Calvin makes haste to inform us that we must not put a wrong construction on his words and come to a "hatred of the present life or ingratitude toward God". On the contrary, this life is among "the blessings of God, which are not to be contemned".[97] And he shows its advantages and benefits. God reveals Himself here as our Father, in the smallest details; we are here preparing for the glory of His kingdom, etc. Furthermore, the earthly life seems despicable to us only in comparison with the heavenly life.[98]

4. However, it must be observed that these utterances are only preliminary. Could one speak of the monastic asceticism of Calvin even if these prefatory statements were all? Certainly not.

Calvin speaks to us "of the right use of earthly blessings". It is here that we find the true nature of his asceticism. Let us read attentively. We do not have to abstain from this world's goods, Calvin declares, not even from those "which seem more conducive to pleasure *(oblectationi)* than to our necessities". On the contrary, we are to use them "as well for our needs as for our delectation *(oblectamentum)*".[99] Such is the exordium of the alleged panegyric on monastic asceticism.

Some good persons among the "Saints" have permitted man to use this world's goods only in so far as necessity demands. Undoubtedly, these Saints were well intentioned; they were none the less mistaken; "they practiced a too great rigor"; they were more "strict" than God's word. And this overstrictness is "very dangerous". Yet it is not necessary to believe them and to imagine that it is unlawful "to add anything to the brown bread and water".[100] This is monastic asceticism, and—its formal condemnation.

There follows a charming passage of good sense, as realistic as poetic: "If we consider for what purpose God created food, we shall find that He wished to provide not only for our necessity, but also for our pleasure and recreation *(oblectamento quoque ac hilaritati)*. So as to raiment, beside necessity, He has regard to that which is proper and becoming *(decorum et honestas)*. As to herbs, trees, and fruits, beside their various useful qualities, He has enhanced them by their beauty *(aspectus gratia)*, and gives us added pleasure in their perfume *(jucunditas odoris)*. If this were not so, the prophet would not have numbered among the divine blessings the wine that rejoiceth man's heart and oil that maketh his face to shine . . . The good qualities that all things have by nature *(naturales rerum dotes)* show us how we ought to enjoy them . . . Do we think that, our Lord having given such beauty to the flowers which present themselves to the sight (*quae ultro in oculos incurreret*), it is not lawful to be touched with pleasure in seeing them? Do we think that He has given them so sweet an odor (*tantam odoris suavitatem*) and does not wish that man should delight to smell them? . . . Have done then with that inhuman philosophy, which . . . not only maliciously (*malignè*) deprives us of the lawful fruit of the divine beneficence, but also cannot be realized without depriving man of all sentiment, and making him like a block of wood."[101]

And Calvin preached this anti-asceticism from his pulpit after having recommended it in his dogmatics. "It is said in Ps. civ., that God has not only given man bread and water for the necessity of life, but that He added as well wine to comfort and rejoice his heart . . . He might easily have made the corn grow for our nourishment without any preceding bloom. He might easily have made fruits and trees without leaves and blossoms. We see that our Lord wills that we should rejoice through all our senses . . . "[102] "The world was created for us, and our God wills not that we should be deprived of anything whatever."[103]

5. Self-denial is a form of asceticism; asceticism is a form of pessimism. But we do not really think it necessary to enter into a detailed discussion of the reasons by which the attempt is made to prove, in spite of everything, that Calvin taught monastic pessimism. Moreover, it would be necessary to define pessimism and the different kinds of pessimism. This would take time and space. If one were to speak of pessimism without particularizing, is there not a Biblical, Christian pessimism,—an evangelical pessimism even? And does this kind of pessimism prevent Christianity from being a doctrine of optimism,—a doctrine of the greatest, the only true optimism that the world has known?

Leaving to our readers the task of combining them, we

cite some of the texts at random. "The world lieth under the power of the evil one" (1 John v. 19); "The wages of sin is death" (Rom. vi. 23); "The sorrow of the world worketh death" (1 Cor. vii. 10). . . . And, indeed, must we not go higher than St. Paul and St. John? Are not the Beatitudes a strange cry of mingled pessimism and optimism? "Blessed are the poor in spirit; blessed are they that mourn; blessed are they that hunger and thirst after righteousness; blessed are they that are persecuted for righteousness sake" (Matt. v. 3, 4, 6, 10).

Then, technical terms are resorted to, scholastic discussions, and all that theological art which consists in contemplating the trees in such a way as not to see the forest. We are told that Calvin's pessimism has all the characteristics of real pessimism; it is eschatological, negative and ascetic . . . The pessimism of Calvin is all that!

We limit ourselves to the consideration for a moment of the first of these sinister words: eschatological. It is one of the great words of present-day theology. What does it mean? Does it mean that the supreme good exists only in the other life?[104] Or, rather, that the felicity of salvation begins to be our heritage in this life, but it is complete only in the other life? Whatever is thought of the first statement, it is the second that Calvin sets forth; and it is difficult to see in the second anything else than an evident truth for every Christian.

Calvin writes: "As to us, already in this earthly pilgrimage (*in hac quoque terrena peregrinatione*) we know what is the only and perfect felicity (*nobis unica et perfecta felicitas in hac quoque terrena peregrinatione nota est*), but in such sort that it inflames [more exactly: this felicity, which inflames] our hearts daily more and more with desire for it (*sui desiderio*), until we shall be satisfied with its full

possession" (*donec plena fruitio nos satiet*).[105] Could one
wish anything more clear?   This happiness of salvation is
not merely eschatological.

   This text annoys the inventors of the pessimism and asceticism, etc., of Calvin.   They summon exegesis to their aid,
and declare that Calvin has in mind here, for this earth,
only an abstract knowledge of perfect happiness.   "This is
not the object of our present pleasure".[106] We shall not stop
here to show that this exegesis does too much violence to the
text; that a knowledge *(nota)* which inflames the heart with
desire (*desiderio corda accendit*), and gives us already a
partial joy (*fruitio*), awaiting complete happiness (*donec
plena*), never was an abstract notion.   But of what use is
this exegesis?   Calvin has himself explained clearly his
thought and his phraseology: "We begin *(incipimus)* here
to enjoy the sweetness of His kindness in His benefits *(divinae benignitatis suavitatem delibare)*, so that our hope and
desire are incited to expect the full revelation *(quo spes ac
desiderium nostrum acuatur ad plenam ejus revelationem ex-
petendam)*."[107]

   Even Schulze is obliged to admit the existence of passages that "seem to contradict his thesis explicitly" (*Man-
ches scheint dem direct zu widersprechen*).[108]   But, really,
what is to be said?   This is to be said, which Troeltsch confesses, that the Reformers did not make this earthly life,
the possessions of this life, ends in themselves, but means to
arrive at the true goal: the possession of God, eternal life
in God.   Only, if this is eschatological pessimism, this eschatological pessimism is found in all the Reformers, as well
as in Calvin; and, indeed, before the Reformers, in St. Paul.
This pretended eschatological pessimism is an authentic
Pauline conception.   "For verily in this tabernacle we
groan, longing to be clothed upon with our habitation which

is from heaven" (2 Cor. v. 2). "For our citizenship is in heaven; from whence also we wait for a Saviour, the Lord Jesus Christ" (Phil. iii. 20). "For me to live is Christ, and to die is gain. But if to live in the flesh—if this is the fruit of my work, then what I shall choose I wot not. But I am in a strait betwixt the two, having the desire to depart and be with Christ, which is far better" (Phil. i. 21-23). "Forgetting the things which are behind and reaching forth to the things which are before, I press on toward the goal, unto the prize of the high calling of God in Christ Jesus" (Phil. iii. 13). "For our light affliction, which is for the moment, worketh for us more and more exceedingly an eternal weight of glory; while we look not at the things which are seeen, but at the things which are not seen: for the things which are seen are temporal; but the things which are not seen are eternal" (2 Cor. iv. 17-18).

Our readers may multiply these citations at will. We only add that in case some objector rejects St. Paul altogether, and proclaims him to be the founder of asceticism and of eschatological monastic pessimism, it matters little. Jesus remains. Is it not He who spoke so often of the necessity for His disciples to deny themselves (Matt. xvi. 24), to give up everything (Luke xiv. 33), to bear their cross (Matt. x. 38), to love Him more than their fathers and mothers (Matt. x. 37), to lose, to hate their own life (Matt. xvi. 25, Lk. xiv. 26), not to lay up treasures on earth (Matt. vi. 19), not to set their hearts on treasures on earth but on treasures in heaven (Matt. vi. 20), to make themselves maimed, halt, blind, if hand, or foot, or eye stays the course toward eternal life (Matt. xvii. 8-9)? "Sell all that thou hast and give alms . . . make for yourselves treasures in heaven. . . . For where your treasure is, there will your heart be also" (Lk. xii. 33-34). "How hardly shall they that have riches enter into the kingdom of God! And the disciples were amazed at his words. But Jesus answereth again and saith unto them, Children, how hard is it for them that trust in riches to enter into the kingdom of God! It is easier for a camel to go through a needle's eye than for a rich man to enter into the kingdom of God. They were astonished exceedingly, saying unto him, then who can be saved? Jesus looking upon them saith: With men it is impossible, but not with God; for all things are possible with God" (Mk. x. 23-27). Is all this different from St. Paul? And had Calvin a different conception than that of St. Paul and Jesus Christ?

The conclusion is always the same: the attacks on Calvin and the Reformation do not strike the Reformers only; they go back to St. Paul and the historic Christ Himself.

6. After what Weber has said of vocation, we may here pass by in complete silence this chief element of the Calvinistic conception. The idea of vocation is one of the principal ideas of the Reformation. But it is only with Calvin and the Calvinists that it has developed its practical and decisive consequences. Giving to the life of every man and to every detail of that life a divine value, it suffices of itself to overturn all the exploitations of the pretended pessimism of Calvin.

But there is another point, which must be insisted upon, for it is upon this point that the accusations of pessimism and asceticism are ultimately based—the more securely, it is believed; I mean Calvin's conception of the body.

It is said: "Calvin especially likes the comparison of the body to a tent (quickly pitched) or even to a prison (besides *carcer* there is also *ergastulum*)."[109] This is true. It might be added that Calvin sees in the deliverance from the body a condition of complete deliverance from sin. "There always remain many infirmities", he says, "while we are shut up in our mortal body (*mole corporis nostri*)."[110] "While we inhabit this prison of our body (*in carcere corporis nostri*) we must always and without ceasing combat the corruption of our nature."[111] But are not these precisely the words and thoughts of St. Paul? "I am carnal, sold under sin. . . . O wretched man that I am, who shall deliver me out of the body of this death?" (Rom. vii. 24).

To tell the truth, Schulze has forgotten to notice the most scornful word that Calvin uses to designate the body, a word that occurs more than once in his Sermons when he is trying to smite as with rod and hammer (these are his own expressions) the hardened consciences of his hearers: "We are enveloped in our bodies, which are but carcases."[112]

It is seen that we conceal nothing. But just where Calvin, in his extravagant way of speaking, most abuses the body, does he most exalt it: "Our bodies, although they are wretched corpses, do not cease to be temples of the Holy Spirit, and God would be adored in them. . . . We are the altars, at which He is worshipped, in our bodies and in our souls."[113]

But let us go further and from words pass to ideas. With the aid of a passage relative to Osiander, it is thought that it can be proved that Calvin excluded the body from what is called "the image of God". This is wrong. What Calvin reproaches Osiander with, is not that he placed the image of God in the soul and in the body, but that he did this "confusedly" (*promiscue*) and "equally" (*tam ad corpus quam ad animam*). As to himself, if he did not do this confusedly and equally, he yet put it in the one no less than in the other. "The image of God embraces the entire dignity, by which man is exalted above all the animal species." And he expressly says: "there is no part of man, including the body itself, in which there is not some luminous spark" of that divine image.[114]

Hence, while the ascetic conception tends to the abasement of the body, the Calvinistic conception tends to respect for and care of the body.

Calvinism makes it the strict duty of the faithful to keep the body clean and healthy, as much as possible. "God deigns to dwell within us; let us endeavor then to walk in such purity of body and soul, that our soul, especially, may be purified from all evil thoughts and affections; and then, that our bodies also may be kept with such decency that we shall not callously commit improprieties before men and be not ashamed; for this would cause us to forget the duty we owe to God."[115] That is to say that there is no place in Calvinism for any St. Labre of repulsive memory (*de pouilleuse memoire*). And this explains how and why it is that the most Calvinistic peoples, the Scotch and the Dutch, are the most noted for their cleanliness.

Cleanliness and health. Health (as far as it depends upon ourselves) is a duty toward God, like cleanliness. Recommendations abound: "We must beware of a too great austerity, for God does not wish that man should commit suicide."[116] Man ought to be as mindful of his health as possible, and this not so much for his own welfare as that he may study to do good."[117] If we are sick, we must use the remedies that are offered us; "it is God's will that we should use them; it is devilish pride that makes us willing to abstain from their use".[118] Is it then "comely for an Apostle of Jesus Christ to exhort a man to drink wine"? Certainly. "In everything and everywhere, even in drinking and eating, God wills that our life should be regulated, to the end that by using His creatures (*choses crées*) we may serve Him, that we should be fit for doing good."[119] *Mens sana in corpore sano.* If there has ever been a philosophy which explained, justified and preached this adage, it is certainly the Christian philosophy of Calvin.

Far from leading to asceticism, this philosophy has led— very logically—to such a union of cleanliness and piety, of joy and health, as alone can make our soul and body do their greatest service for God and humanity. Hence one understands why the body of the Calvinist, not less than his soul, has been so fit for the conquest of the modern world. through all the most intense enterprises of commerce and industry, in the old and in the new world.[120]

Finally, let us note—over against all theologians sufficiently blinded by their prejudices to speak still of the monastic and Platonic asceticism of Calvin—let us note the belief in the resurrection of the body, a belief unknown to the Greek philosophers, and upon which Calvin insists in this wise: "The error of those who imagine that the soul will not resume the body with which it is now clothed, but that a new one will be made for it, is so enormous that we shall regard it as a detestable monster."[121]

Here is a hymn in honor of the body. The body is a temple of the Holy Spirit: "Can it sink into putrefaction without hope of resurrection?"[122] The body is a member of Jesus Christ. God asks that our tongues and our hands worship Him. If He does "such honor to our bodies, what madness is it in mortal man to reduce them to dust without hope that they shall be raised again?" "Shall the body of St. Paul", exclaims Calvin, "which bore the marks of Jesus Christ, which glorified him exceedingly, be deprived of the reward of the crown?"[123]

Schulze is here again disturbed by the text. He is even

obliged to admit "that there is a real difference between the eschatology of Calvin and that of Plato". "But", says he, "it is an unconscious contradiction, that is all." "Calvin was not at all conscious (*er ist sich gar nicht bewusst*) how little this agrees with his small esteem for the body."[124] Let the reader decide.

6. In order to sum up and as it were make all these ideas and opinions concrete, nothing remains but to read the chapter on "Christian Liberty" (and some pages of the Sermons treating of this same subject). This chapter is usually passed over in silence. And undoubtedly it is not written with the lyric charm of Luther's analagous treatise. But it is this, in our view, that gives it its value. There is no question, indeed, of a copy, an imitation. There is no question even of a theme treated over again, but as of necessity, because the plan of the work required it. Calvin here is perfectly original, with a robust, spontaneous and most characteristic originality.

He wishes men to set themselves from the start against all monastic asceticism, as if God took pleasure in these material sacrifices. He shows that the ground is slippery; and that once the foot is set on the slope, one must go to the end. The history of certain Saints proves it. With his virile good sense he writes: "When once the conscience is bridled and held in check (*in laqueum*), it enters an infinite labyrinth and a deep abyss, whence it is not easy to escape. If one begins to doubt whether it is lawful for him to use linen sheets, shirts, handkerchiefs and napkins, he will not long be sure about using hemp, and at last he will vacillate as to the use of tow. For he will wonder if he might not eat without a napkin and do without handkerchiefs. Should he deem a daintier food unlawful, he will at last not dare to eat either bread or common viands

with an assured conscience before God, since it will always
occur to him that he might sustain life with still meaner
food. If he scruples to drink good wine (*suaviori*), he will
afterward not dare to drink the worst with a good conscience, or water that is unusually sweet and pure; in fine,
it will come to this, that he will hold it a great sin to
trample on a straw in his path."[125]   Liberty! Liberty!
says Calvin. We ought, "without scruple of conscience or
trouble of spirit, to make such use of the gifts of God as has
been ordained".[126]

And from theory, Calvin goes on to practice, to examples.
We find in Calvin a man of the 16th century, who loves to
banquet, to make good cheer and to drink a few glasses of
good wine with his friends. "The feast of Nabal was not
blameworthy in itself; the divine law surely permitted him
to invite his friends to a feast (*convivium*), and to treat
them hospitably (*liberalius*). . . . God sometimes permits us to live more freely, more sumptuously (*lautius*), by
special divine favor." Nabal sinned through excess; he
was drunken.

Now Calvin is pitiless toward drunkards. For drunken-
ness turns us into unclean beasts (*sues*). Elsewhere Calvin
expresses himself in this wise: "If a man knows that he
has a weak head, and that he cannot carry three glasses of
wine without being overcome, and then drinks indiscreetly,
is he not a hog?"[127] We notice the "three glasses of wine",
the minimum that harmed the weak heads only, and we
strongly suspect that Calvin did not rank himself among
them.

He takes up again his story of the banquet of Nabal:
"The liberality of God toward the human race is so great,
that He supplies us not only with that which is necessary for
the nourishment of our bodies, but also with that which pro-

vides plenty and pleasure (*jocunditatem*). Thus wine has been given, not only to strengthen man's heart, but also to make him joyful (*ad illum exhilarandum*)." It is only necessary to use these good things in such a way that we can always call upon God and serve Him. "In short, that the gaiety (*hilaritas*) and pleasure (*voluptas*) which we get from wine (*quam ex vino capimus*) may not disturb our worship of God . . . let us use wine and other created things soberly, with temperance, in order that satisfied by them we may receive new strength for the fulfilment of our vocation."[128] Consequently, he altogether approves of the assembling of the sons of Job, and "of the merry time that they had with one another, that they might continue in amity". And in a general way "we should not have scruples or superstitions . . . when we are at table, let us eat in order to be refreshed, as if God were feeding us".[129]

What Calvin says of drinking and eating he repeats with respect to all the other joys of life. And he writes pages full of the most significant realism. Have his critics never read them? "Why are the rich cursed, who have now received their consolation, who are full [*saturati, i. e. rassassiés*], who laugh, who sleep on beds of ivory, who add possession to possession (*agrum agro*), at whose feasts are harps, lutes, tambourines and wine. Surely the ivory and gold and riches are good creatures (*bonae Dei creaturae sunt*), permitted and even appointed for the use of men, and nowhere is laughing forbidden, or being full (*saturari, se rassasier*), or the acquiring of new possessions (*novas possessiones veteribus atque avitis adjungere*), or delight in musical instruments (*concentu musico delectari*), or drinking wine, etc. . . . "[130] Gold, fields, dinners, banquets, concerts; all this is permitted! What becomes of the stereotyped remarks about the sombre, morose and "Franciscan" asceticism of Calvin?

Ritschl wrote in 1880: "As Calvin, personally, did not need any recreation, he saw only pressing temptations to sin in the social forms of recreation and in the luxury that followed them. . . . For this reason he combatted everything that pertained to the gay and free joyousness of life and luxury."[131] These phrases have been circulated from hand to hand, from book to book, like current coin, and they may be found, for example, in the most recent popular work, that of Bess: *Unsere religiösen Erzieher*, 1908. Bess repeats religiously: "This agreed with his personal character, which despised (*verachtete*), which, it may be said, held in horror (*ja zum Teil verabscheute*) all that could refresh and adorn life (*alle Mittel der Erholung und Verschönerung*). He was endowed with a seriousness and with an ability to work that had no need of diversion (*Ablenkung*)."[132]

Pure legend! Caricature, the fruit of ignorance and prejudice. It is sufficient "to use the gifts of God with a pure conscience", to observe "the rule of proper use". Importance does not attach to the things themselves, but to the way in which they are used. "A royal courage often dwells in a coarse and homely garb, and an humble heart is often hidden under silk and velvet." Poverty, a comfortable estate, wealth,—none of these is essential. "The law of Christian liberty . . . is to be content with what we have"; it is to know alike how to bear humiliation and honor, hunger and abundance, poverty and wealth. "If this temperance is wanting, the common and ordinary pleasures are excessive."[133] It would, in truth, be as easy to caricature Calvin as a Rabelaisian *bonvivant,* as to caricature him as a Franciscan monk; as easy, I should say as difficult. Calvin was simply a Christian of the type of Luther and the Reformation, after the fashion of St. Paul and of Christ, a Christian who had for his ideal man created by God, in a world which though fallen is still the handiwork of God.

It is then by a wrong interpretation of certain passages, or by disregarding them under the pretext of unconscious contradiction, when, although wrongly interpreted, they are still vexatious, that the conclusions of the school of Ritschl are formed, to wit, that in Calvinism there is "an undervaluation (*Unterschätzung*) of man's task in the world"; that "as to the work to be done in the world and as to its multiform content, one, from this point of view, could not be much concerned about it"; "that nothing shows more clearly the tendency of morality, in the Calvinistic sense, to turn away from the world (*den Welt abgewandten Character*), than the relation indicated between the chapter in which self-denial is treated, and that in which 'bearing the cross patiently' is spoken of, and likewise the one on 'meditation on the life to come'. . . . As the theatre of our moral preparation for heaven, this life, contemptible in itself, has a value. But this moral preparation becomes a habit of despising life (considered in itself) and a habit of striving after the life to come. This means that this life has this consequence, that while in it we should detach ourselves from it and live for the life to come. Thus the moral earnestness of Calvinistic Christianity does not overcome the mood of the soul which longs for death (*die Stimmung der Todessehnsucht*). On the contrary, that mood finds in it new nourishment."[134]

With a slight modification of the formula of Ritschl we might say that in this appreciation, all that is correct is found in St. Paul; and that what is not found in St. Paul is not correct. But of what use is further discussion amidst

all these subtleties, and the loss of time in correcting the
meaning of the passages cited, or accumulating neglected
ones? This whole conception runs foul of something more
solid even than clear and numerous texts; it encounters
reality, the reality of facts and of all history. The centuries
and whole peoples, in the full sunlight of life, protest
against these adroit or violent feats of the learned in the
half-light of their closets.

Calvinism, lost in the mists of eschatology, living in the
pessimistic expectation of death, paralyzed by the bonds of
asceticism! Where has a Calvinist of this sort ever been
seen? If Calvinism is what Ritschl and Schulze think, there
is only one conclusion: there have never been men less
Calvinistic than the Calvinists! Far from being a man who
seeks retirement or turns from the world and from the
present life, the Calvinist is one who takes possession of the
world; who, more than any other, dominates the world; who
makes use of it for all his needs; he is the man of commerce,
of industry, of all inventions and all progress, even material.

And yet, after having shown this colossal error, we shall
not close with saying it is inexplicable. Not at all; the
explanation, on the contrary, is very easy. The critics of
our Reformation have found themselves confronted with
the contradictions which we have indicated elsewhere. They
are restricted to choosing one of two terms,—that one
which seems to them to justify their theological presupposition, without once asking if there is not some psychological
explanation, capable of harmonizing the apparently contradictory terms, and even of making one the profound
cause of the other. For example, some critics do not comprehend how the doctrine of the subject-will (*serf-arbitre*),
pushed to the extreme by Calvinists, has made of precisely
these Calvinists preëminently the founders of moral aus-

terity and civil liberty. Yet it is a fact, verified by the counter testimony of Pelagianism, which—the party of absolute free-will—leads to the abasement of morality and to social slavery. Very well! As to self-denial in life, and the use of life, exactly the same thing happens and from the same motives, as happened in the case of the subject-will and liberty. In spite of appearances, the former is not the denial of the latter; it is its cause. With Calvin, indeed, self-denial is not a mere negative, privative conception . . . in it we find ourselves simply in the presence of a principle, a law, one of the most important laws of the spiritual and moral world. *Per crucem ad gloriam!* Which sometimes means, through slavery to liberty; and sometimes through self-denial to possession. It is the law which Christ Himself formulated with solemnity and with decisiveness, when He said: "Whosoever would save his life shall lose it: and whosoever shall lose his life for my sake shall find it" (Matt. xvi. 25). And again: "and every one that hath left houses, or brethren, or sisters, or father, or mother, or children, or lands, for my name's sake, shall receive a hundredfold, and shall inherit eternal life" (Matt. xix. 29). And again: "But seek ye first the kingdom of God and His righteousness; and all these things shall be added unto you" (Matt. vi. 33).

We leave out of sight all special intervention by God, all miraculous blessings. The psychological law is as simple as it is incontestable. To renounce everything in order to give everything to God and the brethren,—this is to be in the religious and moral state most fitted to assure liberty of spirit, sureness of action, the employment of the normal, the moral, that is to say, the most efficacious, the most productive means for the domination of the world. Egoism, the passions and vices are not the true means for drawing from the world its hidden resources. Instead of making us masters of the world, they make us slaves. That which rules the world is calmness, self-possession, virtue, and, consequently, piety and faith. In the tempest the pilot who is most certain to save his own life and that of the ship, is not the one who clings most tenaciously to life; it is the one who is so ready to die that he is calm and cool.

Matter brings nothing out of matter. It is the spirit that makes of matter what it will. He who seeks the world for the world, loses it. He who loses it, for Christ's sake, for God's sake, gains it. He who seeks himself, loses himself,—loses himself, as to everything that is not his real self, in his evil desires and mad passions. He who denies himself for the sake of God and the brethren, wins his personality. Self-possession is necessary for self-giving; in the measure in which a man gives himself he takes possession of himself, he gains his true self, his higher, spiritual, moral self, the acting, powerful self. He who denies himself in order to put in the place of himself goodness, Christ, God, becomes a self, creative like God, in every sphere.

But why invoke the example of Calvinism in the history of the old or the new world? There is a more striking example in the history of humanity. Christ is certainly the Being who denied self the most, and what Being has more completely conquered men and the world? "He humbled himself, becoming obedient unto death, even the death of the cross. Wherefore also God highly exalted him and gave him the name, which is above every name; that in the name of Jesus every knee should bow, of *things* in the heaven and *things* on the earth and *things* under the earth" (Phil. ii. 8-10).

Thus it is that the pretended ascetic pessimism of Calvin is, psychologically, the cause of his intense realism; I was about to say, of his *"vitalisme"*. And it is thus that the Reformation in general, and Calvinism in particular, breaking with Romanism and Pelagianism, to reascend to St. Paul, to the Christianity of the Gospel and of Christ, closed the Middle Ages and opened modern times.

THE REFORMATION AND NATURAL LAW

By August Lang

The world of to-day is filled with the conflict about the modern understanding of the Gospel. The decision in this conflict cannot be reached merely through Biblical studies and the investigation of primitive Christianity; there is need also of a thorough acquaintance with the development of the evangelical Church and of the evangelical spirit, as well as with their influence upon the formation of the modern world. In this respect, however, evangelical theology must be pronounced positively backward. The Protestant scholar, who is at home in Babylonia and Assyria, in primitive Christianity, and in the first three centuries, is in Germany no less than in England and America often without a moderately adequate survey of the general development of his own Church. How fragmentary is the exposition in the general Church histories, how narrow and one-sided in the histories of doctrine! How many fields have still received very little cultivation, for example, non-German Protestantism, the great movement of the "Enlightenment" and of Rationalism, Christian life, Protestantism and culture, and the like! In view of this defect, Ernst Tröltsch deserves gratitude on account of the very fact that he has even undertaken such a work as the comparatively full presentation of "Protestant Christianity and the Modern Church", which he offers in the *Kultur der Gegenwart*.[1] His merit becomes greater on account of the fertility of his thought, and especially on account of the real breadth of vision, that has led him not to confine himself one-sidedly to German evangel-

ical Christianity, but rather to attempt also an appreciation especially of Calvin and Calvinism, as well as of the smaller religious parties. Against such merits, it is true, must be set the entirely mistaken fundamental thesis of Tröltsch that Luther and the entire Reformation belong to the Middle Ages. This assertion is rightly contradicted by men of the most various opinions—I name only Böhmer, Loofs, Kattenbusch, Hunzinger.[2]

Little, however, has yet been accomplished towards the refutation of that proposition, which can be regarded only as a catchword, similar to the various clever half-truths that appear in Tröltsch's style. Students of recent history have long been agreed that the close of the seventeenth century, the conclusion of the religious wars, marks the beginning of a new epoch in Church history, the character of which, as Loofs[3] judiciously puts it, "stands in no less sharp contrast with the previous period of the Reformation and Counter-Reformation, than that former period with the Middle Ages, and the Middle Ages with the period of the ancient Church". The peculiarity of the new period is, expressed in one word, what is called, sometimes with pride, sometimes with contempt, "modernism", or "the modern spirit". But if the division is a real one, there arises the question, embarrassing to every evangelical Christian, How is the modern spirit, which, since the seventeenth century, in spite of the check that it received in the nineteenth, has been unfolding itself with ever-increasing vigor, related to the Gospel of the Reformation? How could the age of the Reformation with its conflicts of faith be followed so suddenly by an age whose views about historical criticism and natural science, about politics and social life, are in part directly opposed to the Reformation conception of the world? What forces of the Gospel had a part in the development of the new way of

thinking? What other, unevangelical, tendencies intruded
themselves, and therefore, because they arose, for example,
in Catholicism (and hence in false belief), or in an unbe-
lieving and therefore pernicious development of civilization,
must be combatted and eliminated? Or perhaps the Gospel
of the Reformation is no longer judge over modern progress? Perhaps it is rather the latter that shall decide how
much of the former is still tenable and fit for use?

To these questions, which, although they concern the
systematic theologian as much as the historian, are primarily
historical questions, I desire to make a slight contribution by
examining the relation between the Reformation and Natural
Law. For there can be no doubt that "natural law"—
primarily a school of jurisprudence, usually regarded as
beginning with Hugo Grotius and not till the nineteenth
century replaced by the historical school—was one of the
principal historical factors in the formation of the modern
spirit, a factor whose after-effects are still perceptible in
the most diverse spheres. For not only have the laws of
the evangelical Church itself been influenced thereby, both
in the collegial law of the eighteenth century and also,
though not so strongly, in the modern presbyterial-synodical
constitutions; but especially all the political reversals up to
the French Revolution are most intimately connected with
the natural-law theories. Rousseau's *Contrat social* is the
last great manifest of natural law. This itself is sufficient
to show that natural law was more than a mere political and
legal system; it became also the starting-point for "natural
theology", the broad religious basis of the religion of the
"Enlightenment".

How could this natural law spring up on the ground of
the Reformation, take such deep root and put forth such
wide-spreading branches? Of course, it is far from my

intention to include in the investigation the whole complicated phenomenon of natural law,[4] especially on its juristic and purely political side. My endeavor is only to study the beginnings of natural law on Protestant ground (which in many ways were interwoven with theological points of view), and even in this, I am not attempting anything like completeness, but desire merely, by means of certain chief representatives, to show from the origin of the natural law of the "Enlightenment", how far that movement was influenced whether positively or negatively by the ideas and motives of the Reformation.

I

First of all, there can be no doubt that natural law received at one point in the Reformation theology itself, if not a formal treatment, at least an organic insertion into the general body of its dogmatico-ethical system, namely, in Melanchthon. So early as in the first edition of his *Loci*,[5] that echo of the Gospel of Luther, he mentions the most usual forms (*communissimas formas*) of the *lex naturae* or of the *ius naturale,* as the theologians and jurists were accustomed to set them forth. These he finds in three principal divisions of natural law—concerning the worship of God, concerning the formation of the state and the inviolability of the individual persons guaranteed in the state, and concerning property—and to these he appends a brief notice about the *ius gentium* with its regulations concerning marriage, business, trade and the like. Biblical attestation of the *lex naturae* with its innate moral principles is according to Melanchthon contained in the apostolic dictum, Rom. ii. 15. Nevertheless, he is unwilling at first to concede to natural law any influence upon his system, for, now that human reason has been darkened by the Fall, though the moral faculty of man survives, yet it would be a great mistake to suppose that the material content of the innate moral law can be disengaged from the corruptions that have intruded themselves.[6] So in 1521; but the disposition of the Reformer becomes much more favorable in the editions of the *Loci* subsequent to 1535, after he had turned aside towards synergism. While he recognizes no relation between the *naturalis notitia* and the Gospel, both on account of the character of the Gospel as *mysterium* and on account of the grace that is contained in it, he now sets up the equation: *legem divinam notitias esse nobiscum nascentes sicut aliarum artium principia et demonstrationes.*[7] *Una est lex et natura nota omnibus gentibus et aetatibus.*[8] It is true that emphasis is still placed upon the fact that natural law, especially with regard to the first table, is much obscured, and above all lacks the power for the execution of its commands; yet there is no principial but merely an accidental opposition between the revealed and the natural law. The Decalogue has rather merely the function of elucidating and expounding the law of nature. Accordingly, a number of natural-law principles are again discussed; for example, in the regulations of the Mosaic law about the forbidden degrees in marriage, an element is discovered which, since it belongs to natural law, is therefore binding upon the whole of humanity. In proof is cited the assertion of Scripture that the Canaanites (though they were not subject to the revealed law) were exterminated on account of their incestuous disregard of the marriage laws[9]—an argument which appears afterwards in Hugo Grotius in almost the same form.

With the disquisitions in the *Loci* agrees the frequent mention of natural law in other writings of the Reformer. To select merely one class of instances, I may refer especially to the frequent *Declamationes de dignitate legum.*[10] God, so we hear in these passages, has infused a ray of His eternal wisdom and justice into the nature of men, and however weak that nature has become, God has left even to fallen men so much comprehension of His law that that law rules their outward behavior, indeed in a certain sense their will.[11] This law of nature is best expressed in the Decalogue.[12] Yet all other laws of the nations have issued from these *initia et principia* given by nature, and in spite of their diversity are, in accordance with the character of each nation, good and justifiable, in so far as they *ad illum radium lucis divinae transfusum in mentes hominum congruant, qui vocatur ius naturae, ex quo vult Deus exstrui leges.*[13] Among all the legal systems that have been formed upon the basis of this law of nature, the Roman law deserves the palm; *nusquam extat perfectior et illustrior imago iusticiae quam in his [Romanis] legibus.*[14] Such expressions, it is true, contain nothing about a primitive contract or the like, yet evidently something more is intended than the mere natural faculty for law-making; for natural law is called in to decide the most important legal questions—not merely, for example, in an academic discussion as to whether or no the assassination of Cæsar was justifiable,[15] but also in the extremely important question of practical politics: *an liceat vi resistere Caesari vim iniustam inferenti.* With regard to this question Melanchthon's finding on the basis of natural law in 1530 still runs: *etiam sententiae iniustae iudicio sit obediendum.*[16] Later, on the other hand, in 1537, he expresses quite the opposite opinion: *Evangelium non tollit magistratum et ius naturae;* hence *licita defensio contra inferentem iniustum bellum.*[17]

An example of the variableness of natural-law conceptions! The estimate placed upon the law of nature receives

further light, however, when it is observed that Melanchthon
regards the natural moral law in general as the most valuable product of human reason, indeed as the highest achieve-
ment of philosophical thought. Nevertheless, in the equation
between divine and natural law the point was given, where,
in the orthodox system which was being formed, secular
science, philosophy, law and the like could come into organic
connection with the purely theological principles derived
from the Gospel. Accordingly, Lutheran orthodoxy gives
to the dogmatics and ethics that are derived from Revelation a substructure of natural sciences and arts, which,
it is true, as a lower, secular sphere must allow its truth-
content to be controlled and corrected by the higher, spiritual
sphere. In this connection, even before Grotius, there appeared in Lutheran territory expositions of natural law by
Oldendorp, Hemming, Winkler, which derived their nourishment substantially from the material afforded by Melanchthon's ideas.[18]

Tröltsch, who in his treatise, *Vernunft und Offenbarung
bei Joh. Gerhard und Melanchthon,* first made these relations clear, is unwilling, it is true, to recognize in the whole
phenomenon a creative act of genius on the part of Melanchthon, yet he regards it as a necessary "compromise
between the autonomous reason that was so to speak incar-
nate in the productions of antiquity on the one side, and the
religious spirit of humanity on the other". It was a compromise such as within our circle of culture "cannot be avoided
by any theology", and one cannot refuse a certain admiration
to the grandeur of the plain and straightforward sequence
of thought.[19] We neither desire nor are we able to dispute
this estimate here, but it should at least be said even at this
point that the adjustment thus secured between secular and
theological science remained entirely unfruitful for the fu-

ture. When Lutheran orthodoxy fell to pieces, the new scientific impulses, in quite a special manner those for natural law, came from the West, from the science that had been developed in the Calvinistic camp. A Pufendorf and a Thomasius, as is well known, did not start from Melanchthon or the orthodoxy, but from Grotius and his spiritual kinsmen.

But if the natural-law theories could appeal to Melanchthon as their patron, is the same true for the other Reformers as well? For Luther, this is affirmed by the Paris theologian Eugène Ehrhardt, who has published a special investigation under the title, *"La notion du droit naturel chez Luther."*[20] It is a fact that Luther often speaks of natural law or the law of nature,[21] and Ehrhardt, investigating, though not with absolute completeness, the use of the conception in the writings of the Reformer, believes he has discovered that the conception in Luther also has had its roots in fundamental principles of his theology.[22] This judgment becomes already precarious, however, when it is observed that the notion of natural law, which, it is true, is at all times variable, threatens in the Reformer to lose itself almost altogether in the most diverse interpretations. At one time, he thinks of it as like a law of reason which "issuing from free reason overleaps all books".[23] At another time it is like "natural equity".[24] At another time it is identified out and out with the law of Christian love,[25] when it is said of the law of nature: "which also the Lord declares in Luke vi. 31 and Matt. vii. 12: 'whatsoever ye would that men should do to you, do ye even so to them'."[26] At another time, however, it is again only the law "which also heathen, Turks and Jews must keep", "kept among all heathen in common", which, although it forbids resistance to lawful authority, still is far from making a man a Christian.[27] In expressing himself about its relation to positive law, Luther now places it in the closest relation to Roman law,[28] now regards it as the source of all written law;[29] at another time he distinguishes the natural law as the general moral demands of conscience from Moses' law as the Jew's *Sachsenspiegel,* and yet says just afterwards that the natural laws are nowhere drawn up in such a fine and orderly manner as in Moses.[30] It is of course easy, in connection with Rom. i. 19ff. and ii. 15, to discover a ruling idea in these more or less divergent utterances, but if this idea had, as Ehrhardt supposes, exerted a pervasive and fundamental influence over Luther's ethical, social and political views, Luther would probably have taken occasion to express himself more fully and definitely about the meaning and character of natural law.

Luther's conception of the state, its duties and its relation to the Kingdom of God, is plainly two-fold. On the one side, as is well known, he freed the natural arrangements of life in family and state from the ban of ecclesiastical asceticism; the "civil law and sword" is a divine institution that has its office from God.[31] The state's historical and positive laws have their authority according to the will of God, and no natural law may nullify them. [32] By virtue of the universal priesthood, the civil authority has the right of reformation. It has the right to abolish all abuses that have established themselves in the "Christian body",[33] that is, in state and Church, in case the ecclesiastical authority does not itself make the first move. In correspondence with this positive estimate of the functions of the state, the direction of Church affairs under the new conditions came later, in the evangelical territories, with at least the permission of the Reformer, into the hands of the princes and magistrates.

But alongside of the positive view of the state, stands a

more negative one,[34] and to this indeed Luther has given more frequent expression in his writings. He starts here from a strict separation of the Kingdom of God and the kingdom of the world. There are "two divisions of Adam's children, of which one is in the Kingdom of God under Christ, the other, in the kingdom of the world under the magistrate".[35] The latter is by nature evil through and through. "We are serving here in an inn, where the devil is master, and the world mistress, and all kinds of evil desires are the household; and these all together—master, mistress, and household — are the Gospel's enemies and adversaries. If a man steals thy gold, defames thy honor, remember, in this house, that is the way things go."[36] The civil authority has the commission to check evil in some measure, lest things devour one another.[37] Therefore it is necessary for the bad and the weak; but the Christians, the living members of the body of Christ, have no need of it at bottom. The Gospel "places the outward life altogether in suffering, injustice, a cross, patience and contempt of temporal goods and temporal life"; but where there is "nothing but enduring, no punishment, no law, no sword is needed".[38] "The kingdom of the world is a kingdom of wrath and sternness", "a true forerunner of hell and of eternal death", hence also its "instrument" is a naked sword.[39]

When such a negative view is held of legal institutions, the Scripture cannot of course be the source of their authority. A theologian must teach simply belief in the Lord Christ, and not meddle with secular affairs.[40] "God has subjected and entrusted the civil government to the reason, because that government has to control not the soul's salvation nor eternal goods, but only bodily and temporal possessions."[41] Now Ehrhardt calls up that passage from the treatise, *Von weltlicher Obrigkeit*,[42] in which natural law is

identified with the reason, inasmuch as the reason is the
"law-fountain"[43] of all written law.   From this Ehrhardt
draws the conclusion that Luther saw in natural law or the
law of reason the particular source of all legal institutions.[44]
Luther had to fight against a double opposition, Ehrhardt
continues—against the Catholic theocracy, and against the
theocracy of the letter of Scripture, which the fanatics
sought to establish.   On both sides, he defended the independence of the state—both over against ecclesiastical tute-
lage, and also in recognition of the fact that state and Gospel
belonged to entirely separate spheres of life.   But this independence of the state and of society he secured by represent-
ing the foundation of their legal order to be natural law,
which, in accordance with its origin in the primitive revelation, he could in a certain sense designate also as divine law.
So the idea of natural law, Ehrhardt concludes, becomes a
necessary middle term in the sequence of Luther's thought.[45]

Nevertheless, Ehrhardt is himself obliged to admit that
in his practical instructions for dealing with individual legal
and social questions, the Reformer often did not at all abide
by his notion of natural law as Ehrhardt has conceived it;
not in the attitude of the state with respect to the persecution
of heretics, not with regard to property, marriage, interest
and usury—that is, not in any of the individual questions
that Ehrhardt discusses.   Ehrhardt concludes that Luther
indeed desired to make of his natural law a principle of
social reform, but as soon as he tried to bring this conception into practical use, he had to borrow now from the Old
and New Testaments, now from Roman law, from national
traditions, indeed even from canon law.[46]   It is possible to
go still further and to maintain that, aside from isolated
utterances, Luther's method of reasoning in the practical
concerns of national and social life is based throughout upon

the ethical principles of Christianity and the Bible. He desires to deal with the twelve articles of the peasants, in accordance with their proposal, on the basis of "clear, open, undeniable sayings of Scripture",[47] and so in all the disputed questions before him he treats the Christian-ethical principles derived from God's word as the decisive norm. His only quarrel with the fanatics is that they apply the letter of Scripture to the affairs of the state and of society as a rigid law, without regard for historical development, without recognition of the distinction between the Gospel and legal institutions. Natural law is for him, it is true, a familiar and recognized conception; but everywhere he permits it to play merely a secondary, incidental part. The best proof of this is afforded by the treatise, *Von weltlicher Obrigkeit,* in which Luther delivers himself at great length about the divine right of the civil authority, the limits of its power, the duties of a prince, with interpretation of the Bible texts in point; but takes notice of natural law only at the very end and in an extremely cursory manner.[48]

The above-mentioned antinomy in the thought of Luther about the state is to be judged similarly to the well-known antinomy in his view of the relation between law and Gospel. The *lex moralis* as a wage-agreement between God and man is, according to Luther, abolished for the regenerated man; indeed it is regarded by him as the pernicious, death-dealing, sin-increasing power. On the other hand, as moral obligation it is retained even by Luther, although his expressions are not always perfectly consistent. Indeed faith, Luther says, should procure for the law its true fulfilment.[49] To the former manner of regarding the law is closely related the negative view of the state and of legal institutions as a piece of this world, to which the Christian must with suffering accommodate himself. But accordingly this.

view is supplemented by the valuation of the state and of social relations as divine institutions; where, however, this positive valuation makes itself felt, there also the life of the state is subjected to judgment according to Christian-ethical standards, which are derived not from natural law but from the Scriptures. In this sense, Luther at any rate always taught the so-called *usus civilis* or *politicus* of the revealed law,[50] upon which, as well as upon the New Testament passages about its own divine establishment,[51] the civil power supports its authority for the punishment of evil-doers.[52]

It is true, after all has been said, that the relation between ethics and law, Scripture truth and state institutions, was, in spite of many valuable beginnings, never brought by Luther to a perfectly clear definition; but this lack of clearness should not be exploited for the benefit of natural-law theories. Luther's merit is that he assigned to the state and to law an independent, well-grounded special province. But when it comes to developing that special province, Luther simply uses the ethical principles of the Christian revelation; or else he refers, as, for example, in a fine passage of his *Auslegung des 101. Psalms,*[53] to "God's wonder-workers",[54] whom He raises up now and then and whose mind and heart He endows with the power of separating the "healthy law" from the "diseased law", who either "change the law or so master it, that the whole land thrives and blooms". Luther intimates here that the secular law, so far as it proves itself useful and excellent, is given to the peoples by wise rulers, "heroes of law", who create it by their genius, their endowment from above; accordingly, he would have provided the historical school of jurisprudence of the nineteenth century, long before its appearance, with a convincing justification.

Even less than Luther does Calvin show himself a friend

of natural law.   He holds too strongly the fundamental
Reformation conviction of the universal sinful corruption of
the natural man.   True, he admits in his *Commentary on
Romans*[55] that there is *naturalis quaedam legis intelligentia,
quae hoc bonum atque expetibile dictet, illud autem detes-
tandum,* that *quasdam iustitiae ac rectitudinis conceptiones,
quas Graeci* προλήψεις *vocant, hominum animis esse naturaliter ingenitas.*   These "seeds of righteousness" consist in
the fact that all peoples have a religion, punish adultery,
theft, murder, also lay stress upon fidelity and trust in trade
and intercourse.[56]   Likewise Calvin speaks in the introductory chapters of the *Institutio* of the natural knowledge of
God implanted in the human spirit, but at the same time he
pronounces this knowledge completely corrupted and stifled.
*Hinc rursus facile elicitur quantum ab hac confusa Dei noti-
tia differat, quae solis fidelium pectoribus instillatur pietas,
ex qua demum religio nascitur.*[57]   The natural knowledge of
God serves him only as a dark background to set off in all
the clearer light the knowledge which faith derives from
the revelation of God in Scripture.   Therefore Calvin attributes also to the *lex naturae* as moral standard, in spite of
that passage in the *Commentary on Romans,* only a subordinate value.   Of the three passages where the *Institutio*
mentions the *lex naturae,* it is said of it in the first two
merely that it affords only a very faint foretaste of what is
really well-pleasing to God,[58] and serves only the purpose of
preventing man from pleading before the judgment-seat of
God the excuse of ignorance.[59]   More important is the third
place where it is mentioned, in the last chapter of the *Institutio.*   Here the question under discussion is, Where does a
Christian state secure the ethico-religious standard for its
legislation?   Even Calvin rejects here the unqualified subor-
dination of the state's law to the law of Moses.[60]   He dis-

tinguishes in the revealed law between the ethical principles, which are summed up in the commandment of love to God and one's neighbor, and which for all peoples and all ages represent the eternal rule of righteousness, and the judicial, purely political regulations in the law of Moses (*iudiciorum forma, iudiciariae constitutiones*), which have merely the temporary importance for Israel of confirming love, the eternal law of God, as the foundation of legal enactments and procedure in the Jewish people. From the latter element of the revealed law, Calvin says the other peoples are free, but not from the former. For although laws may be very differently constituted in detail (*legis constitutio*) according to different conditions and circumstances, yet in their ethical tendency they must all exhibit a natural equity (*naturalis aequitas*), as it is demanded by the conscience of man. But since the revealed divine moral law is nothing else than *naturalis legis testimonium*, the best expression of that natural *aequitas,* it contains standard, goal, and limits for the legislation of the peoples and nations.[61] So the nations may indeed make their laws, Calvin says, without reference to Moses, as they think advantageous; only these laws must conform to the eternal fundamental law of love in God's commandment, so that though the form varies, the tendency shall remain the same.[62]

In this sequence of thought the incidental mention of natural law serves merely the purpose of strengthening the Calvinistic principle, that for the state and for law as well as for other things, despite all accidental differences, still the eternal norm is to be found in the rightly understood revelation of the divine will in Scripture. This is in harmony also with the method of the Geneva thinker; natural law plays no part in his judgment of legal and social conditions. It is true that in the collection of his *Consilia*[63] we meet at

one point a remark about the *équité naturelle,* at another
point, one about the *ius naturale,* which are identified both
times with the rule of Christ, "Whatsoever ye would that
men should do to you, do ye even so to them".[64]   Indeed,
in a difficulty, in order to strengthen his view that marriage
with a brother's widow is opposed to the Mosaic law and
therefore forbidden for Christians too, Calvin has recourse
also to the *commune ius gentium* (whereby, however, he
means nothing more than the *naturae honestas*), which
declares that even *ipse naturae sensus* rejects such marriages
as *foeditas.*[65]   Similarly he places the law of Moses and the
commune ius gentium side by side in still another difficulty
about the marriage laws.[66]   Further utterances of that kind,
however, have not come to my notice in my search in the
writings of Calvin for the point now under discussion.
Everywhere else—in the treatment of usury,[67] of the right
of the civil authority,[68] or of the duty of obedience even to
tyrannical rulers,[69] and the like—natural law is passed over
without a word.   Most convincing, however, is the above-
mentioned closing chapter of the *Institutio.* Here the Reformer, in his discussion about the civil authority and the
constitution of the state, about legislation and the position
of the subjects, offers in his way a "Politics".   But in so
doing, he never deserts the method that he employs throughout the whole of the *Institutio*—a method which is based
upon Scripture and the *analogia fidei,* or in this case also
upon the revealed moral law confirmed by the *naturalis
aequitas.* This method he does not sacrifice at a single point
for the benefit of a general ethical ratiocination, certainly
not for natural-law theories of any description.

We may conclude as follows.   All the Reformers recognized of course a natural moral faculty on the ground of
Rom. ii. 15.   But there are also indications that even they,

at that early time, held as a matter of learned tradition some kind of conception of a specific natural law. But in distinction from Melanchthon, Luther attributed to it only a subordinate importance, Calvin almost no importance at all. Finally, the views about the relation of politics, law and equity to the word of God and to Christian ethics were as yet little elucidated, though Calvin was the most positive in hoping to find the foundations for an evangelical Christian conception of the state in the ethical principles of the Bible—which principles, however, are not to be identified off-hand with the Mosaic law.

II

Under such circumstances, how did it happen that it was precisely decided Calvinists who, first among the men of evangelical faith, and so early as the sixteenth century, not merely developed natural law theoretically, but at the same time, as political publicists, made it a weapon in the conflicts of the time? Before we seek the explanation, however, we must briefly recall the fact itself. It is a question here primarily of the so-called "Monarchomachist" writers and jurists—not all of the Reformed faith, but some also Jesuit-Catholic (of the latter we shall speak further on)—who in the religious wars of the sixteenth century drew from the principle of the sovereignty of the people the revolutionary conclusion of a right of active resistance towards contract-breaking rulers. Among the Calvinists, besides the Reformer John Knox[70] should be mentioned particularly the Scotchman George Buchanan, the Frenchmen Hubert Languet (author, under the pseudonym Junius Brutus, of *Vindiciae contra tyrannos*), François Hotman (Francogallia), and Lambert Daneau, and the German Johannes Althusius. The last-named—born in 1557 in the territory of Wittgen-

stein, from 1586 to 1604 teacher of law in the Reformed
University at Herborn, from 1604 till he died syndic of the
city of Emden—gave to the tendencies of the Monarchomachi, in his *Politics,* appearing in 1603, the methodically
scholastic, and at the same time completest and most thor-
ough-going expression.   Otto Gierke, in his book, *Joh.
Althusius und die Entwicklung der naturrechtlichen Staats-
theorien* (Breslau, 1880), has the merit both of rescuing the
teachings of Althusius himself from the dust of oblivion and
of assigning them their place in the general historical development of law from the Middle Ages to the close of the
eighteenth century.   The significance of the questions there
under discussion becomes sufficiently evident from the single remark of Gierke[71] to the effect that a remarkable agreement just in a number of fundamental and distinctive ideas
renders it probable that the *Politics* of Althusius was read
and made use of by Rousseau for his *Contrat social.*

The following is a very rough sketch of the doctrine of
the Monarchomachi concerning the state. We shall disregard their more or less serious differences from each other,
and depend substantially upon the best-defined and most
completely developed doctrines of Althusius.   In the hands
of the Monarchomachi the state loses more and more of its
theocratic character.   True, government is regarded as having its power from God; but it has it indirectly, not directly.
Between it and God there stands a legal transaction of natural law.   For natural law postulates an original natural
condition when there was no state, when men lived in complete freedom and equality, indeed with community of goods.
The state did not take its rise until a double contract had
been freely concluded—the social contract and the governmental contract.   By the social contract—the model of
Rousseau's *Contrat social*—the community of men becomes

for the first time a legal body; as such it then, by the second
contract, delegates the government to the rulers. The
terms of the governmental contract could, it is true, be interpreted in two ways. It might be said, in the first place, as
was done for example by Bodinus, the famous French absolutistic teacher of law, of the end of the sixteenth century, that by this contract the sovereignty was once for all
fully and unconditionally transferred to the ruler. On the
other hand, the original right of the people might be
granted a permanent precedence over against the holder
of the state power. In adopting the latter interpretation
the Monarchomachi are a unit. For them the ruler is
merely the highest officer of the people, holding his office
by contract. His right to exert the power of the state is
independent, it is true, but at the same time conditional and
revocable. He has only a munus *sub conditione et stipula-
tione;* he is merely *mandatarius.*[72] Althusius supported the
limitation of the power of the ruler in his logical radicalism
with the proposition that the sovereignty, the majesty, is by
its definition an indivisible unity, which can belong only to
one of the two powers, the people or the ruler. But since the
prerogatives of sovereignty are as necessary to the nature
and existence of the social organism, *populus universus in
corpus unum symbioticum ex pluribus minoribus consocia-
tionibus consociatus,* as life is an inalienable possession of
every man,[73] therefore in the governmental contract those
prerogatives must have remained in possession of the people.
But beside them there can be no full, unlimited monarchical
sovereignty, but in the last analysis only a chief business-
manager. To this is added still a further deduction, which
again appears in an especially incisive form in Althusius.
As in the governmental contract, so also before that in the
social contract, the individual surrendered only so many

rights as were necessary for the accomplishment of the governmental ends. Therefore there remain to the individual under every form of government certain inalienable rights of man, which from the time of the Monarchomachi on played an ever more important part in various schools of natural law, until in the French Revolution they became, as everyone knows, the battle-cry that moved the peoples. But in order to make the rights of the people effective, there was recognized, even at the beginning and by the Monarchomachi themselves, the need of representatives, estates, or, as Althusius calls them after an expression used incidentally by Calvin,[74] ephors, who represent the people, assist the ruler especially in legislation, and restrain him, by force if necessary, when he exceeds his authority.

One needs only to recall these propositions in order to become conscious of their revolutionary character, but at the same time of the fruitful element in them that could enable them gradually to produce the modern constitutional forms of the state. But the motive which forced the Monarchomachi to these theories is quite plain. Their teaching is confined throughout to the political or legal sphere. Their postulation of the rights of man, their reduction of all social and national life to the individuals as the constitutive factors, involves no contradiction of dogma or revelation. But forced as they were into the fearful battle with the Counter-Reformation, the Reformed Monarchomachi sought merely an adequate justification of the right of resistance against the tyrannical government. Over against a state-power which without hesitation exhausted all means to suppress the Gospel, they too had recourse to the last resort, to civil war. But could that be justified? Now it is true that Calvin in a brief remark at the very end of his *Institutio*[75] had expressed himself to the effect that where

there are popular magistrates, estates, who like the ephors
in Sparta, or the tribunes of the people in Rome, are intended
to champion the rights of the people, these lower officials
are justified in offering resistance to the tyranny of the supreme head of the state.   But this remark, however gladly
it was exploited, seemed far from being sufficient; for Calvin
had placed at the head of his "Politics" as highest principle the duty of passive obedience, and had with all energy
declared this principle to be the clear intention of Scripture.   Therefore, the ground remained uncertain.   Although a way could be found to transcend the mere passive
resistance, simply by the abundant use of the Old Testament,
yet that was continually hindered by the great authority of
the Biblical scholar of Geneva.   Therefore, in order to arrive at a plain and firm position, recourse was taken to natural law.   Here was found what was needed; only on this
foundation could the Old Testament examples of resistance
against tyrannical power develop their full strength; it
was deemed certain that in connection with the natural-law
doctrine of the sovereignty of the people the law of the
Decalogue was at the same time finding its first perfect application to politics.

Yet almost at the same time at which the Monarchomachi,
in order to attain a firm legal foundation for resistance
against the anti-Reformation governments, sanctioned natural law, natural law forced itself forward also out of inter-
confessional conflicts into Reformed Protestantism—I mean,
through the book of the Anglican divine, Richard Hooker,
Of the Laws of Ecclesiastical Polity Eight Books.[76] This
work appeared in a number of parts consecutively—the first
four books in 1594, the very copious fifth book in 1597, the
last three books not till many years after the early death of
the author (1600), under the restoration of Charles II.

The genuineness of the last three books has been questioned, but without sufficient reason, since the same style and the same peculiar type of thinking prevail throughout. Hooker's work has received a sympathetic estimation from Leopold von Ranke in an essay entitled, *Zur Geschichte der politischen Theorien,*[77] principally from the point of view that it was written in defence of the ecclesiastical supremacy of the English king over against Rome. But this judgment gives an entirely incorrect picture of the origin and purpose of the *Ecclesiastical Laws.* The book did not grow out of the conflict with Rome, but out of the spiritual unrest into which the Anglican world under Elizabeth was thrown by the rising Puritanism. Hooker, a man of the second generation (born 1553), the pupil of Bishop Jewel of Salisbury, who was the first defender of the Anglican form of the Church as a happy mean between Catholicism and (Reformed) Protestantism, set himself the task, as he repeatedly reminds us and as the whole content of his book undeniably testifies, of justifying Anglicanism against the criticism of the Puritans and Presbyterians. In this defense it was a question chiefly of the Anglican ceremonies and the Anglican constitution. Accordingly, Hooker deals with the former in books iv and v, and with the latter in books vi-viii (concerning the presbyterial-episcopal constitution and the question of the supremacy) ; the discussions of the separate points are preceded by a philosophical substructure in the first three books: concerning the nature of laws, the authority of Scripture, and the idea of the Church.

The chief lever of the Puritan criticism was the radical Reformed doctrine of Scripture to the effect that absolutely everything must be based upon God's word, that the Scripture alone must decide about doctrine and life, about Church and state. Hooker seeks to oppose these claims first of all by limiting the authority of Scripture. It is true, he approves the rejection of tradition, and also approves the doctrine of the sufficiency of Scripture;[78] but he holds that human aids, the studies of learned men, also councils, are indispensable for the purpose of determining what Scripture teaches.[79] The Scripture is indeed the foundation of all things, but the authority of man is the key that unlocks its meaning. Nor did the opposing party, Hooker claims, have any better right to say that their teaching was the pure truth of God; they too depended in their interpretation of Scripture upon human opinion. Further, Hooker calls attention to the differing character of the contents of Scripture. Of course, everything that is necessary to salvation is revealed in it, but it does not by any means afford a clear precept of the divine will for every trifle of daily life.[80] Indeed, Hooker even ventures the assertion that there are matters which in themselves are indifferent from the ethico-religious point of view.[81] At any rate, not everything in Scripture is eternally obligatory; a great deal in the Bible depends upon the temporary circumstances and was prescribed for those circumstances alone. The Gospel is eternal, but not the rites and ceremonies.[82]

However reasonable many of these propositions may appear to us, Hooker was nevertheless fully conscious that, despite all such means, he could scarcely make it credible, under the dogmatic view of Scripture that then prevailed, that the Anglican ceremonies and a form of government with leanings towards Catholicism could stand before the forum of the Bible as well as could the claims of the Presbyterians. Therefore, he too had recourse to an additional aid, namely, to the law of reason and nature. Even in matters of revelation, we cannot do without the reason; only rational reflection can make us certain what God's word is.

The *testimonium spiritus sancti internum* is not sufficient to insure the authority of the Word; for the operations of the Spirit are by their nature obscure and must be tested by the reason before their genuineness can be settled. For a legislation such as is demanded by the situation of the English people, the mere precepts of the Bible are insufficient; we obtain something useful only from Scripture and reason together.[83] Man has within himself a law of reason, which in every individual case points out what is good, and that, too, with compelling force, so that it must be done.[84] This law of reason corresponds to the operations of nature, it is the law of nature.[85] In it the moral faculty of man finds expression, and it is therefore universally valid; to it the positive laws, which owe their origin to definite legislative acts, whether of a human state or of God, stand related as regulations that cannot be obligatory for ever.[86] Among the latter Hooker includes certain "supernatural duties".[87] The law of nature as the natural light of reason does not, it is true, embrace all necessary laws; above all, it cannot be kept without the continual help and coöperation of God;[88] but still it can be recognized without the assistance of Revelation. Standing upon this theologico-philosophical foundation, Hooker accordingly derives the origin of states purely by natural law from a primitive social contract, from which, it is true, he does not clearly distinguish the governmental contract.[89] With regard to the terms of the latter, however, he maintains, like the Monarchomachi, that the individual did not completely surrender his native right of self-government and that the legislative power still remains in substance in the hands of the community. A king who does not base his laws upon the general consent is a tyrant; the people, moreover, declares its consent through its representatives, the parliaments.[90] But since in Hooker's opinion the Church

is included among the political associations to which laws
are given in this way,[91] he finally ventures the conclusion:
king and parliament have the full right to issue such legal
regulations for the Anglican Church as seem to them suit-
able, and if these regulations turn out to be different from
those of other churches and peoples, this is to be explained
by the requirements of the time and of the nation.

So Hooker found in natural law the most valuable ally
for the defense of Anglicanism against the assaults of the
Puritans. On the other hand, the consequences of this point
of view could not fail to appear. True, the Anglican is
willing to subtract nothing from the absolute necessity of
the supernatural-mystical way of redemption through the
Son of God, and maintains further that the knowledge of
this way is to be obtained only in a supernatural manner.[92]
But if reason and nature alone make it possible to distinguish between the eternally valid elements in Revelation and
the perishable admixtures that were added to it in correspondence to temporary needs, it can readily be seen how
precarious the position has thereby become. This uncertain attitude even diminished Hooker's Protestant firmness
against Rome; the Papal Church also is for him a church
of Christ, although with many errors, which we pray God to
take from her.[93] Thus we have in Hooker, leaving out
of account his opposition to monarchical absolutism, all
the elements which later, in the English Revolution, brought
Anglicism to disaster—the tendency towards Catholicism,
the beginnings of the latitudinarianism of a Laud and of
other high-church representatives of the system of the
Stuarts. But we must not forget that all this grew not
without an inward necessity out of the conflict with Puritanism; for the latter was unable in its rigid Biblicism to adapt
itself to the needs of the ever more consciously active relig-

ious spirit of the English people. The uncompromising *jus divinum* called the *jus naturae* with a certain necessity into the arena.

The English latitudinarianism had on the Continent its more original and more vigorous parallel in Arminianism. But if in England latitudinarianism and natural-law ideas formed a union, so, as everyone knows, the Remonstrant Hugo Grotius became the scientific founder of the modern school of natural law. Nothing more natural than this coincidence! Arminianism was dogmatic criticism, criticism of the one central dogma of Calvinism; and that not on the ground of a strong new religious motive, but on the ground of the humanistic-scientific subjectivity of highly refined culture. This criticism could not stop with one dogma; it had to tone down the entire orthodox-Reformed view of life. To that end, Grotius could scarcely have chosen anything apparently less dangerous and at the same time in its almost unlimited possibilities more effective than his natural law. And yet, however disintegrating the effect of Grotius' *Three Books concerning the Law of War and Peace* upon the early Reformed view of the world and of life, it cannot be emphasized strongly enough that he too followed not only a noble purpose, but also an actual compulsion of circumstances. When in 1625 he published his work in Paris, Germany was bleeding in the Thirty Years' War, the Netherlands also had no certain peace with Spain, and in general frightful wars, both civil and foreign, had torn almost all countries of Europe for fifty years. At that time, in the midst of conflicts, this man raised his voice for law; his expressed purpose was to guide the fighters towards humanity by teaching them that even in war there are legal conditions which must be respected, and that war exists merely to prepare for peace. This purpose, however, appeared impossible of attainment merely by an appeal to the *ius divinum,* the divine commands of justice and peaceful-ness. For the wars of that time were waged just on account of Revelation and the differing interpretations of it; this method of urging peace would have meant simply becoming a partisan to the conflict. Only what belonged to all of humanity in common, only what existed before all parties and was recognized by all, in a word, only natural law seemed adapted to the need. Accordingly Grotius proposed for his book the second task of bringing the principles of natural law, in clear distinction from positive law, into sci-entific form.[94] The title of his book, it is true, called to mind primarily only the *ius gentium,* which had formerly been regarded rather as an appendix to natural law proper.[95] But by skilful arrangement, in accordance with which the first book is devoted to the legal admissibility of war, the second to its causes, and the third to the manner of con-ducting it and to the conclusion of peace, Grotius was able to weave into his exposition almost the entire private and internal law of the state.

The influence of the work is thus explained. For two hundred years after the appearance of the *De iure belli et pacis* of Grotius, almost the whole of jurisprudence was controlled by the natural-law theories. And yet the mighty influence of the book is, on the other hand, a riddle, for even to the eye of a juristic layman the scientific weaknesses of this classical work of jurisprudence become immediately ap-parent. In it the theological element is still predominant to an astonishing degree; the boundaries between law and ethics are scarcely determined at all. But especially, what a variable thing it is after all, this natural law! First of all, the doctrine of popular sovereignty and in general the revo-lutionary tendencies of the natural law of the Monarchomachi are considerably weakened, not without arbitrariness and contradiction. The people, so Grotius maintains, can in the governmental contract very well have surrendered the government to its ruler definitely and finally, just as every man can enter the state of private slavery.[96] Still more does a king who has conquered a people through force hold the right of government as his unconditional and even alienable property.[97] Against a state-power that comes into conflict with natural or divine law, nothing more than passive resistance is in any case justifiable;[98] even the *inferiores magistratus,* the ephors of Althusius, have no higher competence.[99] Here, however, Grotius immediately makes an exception; if the tyranny of the ruler endangers the existence of the state, which was established through the primitive contract, then forcible resistance is permitted as a right of necessity.[100] Especially full of contradiction is the relation of Grotius' natural law to the divine commands. On the one side, he emphasizes the fact that natural law itself, though proceeding from the inward principles of man, is from God;[101] indeed, he even ventures the assertion, "Natural law is so unchangeable that even God cannot change it".[102] In another passage, however, he seems to suggest that, as applied to certain materials, natural law has relaxed its strictness and adapted itself to the customs of the time.[103] Or take another example. Grotius declares as a matter of principle that "God has made the principles [of natural law] clearer through express laws";[104] so the revealed law would be the interpretation of the law of nature. But then again the divine law as something positive and arbitrary stands in contrast with the natural law;[105] indeed, it is repeatedly asserted that natural law and the Gospel (he means the ethical regulations of the Gospel) are by no means identical: it is possible for a thing to be strictly forbidden in the Gospel which is permitted by natural law—for example, polygamy.[106]   Something similar is true of slavery, which the natural law of Grotius permits without scruple.[107]

These examples are sufficient to illustrate the attenuation of the moral judgment, which, already bound up with the casuistic method of Grotius, becomes glaring through the contrast between natural law and Revelation.   Already there is beginning to appear that way of thinking to which reason and nature are everything, Scripture truth nothing but an unimportant historical expression of them.   Yet, however much fault may be found with the undertaking of the learned Remonstrant, that undertaking is primarily to be understood as arising from the necessity of constructing for the religious parties that were lacerating one another some sort of common basis of law and of peace.

After the book of Grotius, natural law began its triumphant course; it penetrated into almost all Protestant movements.   A Hobbes employed it in order to deduce with still greater incisiveness than Bodin the absolute right of absolutism; the Independents, Roger Williams and the poet Milton, by means of it supported their demands for civil and religious liberty.   We have no further interest in following up all the various forms assumed by the natural-law theory; only one classical representative of that theory, the philosopher John Locke, may finally be mentioned in passing. First, however, we may offer some general remarks in explanation of his doctrine, with regard to which the recent book of a French writer, Bastide, affords valuable information.[108]   In spite of Williams, Milton and other Independents, the great English Revolution stands by no means under the standard of natural law.   On the contrary, Weingarten (however antiquated his book on the English churches of the Revolution[109] may be in other respects) is correct in his fundamental thesis, when he sees in the Revolution the last mighty attempt to establish the theocratic principle, and at the same time the crisis of the theocracy.   The Puritan army of the saints fought against the absolutistic, catholicizing and latitudinarian tendencies for divine truth and divine regulation of the Church and state, under the conviction that it was thereby guaranteeing to the conscience the free worship of God.   But when the victory had been won, it became evident in the so-called Barebones Parliament of 1653 that the enthusiasts, in spite of all their faith in the Bible, lacked clear and positive ends and were incapable of establishing the new order of things.   Hence, after Cromwell too had passed away without having established a permanent reorganization, the restoration of the Stuarts became a necessity.   All the achievements of the great conflict would have been lost if the follies of Charles II and James II, and the threatening phantom of the reintroduction of Catholicism, had not for a moment extinguished the internal disputes between Whigs and Tories, and made possible the glorious Revolution of 1688 with the accession of William of Orange. Now, through the Bill of Rights, the aristocratic-constitutional form of government in England was definitely established, and at the same time the religious conditions most happily settled in such a way, that, while Anglicanism continued to be the state Church, the dissenting religious parties were granted a tolerance that was at first limited but later became increasingly extensive.

For the reorganization of England, however, natural law offered the more or less clearly recognized theoretical basis. Natural law appeared as though of its own accord, where the saints of the Barebones Parliament had waited in vain for illumination through the Spirit and through Revelation. The Bill of Rights was in fact such a governmental contract between ruler and subjects as natural law referred to primitive times, and John Locke, the son of a Puritan father as well as the adherent and friend of the latitudinarian, not to say skeptical elder Shaftesbury, justified the Revolution of 1688 with opinions which, although by no means already the common property of the English people, were destined in many respects to become such. Of Locke's writings, there come in question in the first place *The Fundamental Constitutions of Carolina,* and then the *Letter concerning Toleration* and *Two Treatises of Government,* which appeared in 1689 but were in part composed earlier.[110] Like all adherents of natural law, Locke here derives the origin of the state from the social and the governmental contracts. But in so doing he emphasizes, like the Monarchomachi before him, the innate rights of man, "liberty and property"; the primitive men in forming a union surrendered only so much of their rights as is necessary for the protection of life and property. The state is in essence only a legally constituted organization, whose compulsion does not extend further than is required by the above-mentioned tasks, or, as Locke also expresses it, by the common good. Within the state, Locke regards the churches as purely corporations, similar to the guilds or to the learned societies; to them, even including Catholics and Socinians or other free-religious societies, is due complete liberty to constitute their worship, form of government and dogmas as they think best. Only the atheists, whose unbelief endangers the trustworthiness of oaths, as well as all religious movements, which, by transcending the spiritual sphere, threaten the stability and peace of the state, must be suppressed by force. And the troublemakers, Locke thinks, are only the fanatically intolerant, domineering preachers and priests. Thus entered into the modern liberalism at its beginning the hatred of priests and theologians that is still in part characteristic of it.

But, in general, Locke's adjustment between state and
Church certainly cannot give complete satisfaction; the
purpose of the state as it is restricted by Locke is too narrow
and is contradicted by all history.   But still less can the
churches attain a full development on the basis of the mere
right of association—perhaps the Independents might do so,
but certainly not the Calvinists and least of all the Catholics.
In Locke's notion of the Church, too little place is given to
the institutional element, to the recognition that the Church
is primarily a public institution with divine authority and a
divine function.   A closer examination reveals the deeper
cause of these defects in Locke's philosophico-religious position.   As is well known, he is a moderate deist; that is, there
are for him two sources for the apprehension of truth, the
reason and Revelation.   By examining both (in the *Essay
concerning Human Understanding* and *The Reasonableness
of Christianity*), he thinks he has discovered that many
things in life prevent us from attaining certitude; we must
therefore often be satisfied with mere probability.[111]   Our
highest duty is therefore humility and love.   In this way
the demand for tolerance is based upon human weakness.
Therein, however, is revealed the Achilles heel of the entire
system.   The doctrine of universal reason, into which in the
age of Deism and of the "Enlightenment" the natural-law
theories developed more and more, did not fill its adherents
with absolute, impregnable certainty; therefore that doctrine
necessarily dissipated and destroyed more than it built up.
Even in a Locke, a keen eye can detect the seeds of those
destructive tendencies which later in France and the French
Revolution exhibited their fearful explosive power.   But
that ought never to cause us to forget that the natural-law
theories were for the England of the seventeenth century

again to a certain extent a necessity. As circumstances stood, those theories alone were able to conserve the tolerance which was the result of the great Revolution; they have therefore contributed their full share towards the happy reorganization of the civil and ecclesiastical constitution of England.

III

We pause here. We have seen how natural law, despite the rather unfavorable attitude of Calvin, pours itself like an irresistible stream into Reformed Protestantism, attains a decisive importance in its vital problems, becomes fundamental in the political constitutions produced by it, and in general enters as one of the most important factors into the spirit of the "Enlightenment" and of the entire modern period. We are now, I think, in a position to form a final judgment concerning natural law in its relation to the Reformation.

The first thing that I have to notice is that natural law is for the Reformation a part of tradition, more particularly an inheritance from the Catholicism of the Middle Ages. The former fact can be at once surmised, so soon as one observes how much as a matter of course, indeed how naïvely, Luther refers to natural law, and lets it appear in varying colors, without, however, conceding to it any fundamental importance. When Melanchthon assumed an attitude so much more favorable, and permitted the circle of ideas that is connected with natural law and the law of nature to become influential for his entire system, it is certain that his classical leanings contributed largely to that end; but they were not the only motive and not even the proximate occasion. It would be highly incorrect, we believe, to suppose that the ideas of natural law are a humanistic inheritance from the ancient world, which was half received by Melanchthon and then gradually emancipated itself.   It is true, the original source of natural law lies, as we all know, in antiquity.   Socrates, Plato and Aristotle already cherished the notion of a natural law in distinction from the arbitrary laws of men.   The form of these views which was most influential for the future was contained in the Stoic doctrine of the world-reason and the pantheizing law of nature: after Cicero, under Platonic influence, had so modified this doctrine that the natural laws inherent in human nature received at the same time a theonomic, divinely obligating character.[112]   But aside from the fact that such teachings never remained uncontradicted in antiquity, Melanchthon himself at his first mention of the natural laws in the *Loci* of 1521[113] takes his start from the *Theologi* and *Iurisconsulti,* that is, from the schoolmen and jurists of his time, and introduces only by comparison with these the utterances of Plato and Cicero.   However, no matter how Melanchthon's position be conceived, it is impossible that a theory of ancient philosophy should merely on Melanchthon's authority, while the other Reformers were at least indifferent, have revived just after the Reformation with such vigor and exerted such an enduring influence, if it had been dormant during the entire Middle Ages.

Just the opposite is in reality the case.   From the height of the Middle Ages, natural law was a recognized, though, it is true, also an extremely multiform doctrine of ecclesiastical and civil law, as well as of scholastic theology.   So early as the *Decretum Gratiani,* we read: *Ius naturale est commune omnium nationum, eo quod ubique instinctu naturae, non constitutione aliqua habetur, ut viri et feminae conjunctio, liberorum successio et educatio, communis omnium possessio et omnium una libertas, acquisitio eorum,*

quae coelo, terra marique capiuntur.[114]   Natural law is in
the *Decretum* at one time identified with the revealed law
(*quod in lege et evangelio continetur*), more particularly,
with the saying of Christ, "Whatsoever ye would that men
should do to you, do ye even so to them"; at another time
it is assigned an independent place between the divine and
the human law.   With increased weight, though also in
equally uncertain terms,[115] natural-law theories are set forth
by Thomas Aquinas.   In that part of his *Summa Theologiae*
which is devoted to the law, he treats successively the *lex
aeterna, lex naturalis* and *lex humana.*[116]   The law of nature
is *participatio legis aeternae in rationali creatura;*[117] hence
it is contained *primo in lege aeterna, secundario in naturali
judicatorio rationis humanae.*[118]   So it oscillates between
God's command and the law of reason.   From the Gospel
or the *lex nova,* the *lex indita naturalis* differs again through
its lack of the *donum superadditum gratiae.*[119]   Nevertheless, it is the foundation of all human laws, so that if a law
differs from the law of nature, it is no longer law but corruption of the law.[120]

Accordingly, Thomas in the treatise, *De regimine princi-
pum* refers also the origin of the state to the *ius naturale.*
A certain independence is thereby conceded to the state, in
that it is regarded no longer as a product of sin (which was
still the view of Bonaventura), but as the product of a
reasonable impulse in human nature; but at the same time in
that way it is delivered over to the control of Church and
Papacy as constituting the higher sphere of grace and faith.
But under the influence of Thomas, the theories of natural
law became more and more the common property of mediæval thought.   So early as the year 1300, they were seized
upon by the popular political writers, both parties using
them as a weapon in the great conflict between Church and

state—a fact for which Richard Scholz, in his instructive investigations concerning *Die Publizistik zur Zeit Philipps des Schönen,* has produced ample proofs.[121] But, in general, a glance into Gierke's *Althusius* or into the third volume of his *Deutsches Genossenschaftsrecht* is sufficient to show how in the second half of the Middle Ages almost all schools of jurisprudence were permeated by these views. All the individual doctrines that have their roots in natural law—the doctrines of the primitive contract and of the sovereignty of the people, and the principle of representation—existed long before the Reformation in more or less thoroughly-developed forms. The strict curialistic school, as well as the teachings of Marsilius of Padua, which contended for popular freedom and the national state; the adherents of the conciliar idea, as well as pre-Reformers like Wiclif; above all, finally, the humanistic school of jurisprudence, which flourished in Italy and then, in the century of the Reformation, in France, and which was cultivated by teachers and friends of Calvin like Alciati and François de Connan—all these had accustomed themselves to erect their conception of the state upon a natural-law foundation.

But such a unanimity of the jurists, theologians and humanists is by no means accidental, for it is a well-known fact that the entire mediæval Catholic system of faith and life is characterized by the separation between the natural and the supernatural—the two spheres are built up one on top of the other like two stories of a house. The natural is the lower sphere of the secular, the transitory; it too proceeds from the Creator's hand and is therefore not altogether sinful, but it must be held in check by a higher power. The supernatural, on the other hand, is the eternal, holy, divine, it is that which rules the lower sphere and thereby gives it an organic part in the Kingdom of God. For an

example we do not need to go further than the doctrine of
the primitive state of man. The *dona naturae* are supplemented by the *dona supernaturalia.* Similarly, the natural
light of reason, with its natural knowledge of God, is the
lower sphere in comparison with the supernatural revelation.
Saving faith in the latter can be attained only through the
sacramental-magic inpouring of the *illuminatio spiritus.* In
the same way, over against the *lex naturae,* which is merely
explained and elucidated by the *lex Mosis,* stands the *lex
Christi* or the *lex gratiae;* in connection with justification,
over against the *praeparatio ad gratiam* afforded by work-
righteousness, the *infusio gratiae;* in ethics, over against the
praecepta destined for all, the *consilia* of monasticism. The
relation of Church and state is exactly similar. The Church
is the divine establishment, the institute of salvation clothed
with supernatural authority. The state is a mere product
of man's natural social requirement, it proceeded from a
primitive contract by virtue of natural law. It must therefore necessarily subordinate itself to the Church if the ends
of the one *civitas Dei* are to be attained. Indeed, the Church,
being the guardian and interpreter of the natural as well as
of the divine law, can depose those rulers who in her opinion
are infringing the primitive contract, and can summon the
subjects to revolution. Such was the practice of the Curia,
at least when the political situation promised success in
making good the claim; such was the more or less decided
teaching of the theorists.

Natural law with all its political consequences must accordingly, so far as one may speak here at all of religious
and ecclesiastical determination, be regarded, despite its
beginnings in antiquity, as a thoroughly Catholic product.
The proof of this view is made still stronger by the fact that
simultaneously with the Reformed Monarchomachi, Cath-

olic Monarchomachi appeared, among whom the Jesuits like the Spaniard Juan Mariana[122] did not shrink even from directly instigating the assassination of tyrants. But since, on the other hand, the theories of natural law must be regarded as a central doctrine of the "Enlightenment", which has exerted an extensive influence upon the entire spirit of modern times in the political, ethico-religious and intellectual spheres, a prospect is opened up which is diametrically opposed to the historical construction of Tröltsch. Not the Reformation, which in its chief representatives met natural law, if not with out-and-out rejection, at least with cool indifference, is mediæval and Catholic; rather has modern liberalism been influenced in its development by a group of ideas which was an integral part of the mediæval-Catholic view of the world. At the same time we see by this example how little value is to be attributed to such general schemes and catch-words as the one proposed by Tröltsch; for the most part they merely help partisans to establish one-sided judgments.

Yet if natural law has its roots in mediæval Catholicism, that only brings us to the chief question, How could doctrines that were Catholic in spirit be appropriated in Reformation territory at such an early time and with so little hesitation? This might be understood in the case of Hooker, for his opposition to Puritanism brought him still nearer to Rome than the genius of his Church would in itself suggest, so that he cites Thomas Aquinas quite expressly as a witness for his theory.[123] But how is it to be comprehended in the other Protestants, particularly the most anti-Catholic of all, the decided Calvinists? For Melanchthon, no doubt academic tradition and the demands of education exercised the determining influence. He saw how the doctrines of natural law were set forth in all schools, even by those who were neutral in the conflict between the confessions, namely, by the humanists; he found those doctrines taught in the works of ancient writers, like Cicero whom he prized so highly; he heard also how Luther spoke of natural law without opposing it, and even on occasion made use of it in his way—all this no doubt combined to remove Melanchthon's objections, which later on, after he had become a synergist, did not weigh very heavily with him anyhow. The men of the Reformed faith may well have been influenced by certain other things. Perhaps even the variability of the ideas in question, and their remoteness from the central truths of religion which made them appear almost like a mere scientific hypothesis, may have helped to commend them. Furthermore, the theories of natural law could be regarded as a principle of individualism, which would naturally be congenial to the Calvinists. But this was for them certainly not the principal reason, for their individualism had such firm root in their particular type of religion, that it needed no further support. The point of view which was finally decisive for the men of the Reformed confession was rather, we believe, the one which was indicated in our investigation, when we spoke of the inward necessity, the compulsion of circumstances, under which the entrance of natural law in all four of the phases discussed in our second section took place. This inward necessity can be made clear by some such general survey as the following.

The Reformation at its very beginning found itself in the presence of problems and exigencies of indefinite range, first of all, conflicts of purely religious and theological character—doctrinal, liturgical, and constitutional conflicts. What an amount of spiritual strength was consumed even by these conflicts! How much there was which went wrong! What unrest, what losses these conflicts produced! And yet the problems which then appeared could be settled by reference to the fundamental religious principle of Protestantism, and on the whole were in fact settled in a truly Protestant way. Much more difficult and dangerous, however, was a second adjustment, which lay more on the periphery of religious truth and yet was no less necessary—namely the adjustment to the general ethical, political and social problems, to science and art. This adjustment, I say, was unavoidable, for if Protestantism, over against the mediæval-Catholic world, involves a new world-view, then there must necessarily be a Protestant science of politics, a Protestant philosophy and science, a Protestant art. This conclusion cannot be avoided through the assertion that the Reformation achieved just the liberation of the secular activities of the spirit from the control of the mediæval church and their restoration to their own immanent principles; for then that freedom would still have to be grounded more in detail, the boundary-lines would have to be drawn to show where the ethico-religious claims of the Gospel end and the rights of the free spiritual principle begin.

For such an adjustment, however, in the very nature of things, time is required; it cannot be accomplished by one man or by one generation. It was, indeed, a thankworthy undertaking, when Calvin in his *Institutio* did not entirely ignore politics, but the results were of such a kind that they did not give satisfaction even negatively, on the question of the obedience of subjects and the right of resistance, much less positively. But now the tasks and problems of culture came upon the young evangelical Church in a storm. Not so much upon the Lutherans. In their small states, where there was little cultural movement, they were able to settle down and persevere for two centuries on the basis of the theocratic idea as purified by the Reformation, and in analogy to the traditional forms of Church and state, as though all those questions of adjustment were really already settled by Melanchthon's organization of the universities and of the sciences. The Reformed, on the contrary, were obliged to fight the hardest battles for existence; then, after the final victory, they had new states to found both at home and in the wilderness; above all, they had to settle the question of tolerance between the different parties that had arisen in their own camp. But the tasks were met by the will to accomplish them. Calvin had inspired in his disciples that energy of piety, which abhors all half-way measures, which boldly endeavors to make all the affairs of life subject to Christ, the Head and Lord. In this congregation of the elect, the individualism of the Reformation reached its climax, and despite all subjection under God's command, there was developed a thirst for liberty, which tolerated nothing that came in its way except after free and earnest investigation. The chief merit of Calvinism is that it brought men's powers into the liveliest activity, undertook the most diversified tasks with vigorous confidence, and so with impatient energy carried humanity forward on its way. But the impulse to freedom can work itself out to the good of humanity only when it remains conscious of its limitations. But what was needed to keep it within bounds, the firm principles about the relation of the Reformation to the forces of culture—to the state, science and art—was lacking, and how could it be attained all at once in the midst of all the unrest of the time? Regarded in this way, we believe, the appearance of natural law becomes comprehensible. A doctrine of the state constructed on evangelical principles was not in existence. But such a doctrine was imperatively demanded by the need of the time. Men needed to have clearness about the relation of the ruler to the subjects, about the problem of Church and state, about the relation between different churches in the same country. No wonder that in the lack of a conception of the state revised in the light of fundamental evangelical ideas, men had recourse to the political theory taught in the traditional jurisprudence, without heeding the fact that that theory had an origin foreign to the Reformation and involved tendencies and consequences which would lead away from the Reformation. These tendencies, of course, became apparent later in slowly-developing after-effects, and then, especially after the spiritual enervation sustained in the protracted religious wars, they could not fail gradually to dissipate and destroy the Reformation's basis of faith.

Unless all indications are deceptive, the progress of events was similar in the case of other cultural questions. The desire for knowledge, the desire for activity, which was experienced by the individual after he had been liberated through the Reformation, plunged itself into all problems of the spiritual life of man, became absorbed in the traditional manner of their treatment, and was all too quickly satisfied with solutions which were not in agreement with the fundamental ethico-religious factors of the practical religious life of the Reformation. The reaction did not remain absent. The evangelical life of faith became shallower, instead of deepening itself and developing in all directions. Here, however, the opposition between the modern spirit and the Reformation would seem to receive an explanation which grows out of an organic understanding of the historical development. It is not true that the Gospel of the Reformation has been outstripped; but spiritual culture in general has infinitely advanced, while its permeation with ethico-religious principles in the spirit of the Reformation has not kept pace. If it is true that the religious spirit of the

Reformation in passing through Deism, the "Enlightenment" and Rationalism, was moving on a downward path, the reason for its deterioration was that the adjustment between the Reformation and culture was neither brought to a satisfactory conclusion nor even earnestly enough attempted. Nevertheless, we hope that such an adjustment may yet be accomplished; the better it succeeds, so much the more completely will the difficulties of our present religious situation disappear.

CALVIN AND COMMON GRACE

By Herman Bavinck

Christianity has from the beginning laid claim to be the one true religion. Already in the Old Testament the consciousness exists that Jehovah alone is Elohim and that the gods of the heathen are things of naught and vanity; and in the New Testament the Father of Jesus Christ is the only true God, whom the Son reveals and declares, and access to whom and communion with whom the Son alone can mediate. This conviction of the absoluteness of the Christian religion has entered so deeply into the consciousness of the Church that the whole history of Christian doctrine may be viewed as one great struggle for upholding it over against all sorts of opposition and denial. For the life of the Church as well as for every individual man the fundamental question is: What think ye of the Christ? This was the issue in the christological and anthropological controversies of the ancient Church, this the issue at the time of the Reformation and in the age of the "Enlightenment", and this is still the issue at the present day in the spiritual battles witnessed by ourselves. No progress can be marked in this respect: the question of the ages is still the question of our time,—Is Christ a teacher, a prophet, one of the many founders of religions; or is he the Only-begotten from the Father, and therefore the true and perfect revelation of God?

But if Christianity bears such an absolute character, this fact immediately gives rise to a most serious problem. The Christian religion is by no means the sole content of history; long before Christianity made its appearance there existed in

Greece and Rome a rich culture, a complete social organism, a powerful political system, a plurality of religions, an order of moral virtues and actions. And even now, underneath and side by side with the Christian religion a rich stream of natural life continues to flow. What, then, is the relation of Christianity to this wealth of natural life, which, originating in creation, has, under the law there imposed upon it, developed from age to age? What is the connection between nature and grace, creation and regeneration, culture and Christianity, earthly and heavenly vocation, the man and the Christian? Nor can it be said that this problem has now for the first time forced itself upon us, owing to the wide extension of our world-knowledge, the entrance of the heathen nations into our field of vision and the extraordinary progress made by civilization. In principle and essence it has been present through all the ages,—in the struggle between Israel and the nations, in the contest between the Kingdom of Heaven and the world-power, in the warfare between the foolishness of the cross and the wisdom of the world.

To define this relation, Scripture draws certain lines which it is not difficult to trace. It proceeds on the principle that for man God is the supreme good. Whatever material or ideal possessions the world may offer, all these taken together cannot outweigh or even be compared with this greatest of all treasures, communion with God; and hence, in case of conflict with this, they are to be unconditionally sacrificed. "Whom have I in heaven but thee? and there is none upon earth that I desire besides thee." This, however, does not hinder earthly possessions from retaining a relative value. Considered in themselves they are not sinful or unclean; so long as they do not interfere with man's pursuit of the kingdom of heaven, they are to be enjoyed with thanksgiving. Scripture avoids both extremes, no less that of asceticism on the one hand than that of libertinism on the other hand. The recognition of this as a principle appears most clearly in its teaching that all things, the entire world with all its treasures, including matter and the body, marriage and labor, are created and ordained of God; and that Christ, although, when He assumed a true and perfect human nature, He renounced all these things in obedience to God's command, yet through His resurrection took them all back as henceforth purified of all sin and consecrated through the Spirit. Creation, incarnation and resurrection are the fundamental facts of Christianity and at the same time the bulwarks against all error in life and doctrine.

It needs no pointing out, however, that in the first age Christians had to assume a preponderantly negative attitude towards the culture of their time. They were neither sufficiently numerous nor on the whole sufficiently influential in the world to permit of their taking an active, aggressive part in the affairs of state and society, of science and art. Besides this, all institutions and elements of culture were so intimately associated with idolatry and superstition that without offense to conscience it was impossible to take part in them. For the first Christians nothing was to be expected from the Graeco-Roman world but persecution and reproach. Consequently, nothing was left for them but to manifest their faith for the time being through the passive virtues of obedience and patience. Only gradually could the Church rise to the higher standpoint of trying all things and holding fast to that which is good, and adopt an eclectic procedure in its valuation and assimilation of the existing culture.

Often in the past, and again in our own time has the charge been brought against the Christian Church, that in applying this principle, it has falsified the original Gospel.

Harnack finds in the history of doctrine a progressive Hellenizing of original Christianity. Hatch regards the entire Christian cultus, particularly that of the sacraments, in the light of a degeneration from the primitive Gospel. To Sohm the very idea of ecclesiastical law appears contradictory to the essence of the Christian Church. But such assertions partake of gross exaggeration. If in all these respects nothing but degeneration is to be found, it will be easy to show that to a considerable degree the degeneration must have set in with the Apostles and even with the writers of the synoptic Gospels, as has been freely acknowledged by not a few writers of recent date. The Christian Church is indeed charged with having falsified the original Gospel, but those who bring the charge retain practically nothing of this Gospel or are at least unable to say in what this Gospel consisted. It is as a rule made out to have been a simple doctrine of morals with an ascetic tinge. Then the problem arises, how such a Gospel could ever have come into real contact with culture, especially to the extent of suffering corruption from culture. A conception is thus formed, both of the original Gospel and of the attitude of the Christian Church toward pagan culture, which is based wholly on fancy and is at war with all the facts.

For not only is the Gospel not ascetic, but even the Christian Church, at least in its first period, never adopted this standpoint. However much it might be on its guard against paganism, it never despised or condemned natural life as in itself sinful. Marriage and family life, secular calling and military estate, the swearing of the oath and the waging of war, government and state, science and art and philosophy,— all these were recognized from the beginning as divine institutions and as divine gifts. Hence theology early began to form relations with philosophy; the art of painting, as prac-

ticed in the catacombs, attached itself to the symbols and
figures of antiquity; architecture shaped the churches after
pagan models; music availed itself of the tunes which
Graeco-Roman art had produced. On every hand a strong
effort is perceptible to bring the new religion into touch with
all existing elements of culture.

It was possible for the first Christians to do this because
of their firm conviction that God is the Creator of heaven
and earth, who in times past has never left Himself without
witness to the heathen. Not only was there an original revelation, which, though in corrupted form, yet survived in tradition; it was also regarded as probable that certain philosophers had possessed a degree of acquaintance with the writings of the Jews. But in addition to this there existed in
paganism a continued revelation through nature and the reason, in heart and conscience,—an illumination of the Logos,
a speech from the wisdom of God through the hidden working of grace. *Anima naturaliter Christiana,* the man is
older than the philosopher and the poet, Tertullian ex-
claimed, thus formulating a truth which lived in the hearts
of all. No doubt among the heathen this wisdom has in
many respects become corrupted and falsified; they retain
only fragments of truth, not the one, entire, full truth. But
even such fragments are profitable and good. The three sisters, logic, physics and ethics, are like unto the three wise
men from the east, who came to worship in Jesus the perfect
wisdom. The good philosophical thoughts and ethical precepts found scattered through the pagan world receive in
Christ their unity and center. They stand for the desire
which in Christ finds its satisfaction; they represent the
question to which Christ gives the answer; they are the idea
of which Christ furnishes the reality. The pagan world, especially in its philosophy, is a pedagogy unto Christ; Aristotle,

like John the Baptist, is the forerunner of Christ. It be-
hooves the Christians to enrich their temple with the vessels
of the Egyptians and to adorn the crown of Christ, their
king, with the pearls brought up from the sea of paganism.

In saying this, however, we by no means wish to imply
that the attitude of the Church towards the world has at all
times and in every respect measured up to the Church's high
calling. *A priori* it is not to be expected that it should, inasmuch as every human development shows abnormal traits
and the life of every individual Christian is tainted with error and sin. When the Church of Rome maintains that
the Gospel has been preserved by her and unfolded in its
original purity, this claim is made possible only through as-
cribing infallibility to the Church. But by the very act of
subscribing to this dogma, Rome acknowledges that without
such a supernatural gift the development could not have been
kept pure. Further, by attributing this gift to the Pope
alone, Rome admits the possibility of error not only in the
ecclesia discens but also in the *ecclesia docens,* even where
the latter convenes in œcumenical council. And Rome's
confining the effect of this infallible guidance to papal deliverances *ex cathedra* involves the confession that the Roman Catholic system, as a whole, with all its teaching and
practice, enjoys no immunity from corruption. The dogma
of papal infallibility is not the ground or cause, but only one
of the many consequences and fruits of the system. And
this system itself has not grown up from one principle; it
has been developed in the course of the ages by the coöperation of numerous factors,—a development the end of which
has not yet been reached.

Although Roman Catholicism has been built up out of va-
ried, even heterogeneous elements, it nevertheless forms a
compact structure, a coherent view of the world and of life,

shaped in all its parts by a religious principle. This religion embraces in the first place a series of supernatural, inscrutable mysteries, chief among which are the Trinity and
the Incarnation. These truths have been entrusted to the
Church to be preserved, taught and defended. To discharge
these functions the Church, in the person of the Pope, as suc-
cessor of Peter, needs the gift of infallibility. The doctrines
are authoritatively imposed by the Church on all its members. The faith which accepts these mysteries has for its
specific object the Church-dogma; it does not penetrate
through the dogma to the things themselves of which the
dogma is the expression; it does not bring into communion
with God; it does not represent a religious but an intellectual
act, the *assensus,* the *fides historica.* Faith is not a saving
power in itself, but is merely preparatory to salvation; nevertheless, it is something meritorious because and in so far as
it is an act of submission to ecclesiastical authority.

The Church, however, is not merely the possessor of supernatural truth; in the second place it is also the depository
and dispenser of supernatural grace. As the Church doctrine is infinitely exalted above all human knowledge and
science, so the grace kept and distributed by the Church far
transcends nature. It is true this grace is, among other
things, *gratia medicinalis,* but this is an accidental and adven-
titious quality. Before all else it is *gratia elevans,* something added to and elevating above nature. As such it entered into the image of God given to Adam before the Fall,
and as such it again appears in the restoration to that original state. In view of its adding to exalted nature a supernatural element, it is conceived as something material, en-
closed in the sacrament, and as such dispensed by the priest.
Thus every man becomes, for his knowledge of supernatural
truth and for his reception of supernatural grace, that is, for

his heavenly salvation, absolutely dependent on the Church, the priest and the sacrament. *Extra ecclesiam nulla salus.*

But even this grace, which, to be sure, remains subject to loss and recovery until the end of life, does not assure man of attainment to fellowship with God. All it does is to impart to him the power whereby, if so choosing, he may merit, through good works, supernatural salvation, the *visio Dei.* Since work and reward must be proportionate, the good works which merit supernatural salvation must all be of a specific kind and therefore need to be defined and pre-scribed by the Church. The Church, besides being the depos-itory of truth and the dispenser of grace, is in the third place also law-giver and judge. The satisfactions which the Church imposes are according to the character of the sins committed. The rapidity or slowness with which a man at-tains to perfection, how much time he shall spend in purga-tory, how rich a crown he will receive in heaven,—all this depends on the number of extraordinary, supernatural works which he performs. Thus a spiritual hierarchy is created. There exists a hierarchy in the world of angels, and a hier-archy in the ecclesiastical organization, but there is a hier-archy also among the saints on earth and the blessed in heaven. In an ascending scale the saints, divided into or-ders and ranks, draw near to God, and in proportion as they become partakers of the divine nature are admitted to the worship and adoration of the deity.

In view of what has been said it is evident that truth, grace and good works bear, according to Rome, a specific, supernatural character. And because the Church is the God-appointed depository of all these blessings, the relation between grace and nature coincides with that between the Church and the world. The world, the state, natural life, marriage and culture are not sinful in themselves; only

they are of a lower order, of a secular nature, and, unless
consecrated by the Church, easily become an occasion for
sinning.   This determines the function of the Church with
reference to the world.   It is the calling of the Church to
declare unto the world that in itself the world is profane,
but that nevertheless, through the consecration of the
Church, it may become a vehicle of grace.   Renunciation of
the world and sovereignty over the world with Rome spring
from one and the same principle.   The celibacy of the
priesthood and the elevation of marriage to the rank of a
sacrament are branches of the same stem.   The whole hie-
rarchical idea is built on the sharp distinction between
nature and grace.   Where the supernatural character of the
Church and the efficacy of the sacrament and the priestly
office are concerned, this system brooks neither compromise
nor concession; but aside from this, it leaves room for a
great variety of steps and grades, of ranks and orders in
holiness and salvation.   The Church contains members that
belong to it in body only, and members belonging to it with
a part of their powers or with all their powers; it makes
concessions to the weak and worships the saints; a lax morality and a severe asceticism, an active and a contemplative
mode of life, rationalism and supernaturalism, unbelief and
superstition equally find a place within its walls.

Towards the close of the Middle Ages this system had
become corrupt in almost every respect.   In the sphere of
truth it had degenerated into nominalistic scholasticism;
in the sphere of grace into demoralizing traffic in indul-
gences; in the sphere of good works into the immoral life
of priests and monks.   Numerous efforts were made to rem-
edy these faults and to reform the Church from within.
But the Reformation of the sixteenth century differed from
all these attempts in that it not merely opposed the Roman

system in its excrescences but attacked it internally in the foundations on which it rested and in the principles out of which it had been developed. The Reformation rejected the entire system, and substituted for it a totally different conception of *veritas, gratia,* and *bona opera.* It was led to this new conception not through scientific reflections or philosophical speculations, but through earnest, heartfelt concern for the salvation of souls and the glory of God. The Reformation was a religious and ethical movement through and through. It was born out of the distress of Luther's soul.

When a helpless man, out of distress of soul, looks to the Gospel for deliverance, the Gospel will appear to him in a totally new light. All at once it ceases to be a set of supernatural, inscrutable mysteries to be received on ecclesiastical authority, with renunciation of the claims of reason, by meritorious assent. It straightway becomes a new Gospel, good tidings of salvation, revelation of God's gracious and efficacious will to save the sinner, something that itself imparts the forgiveness of sin and eternal life and therefore is embraced by lost man with joy, that lifts him above all sin and above the entire world to the high hope of a heavenly salvation. Hence it is no longer possible to speak of the Gospel with Rome as consisting of supernatural mysteries to be responded to by man in voluntary assent. The Gospel is not law, neither as regards the intellect nor as regards the will; it is in essence a promise, not a demand but a gift, a free gift of the divine favor; nay, in it the divine will itself through the Gospel addresses itself to the will, the heart, the innermost essence of man, and there produces the faith which rests in this divine will and builds on it and puts its trust in it through all perils, even in the hour of death.

By reason of this new conception of the Gospel, which in

principle was but a return to the old, Scriptural conception, it could not be otherwise than that faith also should obtain a totally new significance. If the Gospel is not a *veritas* to which the *gratia* is added later on, but is itself *gratia* in its very origin, the revelation of God's gracious will, and at the same time the instrument for making this will effective in the heart of man, then faith can no longer remain a purely intellectual assent. It must become the confidence in the gracious will of God, produced by God himself in man's heart; a surrender of the whole man to the divine grace; a resting in the divine promise; a receiving of a part in God's favor; admission into communion with him; an absolute assurance of salvation. With Rome, faith is but one of the seven preparations, which lead on to the reception of the *gratia infusa* in baptism, and hence bears no religious character; it is naught but a *fides historica,* which stands in need of the supplement of love in order to become complete and sufficient unto salvation. To the Reformers faith from its very first inception is religious in nature. As *fides justificans salvifica* it differs not in degree but in principle and essence from the *fides historica.* It has for its object God himself, God in Christ, and Christ in the garb of Holy Scripture, *Christum Evangelio suo vestitum;*[1] it is in its essence *firma certaque cognitio,*[2] *cordis magis quam cerebri, et affectus magis quam intelligentiae,*[3] to be defined rather as *certitudo* than as *apprehensio.*[4] Faith places beyond doubt *Dei bonitatem perspicue nobis propositam* and enables us to stand before God's presence *tranquillis animis.*[5] Thus it is seen to be the principle of the true fear of God, for *primus ad pietatem gradus [est] agnoscere Deum esse nobis Patrem, ut nos tueatur, gubernet ac foveat, donec colligat in aeternam haereditatem regni sui.*[6]

To all the Reformers, therefore, there lies behind the

Gospel and behind faith the gracious and efficacious will of God. Nay, more than this, in the Gospel and in faith the divine will is revealed and realized. This is the reason why the religious conception of the Gospel and of faith is with the Reformers most intimately connected with their belief in predestination. We in our time no longer understand this. We have lost the habit of religious thinking, because we feel less for ourselves the personal need of communion with God, and so feel less of the impulse to interpret the world from a religious point of view. Instead, our age has learned to think in the terms of natural science; it has substituted for the divine will the omnipotent law and the omnipotent force of nature, and thus thrown itself into the arms of determinism. It claims to have long since outgrown the belief in predestination. And undoubtedly there exists between these two, however often they may be mixed and confounded, a difference of principle. Determinism is in principle rationalistic; it cherishes the delusion of being able to explain everything from the reign of natural law, holding that all existing things are rational since reason perceives that they could not be otherwise than they actually are. Predestination, on the other hand, is a thoroughly religious conception. While able to recognize natural law and to reckon with the forces of nature, it refuses to rest in this or to consider natural necessity the first and last word of history.

He who has learned to regard communion with God as the supreme good for his own person, must feel bound to work his way back, behind the world and all its phenomena, until he arrives at the will of God. He must seek an explanation of the origin, development and goal of the world-process, which shall be in accordance with that will and hence bear an ethico-religious character. This is the reason that, so soon as a religious movement appears in history, the problem of predestination comes to the front. In a way, this is true of all religions, but it applies with special pertinence to the history of the Christian religion. In proportion as the Christian religion is distinctly experienced and appreciated in its essence as true, full religion, as pure grace, it will also be felt to include, and that directly, without the need of dialectic deduction, the confession of predestination. Hence all the Reformers were agreed on this point. It is true that with Luther it was afterwards, for practical reasons, relegated to the background, but even he never recanted or denied it. It was in the controversy about the *servum* or *liberum arbitrium* that the Reformation and humanism parted ways once for all. Erasmus was and continued to be a Romanist in spite of his ridicule of the monks. As late as 1537 Luther wrote to Capito: *nullum agnosco meum justum librum nisi forte de libero arbitrio et catechismum.* The doctrine of predestination, therefore, is no discovery of Calvin; before Calvin it had been professed by Luther and Zwingli. It sprang spontaneously from the religious experience of the Reformers. If Calvin introduced any modification, it consists in this, that he freed the doctrine from the semblance of harshness and arbitrariness and imparted to it a more purely ethico-religious character.

For, all affinity and agreement notwithstanding, Calvin differed from Luther and Zwingli. He shared neither the emotional nature of the one nor the humanistic inclinations of the other. When, in a manner as yet but very imperfectly known to us, he was converted, this experience was immediately accompanied by such a clear, deep and harmonious insight into Christian truth as to render any subsequent modification unnecessary. The first edition of the *Institutio*

which appeared in March, 1536, was expanded and increased
in the later issues, but it never changed, and the task which,
in his view, the Reformation had to accomplish, remained
from beginning to end his own goal in life. While Luther's
faith was almost entirely absorbed in the *fides justificans,*
and while Zwingli one-sidedly defined faith as *fides vivifi-
cans* or *regenerans,* Calvin widened the conception to that
of *fides salvificans,*—a faith which renews the entire man
in his being and consciousness, in soul and body, in all his
relations and activities, and hence a faith which exercises its
sanctifying influence in the entire range of life, upon Church
and school, upon society and state, upon science and art.
But in order to be able to perform this comprehensive
task,—in order to be truly, always and everywhere a *fides
salvificans,* it was necessary for faith first of all to be fully
assured of itself, and no longer to be tossed to and fro by
every wind of doubt. This explains why, more than with
Zwingli and Luther, faith is with Calvin unshaken conviction, firm assurance.

But if faith is to be such an unshaken assurance it must
rest on a truth removed from all possibility of doubt; it must
attest itself as real by its own witness and power in the
heart of man. A house that will defy the tempest cannot
be built on the sand. Behind faith, therefore, must lie the
truth, the will and act of God. In other words, faith is the
fruit or effect of election; it is the experience of an act of
God. Always and everywhere Calvin recurs to this will of
God. The world with its infinite multitude of phenomena,
with its diversities and inequalities, its disharmonies and
contrasts, is not to be explained from the will of the creature nor from the worth or unworthiness of man. It is
true, inequality and contrast appear most pronounced in
the allotment of man's eternal destiny. They are, however,

by no means confined to this, but show themselves in every
sphere, in the different places of habitation appointed for
men, in the different gifts and powers conferred upon them
in body and soul, in the difference between health and sick-
ness, wealth and poverty, prosperity and adversity, joy and
sorrow, in the varying ranks and vocations, and, last of all,
in the fact itself that men are men and not animals. Let the
opponents of the doctrine of election, therefore, answer the
question, *cur homines sint magis quam boves aut asini, cur,
quum in Dei manu esset canes ipsos fingere, ad imaginem
suam formavit.*[7] The more we reflect upon the world the
more we are forced to fall back upon the hidden will of God
and find in it the ultimate ground for both the existence of
the world and its being what it is. All the standards of
goodness and justice and righteous recompense and retribu-
tion for evil which we are accustomed to apply, prove wholly
inadequate to measure the world. The will of God is, and
from the nature of the case must be, the deepest cause of the
entire world and of all the *varietas* and *diversitas* found in
it. There is no more ultimate ground for this than the
absconditum Dei consilium.[8] The unfathomable mystery of
the world compels the intellect and the heart, theology and
philosophy alike to fall back upon the will of God and seek
rest in it.

It frequently happens, however, that theology and philosophy are not contented with this. They then endeavor,
after the manner of Plato and Hegel, to offer a rational
explanation of the world. Or, while falling back upon the
will of God, they make out of this will a βυθὸς ἄγνωστος,
as is done by Gnosticism, or a blind, irrational and unhappy
will, as is done by Schopenhauer, or an unconscious and
unknowable power, as is done by von Hartmann and Spen-
cer. By his Christian faith Calvin was kept from these

different forms of pantheism. It is true, Calvin upholds with the utmost energy the sovereignty of the divine will over and against all human reasoning. Predestination belongs to the *divinae sapientiae adyta* which man may not enter and in regard to which his curiosity must remain unsatisfied; for they form a labyrinth from which no one can find the exit. Man may not even investigate with impunity the things God meant to keep secret. God wants us to adore, not to comprehend, the majesty of His wisdom.[9] Nevertheless God is not *exlex*. He sufficiently vindicates His justice by convicting of guilt those who blaspheme Him in their own consciences. His will is not absolute power, but *ab omni vitio pura, summa perfectionis regula, etiam legum omnium lex*.[10] And the Gospel reveals to us what is the content, the heart and the kernel, as it were, of this will.

For since the Fall nature no longer reveals to us God's paternal favor. On every side it proclaims the divine curse which cannot but fill our guilty souls with despair. *Ex mundi conspectu Patrem colligere non licet*.[11] Aside from the special revelation in Christ, man has no true knowledge of heavenly things. He is ignorant and blind as respects God, His fatherhood and His law as the rule of life. Especially of the *divinae erga nos benevolentiae certitudo* he is without the faintest consciousness, for human reason neither can attain nor strives to attain to this truth, and therefore fails to understand *quis sit verus Deus, qualisve erga nos esse velit*.[12] And herein precisely consists the essence of God's special revelation in Christ, and this is the central content of the Gospel: God here makes Himself known to us not merely as our *Creator*, but as our *Redemptor*.[13] He does not here tell us what He is, to enable us to indulge in speculation, but causes us to know *qualis sit et quid ejus naturae conveniat*.[14] The *gratuita promissio*, the *promissio misericordiae,* the *liberalis legatio qua sibi Deus mundum reconciliat,*—these constitute the essence of the Gospel and the firm foundation of faith.[15] He is a true believer, who, firmly convinced that God is to him a gracious and loving Father, expects everything from His loving-kindness. *Fidelis non est, nisi qui suae salutis securitati innixus, diabolo et morti confidenter insultet.*[16]

This concentration of the Gospel in the promise of divine mercy not only provided Calvin with a firm footing in the midst of the shifting opinions of his time, but also widened his outlook and enlarged his sympathies, so that, while resolutely standing by his own confession, he nevertheless perpetually mediated the things that made for unity and peace among all the sons of the Reformation. To be sure, the conception usually formed of Calvin differs widely from this. His image as commonly portrayed has for its only features those of cruel severity and despotic intolerance. But such a conception does grave injustice to the Genevan Reformer. Unfortunately, he must be held responsible for the death of Servetus, although in this respect he only stands on a level with the other Reformers, none of whom had entirely outgrown all the errors of their age. But the Calvin who gave his approval to the execution of Servetus is not the only Calvin we know. There is also a far different Calvin, one who was united with his friends in the bonds of the most tender affection, whose heart went out in sympathy to all his suffering and struggling brethren in the faith, one who identified himself with their lot, and supplied them with comfort and courage and cheer in their severest afflictions. We know of a Calvin who without intermission labored most earnestly for the union of the divided Protestants, who sought God in His Word alone and was unwilling to bind himself even to such terms as "Trinity" and "Person", who refused to subscribe to the Nicene and Athanasian creeds, who discountenanced every disruption of the Church on the ground of minor impurities of doctrine, who favored fraternal tolerance in all questions touching the form of worship. There was a Calvin, who, notwithstanding all differences of opinion, cherished the highest regard for Luther, Melanchthon and Zwingli, and recognized them as servants of God; who himself subscribed to the Augsburg Confession and, reserving the right of private interpretation, acknowledged it as the expression of his own faith; who recommended the *Loci* of Melanchthon, although differing from him on the points of free-will and predestination; who refused to confine the invisible Church to any single confession, but recognized its presence wherever God works by His Word and Spirit in the hearts of men.

Still another injustice, however, must be laid to the charge of the average conception of Calvin. Men sometimes speak as if Calvin knew of nothing else to preach but the decree of predestination with its two parts of election and reprobation. The truth is that no preacher of the Gospel has ever surpassed Calvin in the free, generous proclamation of the grace and love of God. He was so far from putting predestination to the front, that in the *Institutio* the subject does not receive treatment until the third book, after the completion of the discussion of the life of faith. It is entirely wanting in the *Confessio* of 1536 and is only mentioned in passing, in connection with the Church, in the *Catechismus Genevensis* of 1545. And as regards reprobation, before accusing Calvin, the charge should be laid against Scripture, against the reality of life, against the testimony of conscience; for all these bear witness that there is sin in the world, and that this awful reality, this *decretum horribile,* cannot have its deepest ground in the free will of

man.   And there are still other features in Calvin's doctrine
of reprobation to which attention should be called.   There
is in the first place the fact that he says so little about the
working of reprobation.   The *Institutio* is a work characterized by great sobriety, wholly free from scholastic ab-
struseness; it everywhere treats the doctrines of faith in the
closest connection with the practice of religion.   This is
especially true of eschatology.   As is well known, Calvin
never could bring himself to write a commentary on the
Apocalypse, and in his *Institutio* he devotes to "the last
things" only a few paragraphs.   He avoids all *spinosae
quaestiones* with reference to the state of glory, and interprets the descriptions given by Scripture of the state of the
lost as symbolical: darkness, weeping, gnashing of teeth,
unquenchable fire, the worm that dies not,—all these serve to
impress upon us *quam sit calamitosum alienari ab omni Dei
societate,* and *majestatem Dei ita sentire tibi adversam ut
effugere nequeas quin ab ipsa urgearis.*[17]   The punishment
of hell consists in exclusion from fellowship with God and
admits of degrees.[18]   In connection with Paul's words, that
at last God will be all in all, it is not forbidden to think of
the devil and the godless, since in their subjection also the
glory of God shall be revealed.[19]

But of even greater significance is it that with Calvin
reprobation does not mean the withholding of all grace.
Although man through sin has been rendered blind to all
the spiritual realities of the kingdom of God, so that a
special revelation of God's fatherly love in Christ and a
specialis illuminatio by the Holy Spirit in the hearts of the
sinners here become necessary,[20] nevertheless there exists
alongside of these a *generalis gratia* which dispenses to all
men various gifts.[21]   If God had not spared man, his fall
would have involved the whole of nature in ruin.[22]   As it

was, God immediately after the Fall interposed, in order by His common grace to curb sin and to uphold in being the *universitas rerum*.[23] For after all sin is rather an *adventitia qualitas* than a *substantialis proprietas,* and for this reason God is *operis sui corruptioni magis infensus quam operi suo*.[24] Although for man's sake the whole of nature is subject to vanity, nevertheless nature is upheld by the hope which God implanted in its heart.[25] There is no part of the world in which some spark of the divine glory does not glimmer.[26] Though it be a metaphorical mode of expression, since God should not be confounded with nature, it may be affirmed in a truly religious sense that nature is God.[27] Heaven and earth with their innumerable wonders are a magnificent display of the divine wisdom.[28]

Especially the human race is still a clear mirror of the operation of God, an exhibition of His manifold gifts.[29] In every man there is still a seed of religion, a consciousness of God, wholly ineradicable, convincing all of the heavenly grace on which their life depends, and leading even the heathen to name God the Father of mankind.[30] The supernatural gifts have been lost, and the natural gifts have become corrupted, so that man by nature no longer knows who and what God seeks to be to him. Still these latter gifts have not been withdrawn entirely from man.[31] Reason and judgment and will, however corrupt, yet, in so far as they belong to man's nature, have not been wholly lost. The fact that men are found either wholly or in part deprived of reason, proves that the title to these gifts is not self-evident and that they are not distributed to men on the basis of merit. None the less, the grace of God imparts them to us.[32] The reason whereby man distinguishes between truth and error, good and evil, and forms conceptions and judgments, and also the will which is inseparable from human nature as

the faculty whereby man strives after what he deems good
for himself,—these raise him above the animals. Consequently it is contrary to Scripture as well as to experience
to attribute to man such a perpetual blindness as would
render him unable to form any true conception.[33]   On the
contrary, there is light still shining in the darkness, men still
retain a degree of love for the truth, some sparks of the
truth have still been preserved.[34]   Men carry in themselves
the principles of the laws which are to govern them individ-
ually and in their association with one another.   They agree
in regard to the fundamentals of justice and equity, and
everywhere exhibit an aptness and liking for social order.[34a]
Sometimes a remarkable sagacity is given to men whereby
they are not only able to learn certain things, but also to
make important inventions and discoveries, and to put these
to practical use in life.[35]   Owing to all this, not only is
an orderly civil society made possible among men, but arts
and sciences develop, which are not to be despised.   For
these should be considered gifts of the Holy Spirit.   It is
true the Holy Spirit as a spirit of sanctification dwells in
believers only, but as a spirit of life, of wisdom and of
power He works also in those who do not believe.   No
Christian, therefore, should despise these gifts; on the contrary, he should honor art and science, music and philosophy
and various other products of the human mind as *praestant-
issima Spiritus dona,* and make the most of them for his own
personal use.[36]   Accordingly, in the moral sphere also distinctions are to be recognized between some men and others.
While all are corrupt, not all are fallen to an equal depth;[37]
there are sins of ignorance and sins of malice.[38]   There is
a difference between Camillus and Catiline.   Even to sinful
man sometimes *speciosae dotes* and *speciales Dei gratiae* are
granted.   In common parlance it is even permissible to say

that one man has been born *bene,* another *pravae naturae.*[39]
Nay, every man has to acknowledge in the talents entrusted
to him a *specialis* or *peculiaris Dei gratia.*[40]   In the diversity
of all these gifts we see the remnants of the divine image
whereby man is distinguished from all other creatures.[41]

In view of all these utterances, which it would be easy to
increase and enforce from the other works of Calvin, it is
grossly unjust to charge the Reformer with narrow-minded-
ness and intolerance.   It is, of course, a different question
whether Calvin himself possessed talent and aptness for all
these arts and sciences to which he accords praise.   But
even if this be not so, even if he did not possess the love
for music and singing which distinguished Luther, this is
not to his discredit, for not only has every genius its limitations, but the Reformers were and had to be by vocation men
of faith, and for having excelled in this they deserve our
veneration and praise, no less than the men of art and
science.   Calvin affirms, it is true, that the virtues of the
natural man, however noble, do not suffice for justification at the judgment-bar of God,[42] but this is due to his
profound conviction of the majesty and spiritual character
of the moral law.   Aside from this, he is more generous in
his recognition of what is true and good, wherever it be
found, than any other Reformer.   He surveys the entire
earth and finds everywhere the evidence of the divine goodness, wisdom and power.   Calvin's theological standpoint
does not render him narrow in his sympathies, but rather
gives to his mind the stamp of catholicity.

This appears with equal clearness from the calling which
he assigns to the Christian.   In regard to this also Calvin
takes his point of departure in the will of God.   To the
Romanist view he brings in principle the same objection that
bears against the pagan conception: the doctrine of the

meritoriousness of good works is a delusion; the monastic vows are an infringement of Christian liberty; the perfection striven after by this method is an arbitrary ideal, set up by man himself. Romanism and paganism both minimize the corruption of human nature, and in the matter of good works start from the free will of man. In contradistinction to this Calvin proceeds on the principle: *nostri non sumus, Dei sumus.* The Christian's life ought to be one continual sacrifice, a perfect consecration to God, a service of God's name, obedience to His law, a pursuit of His glory.[43] This undivided consecration to God assumes on earth largely the character of self-denial and cross-bearing. Paganism knows nothing of this; it merely prescribes certain moral maxims and strives to bring man's life into subjection to his reason or will, or to nature.[44] But the Christian subjects also his intellect and his will and all his powers to the law of God. He does not resign himself to the inevitable, but commits himself to the heavenly Father, who is not like unto a philosopher preaching virtue, but is the Father of our Lord Jesus Christ.[45]

The result is that for Calvin the passive virtues of submission, humility, patience, self-denial, cross-bearing stand in the foreground. Like St. Augustine, Calvin is mortally afraid of pride, whereby man exalts himself above God.[46] His strong insistence upon the inability of man and the bondage of the will is not for the purpose of plunging man into despair, but in order to raise him from his lethargy and to awaken in him the longing for what he lacks, to make him renounce all self-glorying and self-reliance and put all his confidence in God alone.[47] Calvin strips man of everything in order to restore unto him all things in God.[48] *Quanto magis in te infirmus es, tanto magis te suscipit Dominus; nostra humilitas ejus altitudo.*[49] *Humilitas* thus becomes the first virtue; it grows on the root of election;[50] we are continually taught it by God in all the adversity and crucifixion of the present life;[51] it places us for the first time in the proper relation towards God and our fellow-man.[52] For it reconciles us to the fact that this life is for us a land of pilgrimage, full of perils and afflictions, and teaches us to surrender ourselves in all things to the will of God: *Dominus ita voluit, ergo ejus voluntatem sequamur*.[53] It likewise teaches us to love our neighbor, to value the gifts bestowed upon him and to employ our own gifts for his benefit.[54]

Still, it would be a mistake to imagine that according to Calvin the Christian life is confined to the practice of the passive virtues. It is true, he often speaks of despising the present and contemplating the future life.[55] But on considering the times in which Calvin lived, the persecution and oppression to which the Reformation was exposed in well-nigh every country, the bodily and mental suffering the Reformer himself had to endure,—on considering all this we cannot wonder that he exhorts the faithful before all things to the exercise of humility and submission, to patience and obedience, to self-denial and cross-bearing. This has always been so in the Christian Church, and may be traced back to the teaching of Jesus and the Apostles. It does not speak favorably for the depth and intensity of our spiritual life, if we are inclined to find fault with Calvin, the other Reformers, and the martyrs of the Church for this alleged one-sidedness of their faith. It rather should excite our admiration that, in the midst of such circumstances, they so largely kept still an eye open for the positive vocation of the Christian. With Calvin at least the reverse side to the attitude thus criticized is not wanting. Nor does it appear merely after an incidental fashion, by way of appendix to his ethics; it is the outcome of his own most individual principle; its root again lies in his conception of the will of God.

As is universally acknowledged, we owe to Luther the restoration of man's natural calling to a place of honor. Calvin, however, carried this principle enunciated by his predecessors to its furthermost consequences. He viewed the whole of life from the standpoint of the will of God and placed it in all its extent under the discipline of the divine law. It was the common conviction of the Reformers that Christian perfection must be realized not above and outside of, but within the sphere of the calling assigned us by God here on earth. Perfection consists neither in compliance with arbitrary human or ecclesiastical commandments, nor in the performance of all sorts of extraordinary activities. It consists in the faithful discharge of those ordinary daily duties which have been laid by God upon every man in the conduct of life. But much more strongly than Luther, Calvin emphasizes the idea that life itself in its whole length and breadth and depth must be a service of God. Life acquires for him a religious character, is subsumed under and becomes a part of the Kingdom of God. Or, as Calvin himself repeatedly formulates it: Christian life is always and everywhere a life in the presence of God, a walking before His face,—*coram ipso ambulare, ac si essemus sub ejus oculis.*[56]

When, therefore, Calvin speaks of despising the present life, he means by this something far different from what was meant by mediæval ethics. He does not mean that life ought to be fled from, suppressed, or mutilated, but wishes to convey the idea that the Christian should not give his heart to this vain, transitory life, but should possess everything as not possessing it, and put his confidence in God alone.[57]   But life in itself is a *benedictio Dei* and comprises many *divina beneficia.* It is for believers a means to prepare them for the heavenly salvation.[58]   It should be hated only *quatenus nos peccato teneat obnoxios,* and this hatred should never relate to life as such.[59]   On the contrary, this life and the vocation in it given us by God are a part which we have no right to abandon, but which without murmuring and impatience we must faithfully guard, so long as God Himself does not relieve us.[75]   So to view life, as a *vocatio Dei,*—this is the first principle, the foundation of all moral action; this imparts unity to our life and symmetry to all its parts; this assigns to each one his individual place and task, and provides the precious comfort *quod nullum erit tam sordidum ac vile opus, quod non coram Deo resplendeat et pretiosissimum habeatur.*[61]

Thus Calvin sees the whole of life steeped in the light of the divine glory. As in all nature there is no creature which does not reflect the divine perfection, so in the rich world of men there is no vocation so simple, no labor so mean, as not to be suffused with the divine splendor and subservient to the glory of God's name. And Calvin applies this point of view to a still wider range. All the possessions of life are after the same manner rescued from the dishonor to which ascetic moralism had abandoned them. To be sure, he protests against defiling the conscience in the use of these possessions and insists upon it that the Christian shall be actuated by *praesentis vitae contemptu et immortalitatis meditatione.* But he maintains with equal emphasis that all these possessions are gifts of God, designed not merely to provide for our necessities, but also bestowed for our enjoyment and delight. When God adorns the earth with trees and plants and flowers, when He causes the vine to grow which makes glad the heart of man, when He permits man to dig from out the earth the precious metals and stones which shine in the light of the sun,—all this proves that God does not mean to restrict the use of earthly possessions to the relief of our absolute necessities, but has given them to man also for enjoyment of life.[62] Prosperity, abundance and luxury also are gifts of God, to be enjoyed with gratitude and moderation. And Calvin does not want to bind the conscience with regard to this to rigid rules, but expects it freely to regulate itself by the general principles laid down in Scripture for this purpose.[63]

It must be admitted that the Reformer of Geneva did not always adhere in practice consistently to this golden rule. Instead of leaving room for individual liberty he endeavored to bring the entire compass of life under definite rules. The Consistory had for its task *invigilare gregi Domini ut Deus pure colatur* and had to exercise censorship over every improper word and every wrong act; it had to watch over orthodoxy and church-attendance, to be on the lookout for Romish customs and worldly amusements, to oversee domestic life and the education of children; it had to keep its eyes on the tradesman in his store, on the craftsman in his workshop, on the merchant in the market-place, and to subject the entire range of life to the strictest discipline. Even regulations for fire-departments and night-watches, for market-facilities and street-cleaning, for trade and industry, for the prosecution of law-suits and the administration of justice are to be found among Calvin's writings. It is possible to justify all these measures in view of the circumstances under which they were introduced in Geneva. But nobody can deny that Calvin went too far in the creation of a moral police of this kind, that he introduced a régime which, while perhaps necessary and productive of excellent results for that age, is yet unsuited to other times and to different conditions.

But this criticism of Calvin's practice by no means detracts from the glory of the principle proclaimed by him. What he advocates in imitation of Zwingli was not a mere religious and ecclesiastical reform, but a moral reformation embracing the whole of life. Both Zwingli and Calvin waged war not merely against the Judaistic self-righteousness of the Roman Church, but assailed with equal vigor all pagan license. Both desired a national life in all its parts inspired and directed by the principles of the divine Word. And both were led to this view by their theological principle; they took their point of departure in all their thought and activity in God, walked with Him through all of life and brought back to God as an offering all they were and had. Behind everything the sovereign will of God lies hidden and works. The content, the kernel of this will is made known to us in the Gospel; from it we know that God is a merciful and gracious Father, who in spite of all opposition proposes to Himself the salvation of the Church, the redemption of the world, the glorification of His perfections. But this will of God is not an impotent desire, it is omnipotent energy. It realizes itself in the faith of the elect; true faith is an experience of the work of God in one's soul, and for this reason affords unshakable assurance, immovable confidence, the power to surmount all pain and peril through communion with God. Though this gracious and omnipotent will of God is made known in the Gospel alone and experienced in faith only, nevertheless it does not stand isolated, but is encompassed, supported and reinforced by the operation of the same will in the world at large. Special grace is encircled by common grace; the vocation which comes to us in faith is connected and connects us with the vocation presented to us in our earthly calling; the election revealed to us in faith through this faith communicates its power to our entire life; the God of creation and of regeneration is one. Hence the believer cannot rest contented in his faith, but must make it the point of vantage from which he mounts up to the source of election and presses forward to the conquest of the entire world.

History has demonstrated that the belief in election, provided it be genuine, that is, a heartfelt conviction of faith, does not produce careless or Godless men. Especially as developed and professed by Calvin, it is a principle which cuts off all Romish error at the root. Whereas with Rome special revelation consists primarily in the disclosure of certain mysteries, with Calvin it receives for its content the gracious fatherly will of God realizing itself through the Word of revelation. With Rome faith is nothing more than an intellectual assent, preparing man for grace on the principle of *meritum congrui;* with Calvin faith is the reception of grace itself, experience of the power of God, undoubting assurance of God, through and through religious in its nature. With Rome grace chiefly serves the purpose of strengthening the will of man and qualifying him for the performance of various meritorious good works prescribed by the Church; with Calvin the grace received through faith raises man to the rank of an organ of the divine will and causes him to walk in accordance with this will before the presence of God and for the divine glory. The Reformation as begun by Luther and Zwingli, and reinforced and carried through by Calvin, put an end to the Romish supernaturalism and dualism and asceticism. The divine will which created the world, which in the state of sin preserves it through common grace and makes itself known through special grace as the will of a merciful and gracious Father, aims at the salvation of the world, and itself through its omnipotent energy brings about this salvation. Because it thus placed the whole of life under the control of the divine will, it was possible for Calvin's ethics to fall into too precise regulations, into rigorism and puritanism; but in principle his ethics is diametrically opposed to all asceticism, it is catholic and universal in its scope.

In order to prove this by one striking example attention may be called to the fact that mediæval ethics consistently disapproved the principle of usury[64] on the ground of its being forbidden by Scripture and contrary to the unproductive nature of money. Accordingly it looked with contempt upon trade and commerce. Luther, Melanchthon, Zwingli and Erasmus adhered to this view, but Calvin, when this important problem had been submitted to him, formulated in a classic document the grounds on which it could be affirmed that a reasonable interest is neither in conflict with Scripture nor with the nature of money. He took into account the law of life under which commerce operates and declared that only the sins of commerce are to be frowned upon, whereas commerce itself is to be regarded as a calling well-pleasing to God and profitable to society.[65] And this merely illustrates the point of view from which Calvin habitually approached the problems of life. He found the will of God revealed not merely in Scripture, but also in the world, and he traced the connection and sought to restore the harmony between them. Under the guidance of the divine Word he distinguished everywhere between the institution of God and human corruption, and then sought to establish and restore everything in harmony with the divine nature and law. Nothing is unclean in itself; every part of the world and every calling in life is a revelation of the divine perfections, so that even the humblest day-laborer fulfils a divine calling. This is the democratic element in the doctrine of Calvin: there is with God no acceptance of persons; all men are equal before Him; even the humblest and meanest workman, if he be a believer, fills a place in the Kingdom of God and stands as a colaborer with God in His presence. But—and this is the aristocratic, reverse side to the democratic view — every creature and every calling has its own peculiar nature: Church and state, the family and society, agriculture and commerce, art and science are all institutions and gifts of God, but each in itself is a special revelation of the divine will and therefore possesses its own nature. The unity and the diversity in the whole world alike point back to the one sovereign, omnipotent, gracious and merciful will of God.

In this spirit Calvin labored in Geneva. But his activity was not confined to the territory of one city. Geneva was to Calvin merely the center, from which he surveyed the entire field of the Reformation in all lands. When his only child was taken away from him by death, he consoled himself with the thought that God had given him numerous children after the Spirit. And so it was indeed. Through an extensive correspondence he kept in touch with his fellow-laborers in the work of the Reformation; all questions were referred to him; he was the councillor of all the leaders of the great movement; he taught hundreds of men and trained them in his spirit. From all quarters refugees came to Geneva, that bulwark against Rome, to seek protection and support, and afterwards returned to their own lands inspired with new courage. Thus Calvin created in many lands a people who, while made up from all classes, nobles and plain citizens, townspeople and country-folk, were yet one in the consciousness of a divine vocation. In this consciousness they took up the battle against tyranny in Church and state alike, and in that contest secured liberties and rights which are still ours at the present day. Calvin himself stood in the forefront of this battle. Life and doctrine with him were one. He gave his body a living, holy sacrifice, well-pleasing unto God through Jesus Christ. Therein consisted his reasonable service. *Cor Deo mactatum offero.*

CALVIN'S DOCTRINE OF THE KNOWLEDGE OF GOD

By Benjamin B. Warfield

The first chapters of Calvin's *Institutes* are taken up with a comprehensive exposition of the sources and guarantee of the knowledge of God and divine things (Book I, chs. i-ix). A systematic treatise on the knowledge of God must needs begin with such an exposition; and we require no account of the circumstance that Calvin's treatise begins with it, beyond the systematic character of his mind and the clearness and comprehensiveness of his view. This exposition therefore makes its appearance in the earliest edition of the *Institutes* which attempted "to give a summary of religion in all its parts", redacted in orderly sequence; that is to say, which was intended as a text-book in theology. This was the second edition, published in 1539, which was considered by Calvin to be the first which at all corresponded to its title. In this edition this exposition already stands practically complete. Large insertions were made into it subsequently, by which it was greatly enriched as a detailed exposition and validation of the sources of our knowledge of God; but no modifications were made in its fundamental teaching by these additions, and the ground plan of the exposition as laid down in 1539 was retained unaltered throughout the subsequent development of the treatise.

We may observe in the controversies in which Calvin had been engaged between 1536 and 1539 a certain preparation for writing this comprehensive and admirably balanced

statement, with its equal repudiation of Romish and Anabaptist error and its high note of assurance in the face of
the scepticism of the average man of the world.   We may
trace in it the fruits of his eager and exhaustive studies
prosecuted in the interval, as pastor, professor and Protestant statesman; and especially of his own ripening thought
as he worked more and more into detail his systematic view
of the body of truth.   But we can attribute to nothing but
his theological genius the feat by which he set a compressed
apologetical treatise in the forefront of his little book—for
the *Institutes* were still in 1539 a little book, although already expanded to more than double the size of their original form (edition of 1536).   Thus he not only for the
first time supplied the constructive basis for the Reformation movement, but even for the first time in the history
of Christian theology drew in outline the plan of a complete
structure of Christian Apologetics.   For this is the significance in the history of thought of Calvin's exposition of
the sources and guarantee of the knowledge of God, which
forms the opening topic of his *Institutes*.   "Thus", says
Julius Köstlin, after cursorily surveying the course of the
exposition, "there already rises with him an edifice of
Christian Apologetics, in its outlines complete (*fertig*).
With it, he stands, already in 1539, unique (*einzig*) among
the Reformers, and among Christian theologians in general
up to his day.   Only as isolated building-stones can appear in
comparison with this, even what Melanchthon, for example,
offered in the last elaboration of the *Loci* with reference to
the proofs for the existence of God."[1]   In point of fact,
in Augustine alone among his predecessors, do we find anything like the same grasp of the elements of the problem as
Calvin here exhibits; and nowhere among his predecessors
do we find these elements brought together in a constructive

statement of anything like the completeness and systematic balance which he gave to it.

At once on its publication, however, Calvin's apologetical construction became the property of universal Christian thought, and it has entered so vitally into Protestant, and especially Reformed, thinking as to appear now-a-days very much a matter of course. It is difficult for us to appreciate its novelty in him or to realize that it is not as native to every Christian mind as it now seems to us the inevitable adjustment of the elements of the problems raised by the Christian revelation. Familiar as it seems, therefore, it is important that we should apprehend it, at least in its outlines, as it lies in its primary statement in Calvin's pages. So only can we appreciate Calvin's genius or estimate what we owe to him. A very brief abstract will probably suffice, however, to bring before us in the first instance the elements of Calvin's thought. These include the postulation of an innate knowledge of God in man, quickened and developed by a very rich manifestation of God in nature and providence, which, however, fails of its proper effect because of man's corruption in sin; so that an objective revelation of God, embodied in the Scriptures, was rendered necessary, and, as well, a subjective operation of the Spirit of God on the heart enabling sinful man to receive this revelation,—by which conjoint divine action, objective and subjective, a true knowledge of God is communicated to the human soul.

Drawn out a little more into detail, this teaching is as follows. The knowledge of God is given in the very same act by which we know self. For when we know self, we must know it as it is: and that means we must know it as dependent, derived, imperfect and responsible being. To know self implies, therefore, the co-knowledge with self of that on which it is dependent, from which it derives, by the standard of which its imperfection is revealed, to which it is responsible. Of course, such a knowledge of self postulates a knowledge of God, in contrast with whom alone do we ever truly know self: but this only the more emphasises the fact that we know God in knowing self, and the relative priority of our knowledge of two objects of knowledge which we are conscious only of knowing together may for the moment be left undetermined. Meanwhile, it is clear that man has an instinctive and ineradicable knowledge of God, which, moreover, must produce appropriate reactions in his thought, feeling and will, whence arises what we call religion. But these reactions are conditioned by the state of the soul which reacts. Although, then, man cannot avoid possessing a knowledge of God, and this innate knowledge of God is quickened and developed by the richest manifestations of God in nature and providence, which no man can escape either perceiving or so far apprehending, yet the actual knowledge of God which is framed in the human soul is affected by the subjective condition of the soul. The soul, being corrupted by sin, is dulled in its instinctive apprehension of God; and God's manifestation in nature and history is deflected in it. Accordingly the testimony of nature to God is insufficient that sinful man should know Him aright, and God has therefore supernaturally revealed Himself to His people and deposited this revelation of Himself in written Scriptures. In these Scriptures alone, therefore, do we possess an adequate revelation of God; and this revelation is attested as such by irresistible external evidence and attests itself as such by such marks of inherent divinity that no normal mind can resist them. But the sin-darkened minds to which it appeals are not normal minds, but disordered with the awful disease of sin.

What is to give subjective effect in a sin-blinded mind to even a direct revelation from God? The revelation of God is its own credential. It needs no other light to be thrown upon it but that which emanates from itself: and no other light can produce the effect which its own splendor as a revelation of God should effect. But all fails when the receptivity is destroyed by sin. For sinners, therefore, there is requisite a repairing operation upon their souls before the light of the Word itself can accredit itself to them as light. This repairing operation on the souls of sinful men by which they are enabled to perceive light is called the testimony of the Holy Ghost: which is therefore just the subjective action of the Spirit of God on the heart, by virtue of which it is opened for the perception and reception of the objective revelation of God. The testimony of the Spirit cannot, then, take the place of the objective revelation of the Word: it is no revelation in this strict sense. It presupposes the objective revelation and only prepares the heart to respond to and embrace it. But the objective revelation can take no effect on the unprepared heart. What the operation of the Spirit on the heart does, then, is to implant, or rather to restore, a spiritual sense in the soul by which God is recognized in His Word. When this spiritual sense has been produced the necessity of external proofs that the Scriptures are the Word of God is superseded: the Word of God is as immediately perceived as such as light is perceived as light, sweetness as sweetness,—as immediately and as inamissibly. The Christian's knowledge of God, therefore, rests no doubt on an instinctive perception of God native to man as man, developed in the light of a patefaction of God which pervades all nature and history; but particularly on an objective revelation of God deposited in Scriptures which bear in themselves their own evidence of their divine origin, to which every spiritual man responds with the same strength of conviction with which he recognizes light as light. This is the basis which Calvin in his *Institutes* places beneath his systematic exposition of the knowledge of God.

The elements of Calvin's thought here, it will readily be seen, reduce themselves to a few great fundamental principles. These embrace particularly the following doctrines: the doctrine of the innate knowledge of God; the doctrine of the general revelation of God in nature and history; the doctrine of the special revelation of God and its embodiment in Scriptures; the doctrine of the noëtic effects of sin; the doctrine of the testimony of the Holy Spirit. That we may do justice to his thought we must look in some detail at his treatment of each of these doctrines and of the subordinate topics which are necessarily connected with them.

I.   NATURAL REVELATION.

That the knowledge of God is innate (I. iii. 3), naturally engraved on the hearts of men (I. v. 4), and so a part of their very constitution as men (I. iii. 1) that it is a matter of instinct (I. iii. 1, I. iv. 2) and every man is self-taught it from his birth (I. iii. 3), Calvin is thoroughly assured. He lays it down as incontrovertible fact that "the human mind, by natural instinct itself, possesses some sense of a deity" (I. iii. 1, *ad init. et ad fin.; 3,—sensus divinitatis* or *deitatis*),[2] and defends the corollaries which flow from this fact, that the knowledge of God is universal and indelible. All men know there is a God, who has made them, and to whom they are responsible. No savage is sunk so low as to have lost this sense of deity, which is wrought into his very constitution: and the degradation of men's worship is a proof of its ineradicableness—since even such dehumanization as this worship manifests has not obliterated it (I. iii.

1). It is the precondition of all religion, without which no religion would ever have arisen; and it forms the silent assumption of all attempts to expound the origin of religion in fraud or political artifice, as it does also of all corruptions of religion, which find their nerve in men's incurable religious propensities (I. iii. 1). The very atheists testify to its persistence in their ill-concealed dread of the deity they profess to despise (I. iv. 2); and the wicked, strive they never so hard to banish from their consciousness the sense of an accusing deity, are not permitted by nature to forget it (I. iii. 3). Thus the cases alike of the savages, the atheists and the wicked are made contributory to the establishment of the fact, and the discussion concludes with the declaration that it is by this innate knowledge of God that men are discriminated from the brutes, so that for men to lose it would be to fall away from the very law of their creation (I. iii. 3 *ad fin.*).[3]

If the knowledge of God enters thus into the very idea of humanity and constitutes a law of its being, it follows that it is given in the same act of knowledge by which we know ourselves. This position is developed at length in the opening chapter. The discussion begins with a remark which reminds us of Augustine's familiar contention that the proper concern of mankind is the knowledge of God and the soul; to which it is added at once that these two knowledges are so interrelated that it is impossible to assign the priority to either. The knowledge of self involves the knowledge of God and also profits by the knowledge of God: the better we know ourselves the better we shall know God, but also, we shall never know ourselves as we really are save in contrast with God, by whom is supplied the only standard for the formation of an accurate judgment upon ourselves (I. i. 2). In his analysis of the mode of the

implication of the knowledge of God in the knowledge of
self, Calvin lays the stress upon our nature as dependent,
derived, imperfect and responsible beings, which if known at
all must be known as such, and to be known as such must
be known as over against that Being on whom we are
dependent, to whom we owe our being, over against whom
our imperfection is manifest, and to whom we are responsible (I. i. 1). As we are not self-existent, we must recognize ourselves as "living and moving" in Another. We recognize ourselves as products, and in knowing the product
know the cause; thus our very endowments, seeing that they
distil to us by drops from heaven, form so many streams
up which our minds must needs travel to their Fountain-
head. The perception of our imperfections is at the same
time the perception of His perfection; so that our very
poverty displays to us His infinite fulness. Our sense
of dissatisfaction with ourselves directs our eyes to Him
whose righteous judgment we can but anticipate; and when
in the presence of His majesty we realize our meanness and
in the presence of His righteousness we realize our sin, our
perception of God passes into consternation as we recognize
in Him our just Judge.

The emphasis which Calvin places in this analysis upon
the sense of sin and the part it plays in our knowledge
of God, at once attracts attention. It is perhaps above
everything the "miserable ruin" in which we find ourselves, which compels us, according to him, to raise our
eyes towards heaven, spurred on not merely by a sense of
lack but by a sense of dread: it is only, he declares, when
we have begun to be displeased with ourselves that we energetically turn our thoughts Godward. This is already an
indication of the engrossment of Calvin in this treatise with
practical rather than merely theoretical problems. He is

less concerned to show how man as man attains to a knowledge of God, than how man as he actually exists upon the earth attains to it. In the very act of declaring that this knowledge is instinctive and belongs to the very constitution of man as such, therefore, he so orders the exposition of the mode of its actual rise in the mind as to throw the emphasis on a quality which does not belong to man as such, but only to man as actually existing in the world,—in that "miserable ruin into which we have been plunged by the defection of the first man" (I. i. 1). Man as unfallen, by the very necessity of his nature would have known God, the sphere of his being, the author of his existence, the standard of his excellences; but for man as fallen, Calvin seems to say, the strongest force compelling him to look upwards to the God above him, streams from his sense of sin, filling him with a fearful looking forward to judgment.

It is quite obvious that such a knowledge of God as Calvin here postulates as the unavoidable and ineradicable possession of man, is far from a mere empty conviction that such a being as God exists. The knowledge of God which is given in our knowledge of self is not a bare perception, it is a conception: it has content. "The knowledge of ourselves, therefore," says Calvin (I. i. 1 *ad fin.*), "is not only an incitement to seek after God, but becomes a considerable assistance towards finding God." The knowledge of God with which we are natively endowed is therefore more than a bare conviction that God is: it involves, more or less explicated, some understanding of what God is. Such a knowledge of God can never be otiose and inert; but must produce an effect in human souls, in the way of thinking, feeling, willing. In other words, our native endowment is not merely a *sensus deitatis,* but also a *semen religionis* (I. iii. 1, 2; iv. 1, 4; v. 1). For what we call religion is just

the reaction of the human soul to what it perceives God
to be. Calvin is, therefore, just as insistent that religion is
universal as that the knowledge of God is universal. "The
seeds of religion", he insists, "are sown in every heart"
(I. iv. 1 ; v. 1) ; men are propense to religion (I. iii. 2 *med.*) ;
and always and everywhere frame to themselves a religion,
consonant with their conceptions of God.

Calvin's ideas of the origin and nature of religion are set
forth, if succinctly, yet with eminent clearness, in his second
chapter. Wherever any knowledge of God exists, he tells
us, there religion exists. He is not speaking here of a com-
petent knowledge of God such as redeemed sinners have in
Christ. But much less is he speaking of that mere notion
that there is such a Being as God which is sometimes called a
knowledge of God. It may be possible to speculate on "the
essence" of God without being moved by it. But certainly it
is impossible to form any vital conception of God without
some movement of intellect, feeling and will towards Him;
and any real knowledge of God is inseparable from movements of piety towards Him. Piety means reverence and
love to God; and the knowledge of God tends therefore to
produce in us, first, sentiments of fear and reverence; and,
secondly, an attitude of receptivity and praise to Him as
the fountain of all blessing. If man were not a sinner,
indeed, such would be the result: men, knowing God, would
turn to Him in confidence and commit themselves without
reserve to His care,—not so much fearing His judgments,
as making them in sympathetic loyalty their own (I. ii. 2).
And herein we see what pure and genuine religion is: "it
consists in faith, united with a serious fear of God, com-
prehending a voluntary reverence, and producing legitimate
worship agreeable to the injunctions of the law" (I. ii. 2
ad fin.).[4]

The definition of religion to which Calvin thus attains is exceedingly interesting, and that not merely because of its vital relation to the fundamental thought of these opening chapters, but also because of its careful adjustment to the state of the controversy in which he was engaged as a leader of the Reformation. In the first of these aspects, as we have already pointed out, religion is with him the vital effect of the knowledge of God in the human soul; so that inevitably religions will differ as the conceptions of God determining our thought and feeling and directing our life differ. In the estate of purity, the knowledge of God produces reverence and trust: and the religion of sinless man will therefore exhibit no other traits but trust and love. In sinful man, the same knowledge of God must produce, rather, a reaction of fear and hate—until the grace of God intervenes with a message of mercy. Sinful man cannot be trusted, therefore, to form his own religion for himself, but must in all his religious functioning place himself unreservedly under the direction of God in his gracious revelation. In its second aspect, then, we perceive Calvin carefully framing his definition so as to exclude all "will-worship" and to prepare the way for the condemnation of the "formal worship" and "ostentation in ceremonies" which had become prevalent in the old Church. The position he takes up here is essentially that which has come down to us under the name of "the Puritan principle". Religion consists, of course, not in the externalities of worship, but in faith, united with a serious fear of God, and a willing reverence. But its external expression in worship is not therefore unimportant, but is to be strictly confined to what is prescribed by God: to "legitimate worship, agreeable to the injunctions of the law" (I. ii. 2 *ad fin.*). This declaration is returned to and expounded in a striking section of the

fourth chapter (I. iv. 3; *cf*. I. v. 13), where Calvin insists
that "the divine will is the perpetual rule to which true
religion is to be conformed", and asserts of newly-invented
modes of worshipping God, that they are tantamount to
idolatry. God cannot be pleased by showing contempt for
what He commands and substituting other things which
He condemns: and none would dare to trifle in such a manner with Him unless they had already transformed Him in
their minds into another and different Being: and in that
case it is of little importance whether you worship one god
or many.[5]

From this digression for the sake of asserting the "Puritan", that is, the "Reformed", principle with reference to
acceptable worship, it is already apparent that Calvin did
not suppose that men have been left to the *notitia Dei insita*
for the framing of their religion, although he is insistent
that therefrom proceeds a propensity to religion which
already secures that all men shall have a religion (I. ii. 2).
On the contrary, he teaches that to the ineradicable revelation of Himself which He has imprinted on human nature,
God has added an equally clear and abundant revelation of
Himself externally to us. As we cannot know ourselves
without knowing God, so neither can we look abroad on
nature or contemplate the course of events without seeing
Him in His works and deeds (I. v). Calvin is exceedingly
emphatic as to the clearness, universality and convincingness
of this natural revelation of God. The whole world is but
a theatre for the display of the divine glory (I. v. 5); God
manifests Himself in every part of it, and, turn our eyes
whichever way we will, we cannot avoid seeing Him; for
there is no atom of the world in which some sparks of His
glory do not shine (I. v. 1). So pervasive is God in nature,
indeed, that it may even be said by a pious mind that nature

is God (I. v. 5),—though the expression is too readily misapprehended in a Pantheistic (I. v. 5) or Materialistic (I. v. 4) sense to justify its use. Accordingly, no man can escape this manifestation of God; we cannot open our eyes without seeing it, and the language in which it is delivered to us penetrates through even the densest stupidity and ignorance (I. v. 1). To every individual on earth, therefore, with the exclusion of none (I. v. 7), God abundantly manifests Himself (I. v. 2). Each of the works of God invites the whole human race to the knowledge of Him; while their contemplation in the mass offers an even more prevalent exhibition of Him (I. v. 10). And so clear are His footsteps in His providence, that even what are commonly called accidents are only so many proofs of His activity (I. v. 8).

In developing this statement of the external natural revelation of God, Calvin presents first His patefaction in creation (I. v. 1-6), and then His patefaction in providence (I. v. 7-9), and under each head lays the primary stress on the manifestations of the divine wisdom and power (I. v. 2-5, wisdom; 6, power: 8, wisdom and power). But the other attributes which enter into His glory are not neglected. Thus, under the former caption, he points out that the perception of the divine power in creation "leads us to the consideration of His eternity; because He from whom all things derive their origin must necessarily be eternal and self-existent", while we must postulate goodness and mercy as the motives of His creation and providence (I. v. 6). Under the second caption, he is particularly copious in drawing out the manifestations of the divine benignity and beneficence—of His clemency—though he does not scruple also to point to the signs of His severity (I. v. 7, cf. 10). From the particular contemplation of the divine clemency and severity in their peculiar distribution here, indeed, he pauses to draw an argument for a future life when apparent irregularities will be adjusted (I. v. 10).

The vigor and enthusiasm with which Calvin prosecutes his exposition of the patefaction of God in nature and history is worth emphasizing further. He even turns aside (I. v. 9) to express his special confidence in it, in contrast to *a priori* reasoning, as the "right way and the best method of seeking God". A speculative inquiry into the essence of God, he suggests, merely fatigues the mind and flutters in the brain. If we would know God vitally, in our hearts, let us rather contemplate Him in His works. These, we shall find, as the Psalmist points out, declare His greatness and conduce to His praise. Once more, we may observe here the concreteness of Calvin's mind and method, and are reminded of the practical end he keeps continually in view.[6] So far is he from losing himself in merely speculative elaborations or prosecuting his inquiries under the spur of "presumptuous curiosity", that the practical religious motive is always present, dominating his thought. His special interest in the theistic argument is, accordingly, due less to the consideration that it rounds out his systematic view of truth than to the fact that it helps us to the vital knowledge of God. And therefore he is no more anxious to set it forth in its full force than he is to point out the limitations which affect its practical value.[7] In and of itself, indeed, it has no limitations: Calvin is fully assured of its validity and analyses its data with entire confidence: to him nothing is more certain than that in the mirror of His works God gives us clear manifestations both of Himself and of His everlasting dominion (I. v. 11). But Calvin cannot content himself with an intellectualistic contemplation of the objective validity of the theistic argument. So dominated is he by practical interests that he actually attaches to the chapter in which he argues this objective validity a series of sections in which he equally strongly argues the subjective inability of man to receive its testimony. Objectively valid as the theistic proofs are, they are ineffective to produce a just knowledge of God in the sinful heart. The insertion of these sections here is the more striking that they almost seem unnecessary in view of the clear exposition of the noëtic effects of sin which had been made in the preceding chapter (ch. iv),—although, of course, there the immediate reference was to the *notitia Dei insita,* while here it is to the *notitia Dei acquisita.*

Thus, however, our attention is drawn very pointedly to Calvin's doctrine of the disabilities with reference to the knowledge of God which are induced in the human mind by sin. He has, as has just been noted, adverted formally to them twice in these opening chapters of his treatise,—on the earlier occasion (ch. iv) with especial reference to the revelation of God made in the constitution of human nature, and on the later occasion (ch. v, §§ 11-15) with especial reference to the revelation of God made in His works and deeds. Were man in his normal state, he could not under this double revelation, internal and external, fail to know God as God would wish to be known. If he actually comes short of an adequate knowledge of God, therefore, this cannot be attributed to any shortcomings in the revelation of God. Calvin is perfectly clear as to the objective adequacy of the general revelation of God. Men, however, do come short of an adequate knowledge of God; and that not merely some men, but all men: the failure of the general revelation of God to produce in men an adequate knowledge of Him is as universal as is the revelation itself. The explanation is to be found in the corruption of men's hearts by sin, by which not merely are they rendered incapable of reading off the revelation of God which is displayed in His works and deeds, but their very instinctive knowledge of God, embedded in their constitution as men, is dulled and almost obliterated. The energy with which Calvin asserts this is almost startling, and matches in its emphasis that which he had placed on the reality and objective validity of the revelation of God. Though the seeds of religion are sown by God in every heart, yet not one man in a hundred has preserved even these seeds sound, and in no one at all have they grown to their legitimate harvest. All have degenerated from the true knowledge of God, and genuine piety has perished from the earth (I. iv. 1). The light which God has kindled in the breasts of men has been smothered and all but extinguished by their iniquity (I. iv. 4). The manifestation which God has given of Himself in the structure and organization of the world is lost on our stupidity (I. v. 11). The rays of God's glory are diffused all around us, but do not illuminate the darkness of our mind (I. v. 14). So that in point of fact, "men who are taught only by nature, have no certain, sound or distinct knowledge, but are confined to confused principles; they worship accordingly an unknown God" (I. v. 12 *ad fin.*) : "no man can have the least knowledge of true and sound doctrine without having been a disciple of the Scriptures" (I. vi. 2 *ad fin.*) : "the human mind is through its imbecility unable to attain any knowledge of God without the assistance of the Sacred Word" (I. vi. 4 *ad fin.*).

Calvin therefore teaches with great emphasis the bankruptcy of the natural knowledge of God. We must keep fully in mind, however, that this is not due in his view to any inadequacy or ineffectiveness of natural revelation, considered objectively.[8] He continues to insist that the

seeds of religion are sown in every heart (I. v. 1 *ad init.*);
that through all man's corruption the instincts of nature
still suggest the memory of God to his mind (I. v. 2); that
it is impossible to eradicate that sense of the deity which is
naturally engraved on all hearts (I. v. 4 *ad fin.*); that the
structure and organization of the world, and the things
that daily happen out of the ordinary course of nature, that
is under the providential government of God, bear a witness
to God which the dullest ear cannot fail to hear (I. v. 1, 3,
7, esp. II. vi. 1); and that the light that shines from creation, while it may be smothered, cannot be so extinguished
but that some rays of it find their way into the most darkened soul (I. vi. 14). God has therefore never left Himself
without a witness; but, "with various and most abundant
benignity sweetly allures men to a knowledge of Him,
though they persist in following their own ways, their pernicious and fatal errors" (I. vi. 14). The sole cause of the
failure of the natural revelation is to be found, therefore,
in the corruption of the human heart. Two results flow
from this fact. First, it is not a question of the extinction
of the knowledge of God, but of the corruption of the
knowledge of God. And secondly, men are without excuse
for their corruption of the knowledge of God. On both
points Calvin is insistent.

He does not teach that all religion has perished out
of the earth, but only that no "genuine piety" remains
(I. iv. 1 *ad init.*): he does not teach that men retain no
knowledge of God, but no "certain, sound or distinct
knowledge" (I. v. 12 *ad fin.*). The seed of religion remains
their inalienable possession, "but it is so corrupted as to
produce only the worst fruits" (I. v. 4 *ad fin.*). Here we
see Calvin's judgment on natural religion. Its reality he
is quick to assert: but equally quickly its inadequacy—and

that because not merely of a negative incompleteness but also of a positive corruption. Men have corrupted the knowledge of God; and perhaps Calvin might even subscribe the declaration of a modern writer that men's religions are their worst crimes.[9] Certainly Calvin paints in dark colors, the processes by which men form for themselves conceptions of God under the light of nature, or rather, in the darkness of their minds, from which the light of nature is as far as lies in their power excluded. "Their conceptions of God are formed, not according to the representations He gives of Himself, but by the invention of their own presumptuous imaginations" (I. iv. 1 *med.*). They set Him far off from themselves and make Him a mere idler in heaven (I. iv. 2); they invent all sorts of vague and confused notions concerning Him, until they involve themselves in such a vast accumulation of errors as almost to extinguish the light that is within them (I. iv. 4); they confuse Him with His works, until even a Plato loses himself in the round globe (I. v. 11); they even endeavor to deny His very existence (I. v. 12), and substitute demons in His place (I. v. 13). Certainly it is not surprising, then, that the Holy Spirit, speaking in Scripture, "condemns as false and lying whatever was formerly worshipped as divine among the Gentiles", nay, "rejects as false every form of worship which is of human contrivance", and "leaves no Deity but in Mount Zion" (I. v. 13). The religions of men differ, doubtless, among themselves: some are more, some less evil; but all are evil and the evil of none is trivial.

Are men to be excused for this, their corruption of the knowledge of God? Are we to listen with sympathy to the plea that light has been lacking? It is not a case of insufficient light, but of an evil heart. Excuses are vain, for this heart-darkness is criminal. If we speak of ignorance here, we must remember it is a guilty ignorance; an ignorance which rests on pride and vanity and contumacy (I. iv. 1), an ignorance which our own consciences will not excuse (I. v. 15). What! shall we plead that we lack ears to hear what even mute creatures proclaim? that we have no eyes to see what it needs no eyes to see? that we are mentally too weak to learn what mindless creatures teach? (I. v. 15). We are ignorant of what all things conspire to inform us of, only because we sinfully corrupt their message: their insufficiency has its roots in us, not in them; wherefore we are without excuse (I. iv. 1: v. 14-15). Our "folly is inexcusable, seeing that it originates not only in a vain curiosity, but in false confidence, and an immoderate desire to exceed the limits of human knowledge" (I. iv. 1 *ad fin.*). "Whatever deficiency of natural ability prevents us from attaining the pure and clear knowledge of God, yet, since that deficiency arises from our own fault, we are left without any excuse" (I. v. 15).

The natural revelation of God failing thus to produce its legitimate effects of a sound knowledge of God, because of the corruption of men's hearts, we are thrown back for any adequate knowledge of God upon supernatural activities of God communicating His truth to men. It is accordingly in an assertion and validation of these supernatural revelatory operations of God that Calvin's discussion reaches its true center. To this extent his whole discussion of natural revelation—in its inception in the implantation in man of a *sensus deitatis,* in its culmination in the patefaction of God in His works and deeds, and in its failure through the sin-bred blindness of humanity—may be said to be merely introductory to and intended to prepare the way for his discussion of the supernatural operations of God by which

He meets this otherwise hopeless condition of humanity sunk in its corrupt notions of God. These operations obviously must meet a twofold need. A clearer and fuller revelation of God must be brought to men than that which is afforded by nature. And the darkened minds of men must be illuminated for its reception. In other words, what is needed, is a special supernatural revelation on the one hand, and a special supernatural illumination on the other. It is to the validation of this twofold supernatural operation of God in communicating the knowledge of Himself that Calvin accordingly next addresses himself (chs. vi-ix).

One or two peculiarities of his treatment of them attract our notice at the outset, and seem to invite attention, before we enter into a detailed exposition of the doctrine he presents. It is noticeable that Calvin does not pretend that this supernatural provision of knowledge of God to meet men's sin-born ignorance is as universal in its reach as the natural revelation which it supplements and, so far as efficiency is concerned, supersedes. On the contrary, he draws it expressly into a narrower circle. That general revelation "presented itself to all eyes" and "is more than sufficient to deprive the ingratitude of men of every excuse, since", in it, "God, in order to involve all mankind in the same guilt, sets an exhibition of His majesty, delineated in the creatures, before them all without exception" (I. vi. 1 *ad init.*). But His supernatural revelation He grants only "to those whom He intends to unite in a more close and familiar connection with Himself" (*ibid.*); "to those to whom He has determined to make His instructions effectual" (I. vi. 3); in a word, to "the elect" (I. vi. 1; vii. 5 near end). In dealing with the supernatural revelation of God, therefore, Calvin is conscious of dealing with a special operation of the divine grace by means of which God is communicating to those He is choosing to be His people the saving knowledge of Himself. It is observable also that, in speaking of this supernatural revelation, he identifies it from the outset distinctly with the Scriptures (ch. vi). This is in accordance with the practical end and engrossment which, as we have already had occasion to note, dominate his whole discussion. He was not unaware that the special revelation of God antedates the Scriptures: on occasion he speaks discriminatingly enough of this revelation in itself and the Scriptures in which it is embodied. But his mind is less on the abstract truth than on the concrete conditions which surrounded him in his work. Whatever may have been true ages gone, to-day the special revelation of God coalesces with the Scriptures, and he does not occupy himself formally with it except as it presents itself to the men of his own time. The task which he undertakes, therefore, is distinctly to show that men have in the Scriptures a special revelation of God supplementing and so far superseding the general revelation of God in nature; and that God so operates with this His special revelation of Himself as to overcome the sin-bred disabilities of man.

In this state of the case we may perhaps be justified in leaving at this point the logical development of his construction and expounding Calvin's teaching more formally under the heads of his doctrine of Holy Scripture and his doctrine of the Testimony of the Holy Spirit.

II. HOLY SCRIPTURE.

First, then, what was Calvin's doctrine of Holy Scripture?

Under the designation of "Scripture" or "the Scriptures" Calvin understood that body of writings which have been transmitted to us as the divinely given rule of faith and life. In this body of writings, that is to say, in "the Canon

of Scripture", he included all the books of the Old Covenant
which were recognized by the Jewish Church as of divine
gift, and were as such handed down to the Christian Church;
and all the books of the New Covenant which have been
given the Church by the Apostles as its authoritative law-
code. Calvin's attitude towards the canon was thus somewhat
more conservative than, say, Luther's. He knew of no such
distinction as that between Canonical and Deutero-Canon-
ical books, whether in the Old or the New Testament. The
so-called "Apocryphal Books" of the Old Testament, included within the canon by the decrees of Trent, he rejected
out of hand: the so-called "Antilegomena" of the New
Testament he accepted without exception.[10]

The representations which are sometimes made, to the
effect that he felt doubts of the canonicity of some of the
canonical books or even was convinced of their uncanon-
icity,[11] rest on a fundamental misconception of his attitude,
and are wrecked on his express assertions. No doubt he has
not left us commentaries on all the Biblical books, and no
doubt his omission to write or lecture on certain books is not
to be explained merely by lack of time, but involves an act
of selection on his part, which was not unaffected by his
estimate of the relative importance of the several books or
by his own spiritual sympathies.[12] He has also occasionally
employed a current expression, such as, for example, "the
Canonical Epistle of John",[13] when speaking of 1 John,
which, if strictly interpreted, might be thought to imply
denial of the genuineness of certain books of the canon,—
such as 2 and 3 John,—and not merely the momentary or
habitual neglect of them; just as the common use of the
term "the Apostle" of Paul might be said, if similarly strictly
pressed, to imply that there was no other Apostle but he. It
is also true that he expresses himself with moderation when

adducing the evidence for the canonicity of this book or that, and in his modes of statement quite clearly betrays his recognition that the evidence is more copious or more weighty in some cases than in others.

But he represents the evidence as sufficient in all cases and declares with confidence his conclusion in favor of the canonicity of the whole body of books which make up our Bible, and in all his writings and controversies acts firmly on this presupposition. How, for example, is it possible to contend that some grave reason connected with doubts on his part of their canonical authority underlies the failure of Calvin to comment on "the three books attributed to Solomon, particularly the Song of Songs",[14] in the face of the judgment of the ministers of Geneva with regard to Castellion, which is thus reported by Calvin himself over his signature.[15] "We unanimously judged him one who might be appointed to the functions of the pastor, except for a single obstacle which opposed it. When we asked him, according to custom, whether he was in accord with us on all points of doctrine, he replied that there were two on which he could not share our views: one of them . . . being our inscribing the Song of Solomon in the number of sacred books. . . . We conjured him first of all, not to permit himself the levity of treating as of no account the constant witness of the universal Church; we reminded him that there is no book the authenticity of which is doubtful, about which some discussion has not been raised; that even those to which we now attach an undisputed authenticity were not admitted from the beginning without controversy; that precisely this one is one which has never been openly repudiated. We also exhorted him against trusting unreasonably in his own judgment, especially where nothing was toward which all the world had not been aware of before he was born. . . . All these arguments having no effect on him, we thought it necessary to consider among ourselves what we ought to do. Our unanimous opinion was that it would be dangerous and would set a bad precedent to admit him to the ministry in these circumstances. . . . We should thus condemn ourselves for the future to raise no objection to another, should one present himself and wish similarly to repudiate Ecclesiastes or Proverbs or any other book of the Bible, without being dragged into a debate as to what is and what is not worthy of the Holy Spirit."[16] Not merely the firmness with which Calvin held to the canonicity of all the books of our Bible, but the importance he attached to the acceptance of the canonical Scriptures in their integrity, is made perfectly clear by such an incident; and indeed so also are the grounds on which he accepted these books as canonical.

These grounds, to speak briefly, were historico-critical. Calvin, we must bear in mind, was a Humanist before he was a Reformer,[17] and was familiar with the whole process of determining the authenticity of ancient documents. If then he received the Scriptures from the hands of the Church, not indulging himself in the levity of treating the constant witness of the universal Church as of no account, he was nevertheless not disposed to take "tradition" uncritically at its face value. His acceptance of the canon of the Church was therefore not a blind but a critically mediated acceptance. Therefore he discarded the Apocrypha: and if he accepted the Antilegomena it was because they commended themselves to his historico-critical judgment as holding of right a place in the canon. The organon of his critical investigation of the canon was in effect twofold. He inquired into the history of the books in question. He inquired into their internal characteristics. Have they come down to us from the Apostolic Church, commanding either unbrokenly or on the whole the suffrages of those best informed or best qualified to judge of their canonical claims? Are they in themselves conformable to the claims made for them of apostolic, which is as much as to say, divine origin? It was by the application of this twofold test that he excluded the Apocrypha of the Old Testament from the canon. They had in all ages been discriminated from the canonical books, and differ from them as the writing of an individual differs from an instrument which has passed under the eye of a notary and been sealed to be received of all.[18] Some fathers, it is true, deemed them canonical; even Augustine was of that way of thinking, although he had to allow that opinions differed widely upon the matter. Others, however, could admit them to no higher rank than that of "ecclesiastical books", which might be useful to read but could not supply a foundation for doctrine; among such were Jerome and Rufinus.[19] And, when we observe their contents, no sane mind will fail to pass judgment against them.[20] Rome may, indeed, find her interest in defending them, for she may discover support in them for some of her false teachings. But this very fact is their condemnation. "I beg you to observe", he says of the closing words of 2 Maccabees, where the writer sets his hope in his own works: "I beg you to observe how far this confession falls away from the majesty of the Holy Spirit"[21]— that is to say, from the constant teaching of Holy Scripture.

And it was by the application of the same two-fold test that he accredited the Antilegomena of the New Testament as integral parts of the canon. In the "Preface" which he has prefixed to 2 Peter, for example, he notes that Eusebius speaks of some who rejected it. "If it is a question", he adds, "of yielding to the simple authority of men, since Eusebius does not name those who brought the matter into doubt, no necessity seems to be laid on us to credit these unknown people. And, moreover, he adds that afterwards it was generally received without contradiction. . . . It is a matter agreed upon by all, of common accord, that there is nothing in this Epistle unworthy of Saint Peter, but that, on the contrary, from one end of it to the other, there are apparent the force, vehemence and grace of the Spirit with which the Apostles were endowed. . . . Since, then, in all parts of the Epistle the majesty of the Spirit of Christ is clearly manifest, I cannot reject it entirely, although I do not recognize in it the true and natural phrase of Saint Peter."[22] To meet the difficulty arising from the difference of the style from that of 1 Peter, he therefore supposed that the Epistle is indeed certainly Peter's, since otherwise it would be a forgery, a thing inconceivable in a book of its high character,[23] but was dictated in his old age to some one of his disciples, to whom it owes its peculiarities of diction. Here we have an argument conducted on the two grounds of the external witness of the Church and the internal testimony of the contents of the book: and these are the two grounds on which he everywhere depends. Of the Epistle of Jude he says:[24] "Because the reading of it is very useful, and it contains nothing that is not in accord with the purity of the apostolic doctrine; because also it has long been held to be authentic by all the best men, for my part, I willingly place it in the number of the other epistles." In other cases the external evidence of the Church is not explicitly mentioned and the stress of the argument is laid on the Apostolic character of the writing as witnessed by its contents. He receives Hebrews among the Apostolic Epistles without difficulty, because nowhere else is the sacrifice of Christ more clearly or simply declared and other evangelical doctrines taught: surely it must have been due to the wiles of Satan that the Western Church so long doubted its canonicity.[25] James seems to him to contain nothing unworthy of an Apostle of Christ, but to be on the contrary full of good teaching, valuable for all departments of Christian living.[26] For the application of this argument he of course takes his start from the Homologoumena, which gave him the norm of Apostolic teaching which he used for testing the other books. It must not be supposed that he received even these books, however, without critico-historical inquiry: but only that the uniform witness of the Church to their authority weighed with him above all grounds of doubt. It was, in a word, on the basis of a purely scientific investigation that Calvin accredited to himself the canon. It had come down to him through the ages, accredited as such by the constant testimony of its proper witnesses: and it accredited itself to critical scrutiny by its contents.[27]

The same scientific spirit attended Calvin in his dealing with the text of Scripture. As a Humanist he was familiar with the processes employed in settling the texts of classical authors; and naturally he used the same methods in his determination of the text of the Biblical books. His practice here is marked by a combination of freedom and sobriety; and his decisions, though often wrong, as they could not fail to be in the state of the knowledge of the transmission of the New Testament text at the time, always manifest good sense, balance and trained judgment. In his remarks on the pericope of the adulteress (Jno. vii. 53-viii. 11), we meet the same circle of ideas with which we are familiar from his remarks on the Antilegomena. "Because it has always been received by the Latin Churches and is found in many of the Greek copies and old writers, and contains nothing which would be unworthy of an apostolical spirit, there is no reason why we should refuse to take our profit from it."[28]   He accepts the three-witness passage of 1 Jno. v. 7. "Since the Greek codices do not agree with themselves", he says, "I scarcely dare reach a conclusion. Yet, as the context flows most smoothly if this clause is added, and I see that it stands in the best codices and those of the most approved credit, I also willingly adopt it." When puzzled by difficulties, he, quite like the Humanist dealing with a classical text, feels free to suggest that there may be a "mendum in voce". This he does, for example, in Matt. xxiii. 35, where he adduces this possibility among others; and still more instructively in Matt. xxvii. 9, where he just as simply assumes "Jeremiah" to be a corrupt reading[29] as his own editors assume that the "Apius" which occurs in the French version of the *Institutes* in connection with Josephus is due to a slip of his translators, not of his own—remarking: "It is evident that it cannot be Calvin who translated this passage."[30]   His assurance that it cannot be the Biblical writer who stumbles leads him similarly to attribute what seems to him a manifest error to the copyists. It is only, however, in such passages as these that he engages formally in textual emendation. Ordinarily he simply follows the current text, although he is, of course, not without an intelligent ground for his confidence in it.[31]   As we cursorily read his commentaries we feel ourselves in the hands of one who is sanely and sagely scrutinizing the text with which he is dealing from the point of view of a scholar accustomed to deal with ancient texts, whose confidence in its general integrity represents the well-grounded conclusion of a trained judgment. His occasional remarks on the text, and his rare suggestion of a corruption, are indicia of the alertness of his general scrutiny of the text and serve to assure us that his acceptance of it as a whole as sound is not merely inert acquiescence in tradition, but represents the calm judgment of an instructed intelligence.

INSPIRATION OF SCRIPTURE.

Now, these sixty-six books of canonical Scriptures handed down to us, in the singular providence of God,[32] in a sound text which meets the test of critical scrutiny, Calvin held to be the very Word of God. This assertion he intended in its simplest and most literal sense. He was far from overlooking the fact that the Scriptures were written by human hands: he expressly declares that, though we have received them from God's own mouth, we have nevertheless received them "through the ministry of men".[33] But he was equally far from conceiving that the relation of their human authors to their divine author resembled in any degree that of free intermediaries, who, after receiving the divine word, could do with it what they listed.[34] On the contrary, he thought of them rather as notaries (IV. vii. 9), who set down in authentic registers (I. vi. 3) what was dictated to them (*Argumentum in Ev. Joh.*).[35] They wrote, therefore, merely as the organs of the Holy Ghost, and did not speak *ex suo sensu*, not *humano impulsu*, not *sponte sua*, not *arbitrio suo*, but set out only *quae coelitus mandata fuerant*.[36] The diversity of the human authors thus disappears for Calvin before the unity of the Spirit, the sole responsible author of Scripture, which is to him therefore not the *verba Dei*, but emphatically the *verbum Dei*.[37] It is *a Deo* (*Inst.* I. vii. 5); it has "come down to us from the very mouth of God" (I. vii. 5);[38] it has "come down from heaven as if the living words of God themselves were heard in it" (I. vii. 1);[39] and "we owe it therefore the same reverence which we owe to God Himself, since it has proceeded from Him alone, and there is nothing human mixed with it"

(Com. on 2 Tim. iii. 16).[40] According to this declaration the Scriptures are altogether divine, and in them, as he puts it energetically in another place, "it is God who speaks with us and not mortal men" (Com. on 2 Pet. i. 20).[41] Accordingly, he cites Scripture everywhere not as the word of man but as the pure word of God. His "holy word" is "the scepter of God", every statement in which is "a heavenly oracle" which "cannot fail" (*Dedicatory Epistle* to the *Institutes*): in it God "opens His own sacred mouth" to add His direct word to the "voice" of His mute creatures (I. vi. 1). To say "Scripture says" and to say "the Holy Ghost says" is all one. We contradict the Holy Spirit, says Calvin—meaning the Scriptures—when we deny to Christ the name of Jehovah or anything which belongs to the majesty of Jehovah (I. xiii. 23). "The Holy Spirit pronounces", says he, . . . "Paul declares . . . the Scriptures condemn . . . wherefore it is not surprising if the Holy Spirit reject"—all in one running context, meaning ever the same thing (I. v. 13): just as in another context he uses interchangably the "commandments of Christ" and the "authority of Scripture" of the same thing. (*Dedicatory Epistle*).

It may be that Calvin has nowhere given us a detailed discussion of the mode of the divine operation in giving the Scriptures. He is sure that they owe their origin to the divine gift (I. vi. 1, 2, 3) and that God has so given them that they are emphatically His word, as truly as if we were listening to His living voice speaking from heaven (I. vii. 1): and, as we have seen, he is somewhat addicted to the use of language which, strictly taken, would imply that the mode of their gift was "dictation". The Scriptures are 'public records' (I. vi. 2), their human authors have acted as 'notaries' (IV. viii. 9) who have set down nothing of their own, but only what has been dictated to them, so that there appears no admixture of what is human in their product (on 2 Tim. iii. 16).[42] It is not unfair to urge, however, that this language is figurative; and that what Calvin has in mind is not to insist that the mode of inspiration was dictation, but that the result of inspiration is as if it were by dictation, viz., the production of a pure word of God free from all human admixtures. The term "dictation" was no doubt in current use at the time to express rather the effects than the mode of inspiration.[43] This being allowed, it is all the more unfair to urge that, Calvin's language being in this sense figurative, he is not to be understood as teaching that the effect of inspiration was the production of a pure word of God, free from all admixture of human error. This, on the contrary, is precisely what Calvin does teach, and that with the greatest strenuousness. He everywhere asserts that the effects of inspiration are such that God alone is the responsible author of the inspired product, that we owe the same reverence to it as to God Himself, and should esteem the words as purely His as if we heard them proclaimed with His living voice from heaven; and that there is nothing human mixed with them. And he everywhere deals with them on that assumption.

It is true that men have sought to discover in Calvin, particularly in his *Harmony of the Gospels,* acknowledgments of the presence of human errors in the fabric of Scripture.[44] But these attempts rest on very crass misapprehensions of Calvin's efforts precisely to show that there are no such errors in the fabric of Scripture. When he explains, for example, that the purpose "of the Evangelists"—or "of the Holy Spirit", for he significantly uses these designations as synonyms—was not to write a chronologically exact record, but to present the general essence of things, this is not to allow that the Gospels err humanly in their record of the sequences of time, but to assert that they intend to give no sequences of time and therefore cannot err in this regard. When again he suggests that an "error" has found its way into the text of Matt. xxvii. 9 or possibly into Matt. xxiii. 35, he is not speaking of the original, but of the transmitted text;[45] and it would be hard if he were not permitted to make such excursions into the region of textual criticism without laying himself open to the charge of denying his most assured conviction that nothing human is mixed with Scripture.   In point of fact, Calvin not only asserts the freedom of Scripture as given by God from all error, but never in his detailed dealing with Scripture allows that such errors exist in it.[45a]

If we ask for the ground on which he asserts this high doctrine of inspiration, we do not see that any other reply can be given than that it was on the ground of the teaching of Scripture itself.   The Scriptures were understood by Calvin to claim to be in this high sense the Word of God; and a critical scrutiny of their contents brought to him nothing which seemed to him to negative this claim.   There were other grounds on which he might and did base a firm confidence in the divine origin of the Scriptures and the trustworthiness of their teaching as a revelation from God. But there were no other grounds on which he could or did rest his conviction that these Scriptures are so from God that there is nothing human mixed with them, and their every affirmation is to be received with the deference which is due to the living voice of God speaking from heaven.   On these other grounds Calvin was led to trust the teaching of the Scriptures as a divine revelation: and he therefore naturally trusted their teaching as to their own nature and inspiration.

Such, then, are the Scriptures as conceived by Calvin: sixty-six sacred books, "dictated" by God to His "notaries" that they might, in this "public record", stand as a perpetual special revelation of Himself to His people, to supplement or to supersede in their case the general revelation which He gives of Himself in His works and deeds, but which is rendered ineffective by the sin-bred disabilities of the human soul. For this, according to Calvin, is the account to give of the origin of Scripture, and this the account to give of the function it serves in the world. It was because man in his sinful imbecility was unable to profit by the general revelation which God has spread before all eyes, so that they are all without excuse (I. vi. 1), that God in His goodness gave to "those whom He intended to unite in a more close and familiar connection with Himself", a special revelation in open speech (I. vi. 1). And it was because of the mutability of the human mind, prone to errors of all kinds, corrupting the truth, that He committed this His special revelation to writing, that it might never be inaccessible to "those to whom He determined to make His instructions effectual" (I. vi. 3). In Calvin's view, therefore, the Scriptures are a documentation of God's special revelation of Himself unto salvation (I. v. 1 *ad init.*); but a documentation cared for by God Himself, so that they are, in fine, themselves the special revelation of God unto salvation in documentary form (I. vi. 2, 3). The necessity for the revelation documented in them arises from the blindness of men in their sin: the necessity for the documentation of this revelation arises from the instability of men, even when taught of God. We must conceive of special revelation, and of the Scriptures as just its documentation, therefore, as not precisely a cure, but rather an assistance to man dulled in his sight so as not to be able to perceive God in His general revelation. "For", says Calvin, "as persons who are old, or whose eyes have somehow become dim, if you show them the most beautiful book, though they perceive that something is written there, can scarcely read two words together, yet by the aid of spectacles will begin to read distinctly,—so the Scripture . . . " etc. (I. vi. 1). The function of Scripture thus, as special revelation documented, is to serve as spiritual spectacles to enable those of dulled spiritual sight to see God.

Of course, the Scriptures do more than this. They not only reveal the God of Nature more brightly to the sin-darkened eye; they reveal also the God of Grace, who may not be found in nature. Calvin does not overlook this wider revelation embodied in them: he particularly adverts to it (I. vi. 1). But he turns from it for the moment as less directly germane to his present object, which is to show that without the "spectacles" of Scripture, sinful man would not be able to attain to a sound knowledge of even God the Creator. It is on this, therefore, that he now insists. It was only because God revealed Himself in this special, supernatural way to them, that our first fathers—"Adam, Noah, Abraham and the rest of the patriarchs"—were able to retain Him in their knowledge (I. vi. 1). It was only through this special revelation, whether renewed to them by God, or handed down in tradition "by the ministry of men", that their posterity continued in the knowledge of God (I. vi. 2). "At length, that the truth might remain in the world in a continual course of instruction to all ages, God determined that the same oracles which He deposited with the patriarchs, should be committed to public records"—first the Law, then the Prophets, and then the books of the New Covenant (I. vi. 2, 3). It is now, therefore, only through these Scriptures that man can attain to a true knowledge of God. The revelation of God in His works is not useless: it makes all men without excuse; it provides an additional though lower and less certain revelation of God to His people—to a consideration of which all should seriously apply themselves, though they should principally attend to the Word (I. vi. 2). But experience shows that without the Word the sinful human mind is too weak to reach a sound knowledge of God, and therefore without it men wander in vanity and error. Calvin seems to speak sometimes almost as if the Scriptures, that is special revelation, wholly superseded general revelation (I. v. 12 *ad fin.;* vi. 2 *ad fin.;* 4 *ad fin.*). More closely scrutinized it becomes evident, however, that he means only that in the absence of Scripture, that is of special revelation, the general revelation of God is ineffective to preserve any sound knowledge of Him in the world: but in the presence of Scripture, general revelation is not set aside, but rather brought back to its proper validity. The real relation between general and special revelation, as the matter lay in Calvin's mind, thus proves to be, not that the one supersedes the other, but that special revelation supplements general revelation indeed, but in the first instance rather repeats and by repeating vivifies and vitalizes general revelation, and flows confluently in with it to the one end of both, the knowledge of God (I. vi. 2). What special revelation is, therefore,—and the Scriptures as its documentation—is very precisely represented by the figure of the spectacles. It is aid to the dulled vision of sinful man, to enable it to see God.

The question forcibly presents itself, however, whether "spectacles" will serve the purpose here. Has not Calvin painted the sin-bred blindnes: of men too blackly to encourage us to think it can be corrected by such an aid to any remainders of natural vision which may be accredited to them? The answer must be in the affirmative. But this only opens the way to point out that Calvin does not present special revelation, or the Scriptures as special revelation documented, as the entire cure, but places by the side of it the *testimonium Spiritus Sancti*. Special revelation, or Scripture as its documented form, provides in point of fact, in the view of Calvin, only the objective side of the cure he finds has been provided by God. The subjective side is provided by the *testimonium Spiritus Sancti*. The spectacles are provided by the Scriptures: the eyes are opened that they may see even through these spectacles, only by the witness of the Spirit in the heart. We perceive, then, that in Calvin's view the figure of the spectacles is a perfectly just one. He means to intimate that special revelation alone will not produce a knowledge of God in the human soul: that something more than external aid is needed before the soul can see: and to leave the way open to point out what further is required that sinful man may see God. Sinful man, we say again: for the whole crux lies there. Had there been no sin, there would have been no need of even special revelation. In the light of the splendid revelation of Himself which God has displayed in the theatre of nature, man with his native endowment of instinctive knowledge of God would have bloomed out into a full and sound knowledge of Him. But with sinful man, the matter is wholly different. He needs more light and he needs something more than light—he needs the power of sight.[46] That we may apprehend Calvin's thought, therefore, we must turn to the consideration of his doctrine of the Testimony of the Spirit.

III. THE TESTIMONY OF THE SPIRIT.

What is Calvin's doctrine of the Testimony of the Spirit?

The particular question to which Calvin addresses himself when he turns to the consideration of what he calls the testimony of the Spirit concerns the accrediting of Scripture, not the assimilation of its revelatory contents. The reader cannot fail to experience some disappointment at this. The whole development of the discussion hitherto undoubtedly fosters the expectation, not, indeed, of an exclusive treatment of the assimilation of special revelation by sinful man—for both problems are raised by it and the two problems are at bottom one and their solution one—but certainly of some formal treatment of it, and indeed of such a treatment of the double problem that the stress should be laid on this. Calvin, however, is preoccupied with the problem of the accrediting of Scripture. This is due in part, doubtless, to its logical priority: as he himself remarks, we cannot "be established in the belief of the doctrine, till we are indubitably persuaded that God is its Author" (I. vii. 4 *ad init.*). But it was rendered almost inevitable by the state of the controversy with Rome, who intrenched herself in the position that the Protestant appeal to Scripture as over against the Church was inoperative, seeing that it is only by the Church that the Scriptures can be established in authority: for who but the Church can assure us that these Scriptures are from God, or indeed what books enter into the fabric of Scripture, or whether they have come down to us uncorrupted? As a practical man writing to practical men for a practical purpose, Calvin could not fail, perhaps, to give his primary attention to the aspect of the problem he had raised which was most immediately pressing. But this scarcely prepares us for the almost total neglect of its other aspect, with the effect that the construction of his general doctrine is left with a certain appearance of incompleteness. Not really incomplete; for the solution of the one problem is, as we have already suggested, the solution of the other also; and even the cursory reader—or perhaps we may say especially the cursory reader—may well be trusted to feel this as he is led on through the discussion, particularly as there are not lacking repeated suggestions of it, and the discussion closes with a direct reference to it and a formal postponement of the particular discussion of the other aspect of the double problem to a later portion of the treatise. "I pass over many things for the present", says Calvin, "because this subject will present itself for discussion in another place. Only, let it be known here that that alone is true faith which the Spirit of God seals in our hearts. And with this one reason every reader of docility and modesty will be satisfied" (I. vii. 5, near the end). That is as much as to say, This whole subject is only one application of the general doctrine of faith; and as the general doctrine of faith is fully discussed at another place in this treatise, we may content ourselves here with the somewhat incomplete remarks we have made upon this special application of that doctrine; we only need to remind the reader that there is no true faith except that which is begotten in the soul by the Holy Spirit.

We can scarcely wonder that Calvin contents himself with this simple reference of the topic now engaging his attention, as a specific case, to the generic doctrine of faith, when we pause to realize how nearly this simple reference of it, as a species to its genus, comes to a sufficient exposition of it. We shall stop now to signalize only two points which are involved in this reference, the noting of which will greatly facilitate our apprehension of Calvin's precise meaning in his doctrine of the testimony of the Spirit to the divinity of Scripture, which is the question that more particularly engages his attention here. This doctrine is no isolated doctrine with Calvin, standing out of relation with the other doctrines of his system: it is but one application of his general doctrine of faith; or to be more specific, one application of his general doctrine of the function of the Holy Spirit in the production of faith. Given Calvin's general doctrine of the work of the Holy Spirit in applying salvation, and his specific doctrine of the *testimonium Spiritus Sancti* in the attestation of Scripture, and in the applying of its doctrine as well, was inevitable. It is but one application of the general doctrine that there is no true faith except that which the Spirit of God seals in our hearts. For Calvin in this doctrine—and this is the second point we wish to signalize—has in mind specifically "true faith". He is not asking here how the Scriptures may be proved to be from God. If that had been the question he was asking, he would not have hesitated to say that the testimony of the Church is conclusive of the fact. He does say so. "The universal judgment of the Church" (I. vii. 3 *ad fin.*) he represents as a very useful argument, "the consent of the Church" (I. viii. 12 *ad init.*) as a very important consideration, in establishing the divine origin of the Scriptures: although, of course, he does not conceive the Church as lending her authority to Scripture "when she receives and seals it with her suffrage", but rather as performing a duty of piety to herself in recognizing what is true apart from her authentication, and treating it with due veneration (I. vii. 2 *ad fin.*). For what is more her duty than "obediently to embrace what is from God as the sheep hear the voice of the shepherd"?[47] Were it a matter of proving the Scriptures to be the Word of God, Calvin would, again, have been at no loss for rational arguments which he was ready to pronounce irresistible. He does adduce such arguments and he does pronounce them irresistible. He devotes a whole chapter to the adduction of these arguments (ch. viii),—such arguments as these: the dignity of the subject-matter of Scripture—the

heavenliness of its doctrine and the consent of all its parts—
(§ 1), the majesty of its style (§ 2), the antiquity of its
teaching (§ 3), the sincerity of its narrative (§ 4), its
miraculous accompaniment, circumstantially confirmed (§§
5, 6), its predictive contents authenticated by fulfilment
(§§ 7, 8), its continuous use through so many ages (§§
9-12), its sealing by martyr blood (§ 13) : and these arguments he is so far from considering weak and inconclusive
(I. viii. 13 *med.*) that he represents them rather as capable
of completely vindicating the Scriptures against all the subtleties of their calumniators (*ibid.*).   Nay, he declares that
the proofs of the divine origin of the Scriptures are so
cogent, as "certainly to evince, if there is a God in heaven,
that He is the author of the Law, and the Prophecies, and
the Gospel" (I. vii. 4, near the beginning) ; as to extort
with certainty from all who are not wholly lost to shame,
the confession of the divine gift of the Scriptures (*ibid.*).[48]
"Though I am far from possessing any peculiar dexterity"
in argument "or eloquence", he says, "yet were I to contend
with the most subtle despisers of God, who are ambitious to
display their wit and their skill in weakening the authority
of Scripture, I trust I should be able without difficulty to
silence their obstreperous clamor" (*ibid.*).   But objective
proofs—whether the conclusive testimony of witnesses, or
the overwhelming evidence of rational considerations,—be
they never so cogent,[49] he does not consider of themselves
capable of producing "true faith".   And it is "true faith",
we repeat, that Calvin has in mind in his doctrine of the
testimonium Spiritus Sancti.   If it seemed to him a small
matter that man should know that God is if he did not know
what God is, it equally seemed to him a small matter that
man should know what God is, in the paradigms of the intellect, if he did not really know this God in the intimacy of

communion which that phrase imports. And equally it seemed to him utterly unimportant that a man should be convinced by stress of rational evidence that the Scriptures are the Word of God, unless he practically embraced these Scriptures as the Word of God and stayed his soul upon them. The knowledge of God which Calvin has in mind in this whole discussion is, thus, a vital and vitalizing knowledge of God, and the attestation of Scripture which he is seeking is not an attestation merely to the intelligence of men, compelling from them perhaps a reluctant judgment of the intellect alone (since those convinced against their will, as the proverb has it, are very apt to remain of the same opinion still), but such an attestation as takes hold of the whole man in the roots of his activities and controls all the movements of his soul.

This is so important a consideration for the exact apprehension of Calvin's doctrine that it may become us to pause and assure ourselves of the simple matter of fact from the language which Calvin employs of it in the course of the discussion. We shall recall that from the introduction of the topic of special revelation he has in mind and keeps before his readers' mind its destination for the people of God alone. The provisions for producing a knowledge of God, consequent on the inefficiency of natural revelation, Calvin is careful to explain, are not for all men, but for "the elect" (I. vi. 1), or, as they are more fully described, "those whom God intends to unite in a more close and familiar connection with Himself" (*ibid.*), "those to whom He determines to make His instructions effectual" (I. vi. 3). From the first provisions of His supernatural dealings, therefore, He "intends to make His instructions effectual". More pointedly still he speaks of the *testimonium Spiritus Sancti* as an act in which "God deigns to confer a singular power on His elect, whom He distinguishes from the rest of mankind" (I. vii. 5).[50] This singular power, now, is nothing else but "saving faith", and Calvin speaks of it in all the synonymy of "saving faith". He calls it "true faith" (I. vi. 5), "sound faith" (I. vii. 4), "firm faith" (I. viii. 13), "the faith of the pious" (I. vii. 3), "the certainty of the pious" (I. vii. 3), "that assurance which is essential to true piety" (I. vii. 4), "saving knowledge" (I. viii. 13), "a solid assurance of eternal life" (I. vii. 1). It is the thing which is naturally described by this synonymy which Calvin declares is not produced in the soul except by the testimony of the Holy Spirit. This obviously is nothing more than to declare that that faith which lays hold of Christ unto eternal life is the product of the Holy Spirit in the heart, and that it is one of the exercises of this faith to lay hold of the revelation of this Christ in the Scriptures with assured confidence, so that it is only he who is led by the Spirit who embraces these Scriptures with "sound faith", that is, "with that assurance which is essential to true piety" (I. vii. 4). What Calvin has in mind, in a word, is simply an extended comment on Paul's words: "the natural man receiveth not the things of the Spirit of God . . . but he that is spiritual judgeth all things" (1 Cor. ii. 14, 15).[51]

Calvin does not leave us, however, to gather from general remarks referring it to its class or to infer from its general effects, what he means by the testimony of the Spirit of God to the divinity of Scripture, but describes for us its nature and indicates the mode of its operation and specific effects with great exactitude.[52] He tells us that it is a "secret" (I. vii. 4), "internal" (I. vii. 13), "inward" (I. vii. 5) action of the Holy Spirit on the soul, by which the soul is "illuminated" (I. vii. 3, 4, 5), so as to perceive their true quality in the Scriptures as a divine book. We may call

this " an inward teaching" of the Spirit which produces
"entire acquiescence in the Scriptures", so that they are
self-authenticating to the mind and heart (I. vii. 5); or we
may call it a "secret testimony of the Spirit", by which our
minds and hearts are convinced with a firmness superior to
all reason that the Scriptures are from God (I. vii. 4).   In
both instances we are using figurative language.   Precisely
what is produced by the hidden internal operation of the
Spirit on the soul is a new spiritual sense (*sensus*, I. vii. 5,
near end), by which the divinity of Scripture is perceived
as by an intuitive perception.   "For the Scripture exhibits
as clear evidence of its truth, as white and black things do
of their color, and sweet and bitter things of their taste"
(I. vii. 2, end): and we need only a sense to discern its
divine quality to be convinced of it with the same immediacy
and finality as we are convinced by their mere perception of
light or darkness, of whiteness or blackness, of sweetness
or bitterness (*ibid.*).   No conclusions based on "reasoning"
or "proofs" or founded on human judgment can compare in
clearness or force with such a conviction, which is instinctive and immediate   and   finds   its   ultimate   ground   and
sanction in the Holy Spirit who has wrought in the heart
this spiritual sense which so functions in recognizing the
divine quality of Scripture.   Illuminated by the Spirit of
God, we believe, therefore, not on the ground of our own
judgment, or on the ground of the judgment of others, but
with a certainty above all human judgment, by a spiritual
intuition.[53]   With the utmost explicitness Calvin so describes this instinctive conviction in a passage of great
vigor: "It is, therefore", says he, "such a persuasion as
requires no reasons; such a knowledge as is supported by the
highest reason and in which the mind rests with greater
security and constancy than in any reasons; in fine, such a

sense as cannot be produced but by a revelation from
heaven" (I. vii. 5).[54] Here we are told that it is a *persuasio,* or rather a *notitia,* or rather a *sensus.* It is a persuasion which does not require reasons,—that is to say, it is
a state of conviction not induced by arguments, but by direct
perception: it is, that is to say, a knowledge, a direct perception in accord with the highest reason, in which the mind
rests, with an assurance not attainable by reasoning; or to
be more explicit still, it is a sense which comes only from
divine gift. As we have implanted in us by nature a sense
which distinguishes between light and darkness, a sense
which distinguishes between sweet and bitter, and the verdict of these senses is immediate and final; so we have
planted in us by the creative action of the Holy Spirit a
sense for the divine, and its verdict, too, is immediate and
final: the spiritual man discerneth all things. Such, in
briefest outline, is Calvin's famous doctrine of the testimony of the Spirit.

MODE OF THIS TESTIMONY.

Certain further elucidations of its real meaning and
bearing appear, however, to be necessary, to guard against
misapprehension of it. When we speak of an internal testimony of the Holy Spirit, it is evident that we must conceive it as presenting itself in one of three ways. It may be
conceived as of the nature of an immediate revelation to
each man to whom it is given. It may be conceived as of the
nature of a blind conviction produced in the minds of its
recipients. It may be conceived as of the nature of a
grounded conviction, formed in their minds by the Spirit,
by an act which rather terminates immediately on the faculties, enabling and effectively persuading them to reach a
conviction on grounds presented to them, than produces the

conviction itself, apart from or without grounds. In which of these ways did Calvin conceive the testimony of the Spirit as presenting itself?

Certainly not the first. The testimony of the Spirit was not to Calvin of the nature of a propositional "revelation" to its recipients. Of this he speaks perfectly explicitly, and indeed in his polemic against Anabaptist mysticism insistently. He does indeed connect the term "revelation" with the testimony of the Spirit, declaring it, for example, such a sense (*sensus*) as can be produced by nothing short of "a revelation from heaven" (I. vii. 5, near end). But his purpose in the employment of this language is not to describe it according to its nature, but to claim for it with emphasis a heavenly source: he means merely to assert that it is not earth-born, but God-wrought, while at the same time he intimates that in its nature it is not a propositional revelation, but an instinctive "sense". That he did not conceive of it as a propositional revelation is made perfectly clear by his explicit assertions at the opening of the discussion (I. vii. 1 *ad init.*), that we "are not favored with daily oracles from heaven", and that the Scriptures constitute the sole body of extant revelations from God. It is not to supersede nor yet to supplement these recorded revelations that the testimony of the Spirit is given us, he insists, but to confirm them (I. ix. 3): or, as he puts it in his polemic against the Anabaptists, "The office of the Spirit which is promised us is not to feign new and unheard of revelations, or to coin a new system of doctrine, which would seduce us from the received doctrine of the Gospel, but to seal to our minds the same doctrine which the Gospel delivers" (I. ix. 1 *ad init.*).

In this polemic against the Anabaptists (ch. ix) he gives us an especially well-balanced account of the relations which in his view obtain between the revelation of God and the witness of the Spirit. If he holds that the revelation of God is ineffective without the testimony of the Spirit, he holds equally that the testimony of the Spirit is inconceivable without the revelation of God embodied in the Word. He even declares that the Spirit is no more the agent by which the Word is impressed on the heart than the Word is the means by which the illumination of the Spirit takes effect. "If apart from the Spirit of God we are utterly destitute of the light of truth", he says (I. ix. 3 *ad fin.*), "equally the Word is the instrument by which the Lord dispenses to believers the illumination of the Spirit." So far as the knowledge of the truth is concerned, we are as helpless, then, without the Word as we are without the Spirit, for the whole function of the Spirit with respect to the truth is, not to reveal to us the truth anew, much less to reveal to us new truth, but efficaciously to confirm the Word, revealed in the Scriptures, to us, and efficaciously to impress it on our hearts (I. ix. 3). This Calvin makes superabundantly plain by an illustration and a didactic statement of great clearness. The illustration (I. ix. 3) is drawn from our Lord's dealings with His two disciples with whom after His rising He walked to Emmaus. "He opened their understandings", Calvin explains, "not that rejecting the Scriptures they might be wise of themselves, but that they might understand the Scriptures." Such also, he says, is the testimony of the Spirit to-day: for what is it—and this is the didactic statement to which we have referred—but an enabling of us by the light of the Spirit to behold the divine countenance in the Scriptures that so our minds may be filled with a solid reverence for the Word (I. ix. 3)? Here we have the nature of the testimony of the Spirit, and its manner of working and its effects, announced to us in a single clause. It is an illumination of our minds, by which we are enabled to see God in the Scriptures, so that we may reverence them as from Him.

Other effect that this Calvin explicitly denies to the testimony of the Spirit and defends his denial from the charge of inconsistency with the stress he has previously laid upon the necessity of this testimony (I. ix. 3). It is not to deny the necessity of this work of the Spirit, he argues, to confine it to the express confirmation of the Word and of the revelation contained therein. Nor is it derogatory to the Spirit to confine His operations now to the confirmation of the revealed Word. While on the other hand to attribute to Him repeated or new revelations to each of the children of God, as the mystics do, is derogatory to the Word, which is His inspired product. To lay claim to the possession of such a Spirit as this, he declares, is to lay claim to the possession of a different Spirit from that which dwelt in Christ and the Apostles—for their Spirit honored the Word—and a different spirit from that which was promised by Christ to His disciples—for this Spirit was "not to speak of Himself". It is to lay claim to a Spirit for whose divine mission and character, moreover, we lack all criterion—for how can we know that the Spirit that speaks in us is from God, save as He honors the Word of God (I. ix. 1 and 2)? From all which it is perfectly plain not only that Calvin did not conceive the testimony of the Spirit as taking effect in the form of propositional revelations, but that he did conceive it as an operation of God the Holy Spirit in the heart of man which is so connected with the revelation of God in His Word, that it manifests itself only in conjunction with that revelation.

Calvin's formula here is, The Word and Spirit.[55] Only in the conjunction of the two can an effective revelation be

made to the sin-darkened mind of man.[56] The Word supplies the objective factor; the Spirit the subjective factor:
and only in the union of the objective and subjective factors
is the result accomplished. The whole objective revelation
of God lies, thus, in the Word. But the whole subjective
capacitating for the reception of this revelation lies in the
will of the Spirit. Either, by itself, is wholly ineffective to
the result aimed at—the production of knowledge in the
human mind. But when they unite, knowledge is not only
rendered possible to man: it is rendered certain. And therefore it is that Calvin represents the provision for the
knowledge of God both in the objective revelation in the
Word and in the subjective testimony of the Spirit as destined by God not for men at large, but specifically for His
people, His elect, those "to whom He determined to make
His instructions effectual" (I. vi. 3). The Calvinism of
Calvin's doctrine of religious knowledge comes to clear
manifestation here; and that not merely because of its implication of the doctrine of election, but also because of its
implication of Calvin's specific doctrine of the means of
grace. Already in his doctrine of religious knowledge, we
find Calvin teaching that God is known not by those who
choose to know Him, but by those by whom He chooses to
be known: and this simply because the knowledge of God
is God-given, and is therefore given to whom He will. Men
do not wring the knowledge of God from a Deity reluctant
to be known: God imparts the knowledge of Himself to
men reluctant to know Him: and therefore none know
Him save those to whom He efficaciously imparts, by His
Word and Spirit, the knowledge of Himself. "By His
Word and Spirit",—therein is expressed already the fundamental formula of the Calvinistic doctrine of the "means of
grace". In that doctrine the Spirit is not, with the Luth-

erans, conceived as in the Word, conveyed and applied wherever the Word goes: nor is the Word, with the mystics, conceived as in the Spirit always essentially present where-ever He is present in His power as a Spirit of revelation and truth. The two are severally contemplated, as separable factors in the one work of God in producing the knowledge of Himself, which is eternal life, in the souls of His people; separable factors which must both, however, be present if this knowledge of God is to be produced. For it is the function of the Word to set before the soul the object to be believed; and it is the function of the Spirit to quicken in the soul belief in this object: and neither performs the work of the other or its own work apart from the other.

It still remains, however, to inquire precisely how Calvin conceived the Spirit to operate in bringing the soul to a hearty faith in the Word as a revelation from God. Are we to understand him as teaching that the Holy Spirit by His almighty power creates, in the souls of those whom God has set upon to bring to a knowledge of Him, an entirely ungrounded faith in the divinity of the Scriptures and the truth of their contents, so that the soul embraces them and their contents with firm confidence as a revelation from God wholly apart from and in the absence of all *indicia* of their divinity or of the truth of their contents? So it has come to be very widely believed; and indeed it may even be said that it has become the prevalent representation that Calvin taught that believers have within themselves a witness of the Spirit by which they are assured of the divinity of Scripture and the truth of its contents quite apart from all other evidence. The very term, "the testimony of the Spirit", is adduced in support of this representation, as setting a divine witness to the divinity of Scripture over against other sources of evidence, and of course superseding them: and appeal is made along with this to Calvin's strong assertions of the uselessness and even folly of plying men with "the proofs" of the divine origin of Scripture, seeing that, it is said, in the absence of the testimony of the Spirit such "proofs" must needs be ineffective, and in the presence of that effective testimony they cannot but be adjudged unnecessary. What can he mean, then, it is asked, but that the testimony of the Holy Spirit is sufficient to assure us of the divinity of Scripture apart from all *indicia,* and does its work entirely independently of them?

The sufficient answer to this question is that he can mean—and in point of fact does mean—that the *indicia* are wholly insufficient to assure us of the divinity of Scripture apart from the testimony of the Spirit; and effect no result independently of it. This is quite a different proposition and gives rise to quite a different series of corollaries. Calvin's dealing with the *indicia* of the divinity of Scripture has already attracted our attention in one of its aspects, and it is quite worthy of renewed scrutiny. We have seen that he devotes a whole chapter to their exposition (ch. viii) and strongly asserts their objective conclusiveness to the fact of the divine origin of Scripture (I. vii. 4). Nor does he doubt their usefulness whether to the believer or the unbeliever. The fulness and force of his exposition of them is the index to his sense of their value to the believer: for he adduces them distinctly as confirmations of believers in their faith in the Scriptures (I. viii. 1, 13), and betrays in every line of their treatment the high significance he attaches to them as such. And he explicitly declares that they not only maintain in the minds of the pious the native dignity and authority of Scripture, but completely vindicate it against all the subtleties of calumniators (I. viii. 13). No man of sound mind can fail to confess on their basis that it is God who speaks in Scripture and its doctrine is divine (I. vii. 4). It is a complete misapprehension of Calvin's meaning, then, when it is suggested that he represents the *indicia* of the divinity of Scripture as inconclusive or even as ineffective.[57] Their conclusiveness could not be asserted with more energy than he asserts it: nor indeed could their effectiveness—their effectiveness in extorting from the unbeliever the confession of the divinity of Scripture and in rendering him without excuse in refusing the homage of his mind and heart to it—in a word, will he, nill he, convincing his intellect of its divinity; their effectiveness also in confirming the believer in his faith and maintaining his confidence intact. This prevalent misapprehension of Calvin's meaning is due to neglect to observe the precise thing for which he affirms the *indicia* to be ineffective and the precise reason he assigns for this ineffectiveness. There is only one thing which he says they cannot do: that is to produce "sound faith" (I. vii. 4), "firm faith" (I. viii. 13),—that assurance which is essential to "true piety" (I. vii. 4). And their failure to produce "sound faith" is due solely to the subjective condition of man, which is such that a creative operation of the Holy Spirit on the soul is requisite before he can exercise "sound faith" (I. vi. 4; viii. 1, 13). It is the attempt to produce this "sound faith" in the heart of man, not renewed for believing by the creative operation of the Holy Spirit, which Calvin pronounces preposterous and foolish. "It is acting a preposterous part", he says, "to endeavor to produce *sound faith* in the Scriptures by disputations": objections may be silenced by such disputations, "but this will not fix in men's hearts *that assurance which is essential to true piety*"; for religion is not a matter of mere opinion, but a fundamental change of attitude towards God (I. vii. 4). It betrays,

therefore, great folly to wish to demonstrate to infidels
that the Scriptures are the Word of God, he repeats in
another place, obviously with no other meaning, "since
this cannot be known without faith", that is, as the context
shows, without the internal working of the Spirit of God
(I. viii. 13 *ad fin.*).

That Calvin should thus teach that the *indicia* are incapable of producing "firm faith" in the human heart, disabled
by sin, is a matter of course: and therefore it is a matter
of course that he should teach that the *indicia* are ineffective
for the production of "sound faith" apart from the internal
operation of the Spirit correcting the sin-bred disabilites of
man, that is to say, apart from the testimony of the Spirit.
But what about the *indicia* in conjunction with the testimony
of the Spirit? It would seem to be evident that, on Calvin's
ground, they would have their full part to play here, and
that we must say that, when the soul is renewed by the Holy
Spirit to a sense for the divinity of Scripture, it is through
the *indicia* of that divinity that it is brought into its proper
confidence in the divinity of Scripture. In treating of the
indicia, Calvin does not, however, declare this in so many
words. He sometimes even appears to speak of them rather
as if they lay side by side with the testimony of the Spirit
than acted along with it as co-factors in the production of
the supreme effect. He speaks of their ineffectiveness in
producing sound faith in the unbeliever: and of their value
as corroboratives to the believer: and his language would
sometimes seem to suggest that therefore it were just as well
not to employ them until after faith had formed itself under
the testimony of the Spirit (I. viii. 1, 13). Of their part in
forming faith under the operation of the testimony of the
Spirit he does not appear explicitly to speak.[58]

Nevertheless, there are not lacking convincing hints that

there was lying in his mind all the time the implicit understanding that it is through these *indicia* of the divinity of
Scripture that the soul, under the operation of the testimony
of the Spirit, reaches its sound faith in Scripture, and that
he has been withheld from more explicitly stating this only
by the warmth of his zeal for the necessity of the testimony
of the Spirit which has led him to a constant contrasting of
this divine with those human "testimonies". Thus we find
him repeatedly affirming that these *indicia* will produce no
fruit *until* they be confirmed by the internal testimony of the
Spirit (I. vii. 4, 5; viii. 1, 13). "Our reverence may be
conciliated by the internal majesty of Scripture, but it never
seriously affects us, *till* it is confirmed by the Spirit in our
hearts" (I. vii. 5). *"Without this certainty,* in vain will the
authority of Scripture be either defended by arguments or
established by the consent of the Church, or of any other
supports: since without the foundation be laid, it remains
in perpetual suspense" (I. viii. 1). The *indicia* "are *alone*
not sufficient to produce firm faith in the Scriptures, *till* the
heavenly Father, discovering His own power therein, places
its authority above all controversy" (I. viii. 13). It is,
however, in his general teaching as to the formation of
sound faith in the divinity of Scripture that we find the
surest indication that he thought of the *indicia* as co-
working with the testimony of the Spirit to this result.
This is already given, indeed, in his strenuous insistence
that the work of the Spirit is not of the nature of a revelation, but of a confirmation of the revelation deposited in the
Scriptures, especially when this is taken in connection with
his teaching that Scripture is self-authenticating. What the
Spirit of God imparts to us, he says, is a *sense* of divinity:
such a sense discovers divinity only where divinity is and
only by a perception of it,—a perception which of course

rests on its proper *indicia*. It is because Scripture "exhibits the plainest evidence that it is God who speaks in it" that the newly awakened *sense* of divinity quickened in the soul, recognizes it as divine (I. vii. 4). The senses do not distinguish light from darkness, white from black, sweet from bitter,—to use Calvin's own illustration (I. vii. 2),—save by the mediation of those *indicia* of light and darkness, whiteness and blackness, sweetness and bitterness, by which these qualities manifest themselves to the natural senses: and by parity of reasoning we must accredit Calvin as thinking of the newly implanted spiritual sense discerning the divinity of Scripture only through the mediation of the *indicia* of divinity manifested in Scripture. To taste and see that the Scriptures are divine is to recognize a divinity actually present in Scripture; and of course recognition implies perception of *indicia,* not attribution of a divinity not recognized as inherent. Meanwhile it must be admitted that Calvin has not at this point developed this side of his subject with the fulness which might be wished, but has left it to the general implications of the argument.

OBJECT TESTIFIED TO.

Closely connected with the question of the mode in which Calvin conceived the testimony of the Spirit to be delivered, is the further question of the matters for which he conceived that testimony to be available. On the face of it, it would seem that he conceived it directly available solely for the divinity of the Scriptures and therefore for the revelatory character of their contents. So he seems to imply throughout the discussion, and, indeed, to assert repeatedly. Nevertheless, there is a widespread impression abroad that he appealed to it to determine the canon of Scripture too,[59] and indeed also to establish the integrity of its text. This impression is generally, though not always, connected with the view that Calvin conceived the mode of delivery of the testimony of the Spirit to be the creation in the soul of a blind faith, unmotived by reasons and without rooting in grounds; and it has been much exploited of late years in the interests of a so-called "free" attitude towards Scripture, which announces itself as following Calvin when it refuses to acknowledge as authoritative Scripture any portion of or element in the traditionally transmitted Scriptures which does not spontaneously commend itself to the immediate religious judgment as divine. Undoubtedly this is to reverse the attitude of Calvin towards the traditionally transmitted Scriptures, and it is difficult to believe that two such diametrically contradictory attitudes towards the Scriptures can be outgrowths of the same principial root. In point of fact, moreover, as we have already seen, not only does Calvin not conceive the mode of the delivery of the testimony of the Spirit to be by the creation of a blind and unmotived faith, but, to come at once to the matter more particularly in hand, he does not depend on the testimony of the Spirit for the determination of canonicity or for the establishment of the integrity of the text of Scripture. So far from discarding the *via rationalis* here, he determines the limits of the canon and establishes the integrity of the transmission of Scripture distinctly on scientific, that is to say, historico-critical grounds. In no case of his frequent discussion of such subjects does he appeal to the testimony of the Spirit and set aside the employment of rational and historical argumentation as invalid or inconclusive; always, on the contrary, he adduces the evidence of valid tradition and apostolicity of contents as conclusive of the fact. It is hard to believe that such a consequent mind could have lived unconsciously in such an inconsistent attitude towards a question so vital to him and his cause.[60]

So far as support for the impression that Calvin looked to the testimony of the Spirit to determine for him the canon of Scripture and to assure him of its integrity is derived from his writings, it rests on a manifest misapprehension of a single passage in the *Institutes,* and what seems to be a misassignment to him of a passage in the old French Confession of Faith.

The passage in the *Institutes* is a portion of the paragraphs which are devoted to repelling the Romish contention that " the Scriptures have only so much weight as is conceded to them by the suffrages of the Church; as though the eternal and inviolable truth of God depended on the arbitrary will of men" (I. vii. 1). "For thus", Calvin says— and this is the passage which is appealed to—"For thus, dealing with the Holy Spirit as a mere laughing stock (*ludibrium*), they ask, Who shall give us confidence that these [Scriptures] have come from God,—who assure us that they have reached our time safe and intact,—who persuade us that one book should be received reverently, another expunged from the number (*numero*)—if the Church should not prescribe a certain rule for all these things? It depends, therefore, they say, on the Church, both what reverence is due to Scripture, and what books should be inscribed (*censendi sint*) in its catalogue (*in ejus catalogo*)" (I. vii. 1). This passage certainly shows that the Romish controversialists in endeavoring to prove that the authority of Scripture is dependent on the Church's suffrage, argued that it is only by the Church that we can be assured even of the contents of Scripture and of its integrity,—that its very canon and text rest on the Church's determination. But how can it be inferred that Calvin's response to this argument would take the form: No, of these things we can be assured by the immediate testimony of the Spirit? In point of fact, he says nothing of the kind, and the inference does not lie in the argument. What he says is that the Romish method of arguing is as absurd as it is blasphemous, a mere cavil (I. vii. 2), as well as derogatory to the Holy Spirit. The Holy Spirit, he says, assures us that in the Scriptures God speaks to us. To bid us pause on the ground that it is only the Church who can assure us that this or that book belongs to the body of the Scriptures, that the text has been preserved to us intact and the like, is to interpose frivolous objections, and can have no other end than to glorify the Church at the expense of souls. Accordingly, he remarks that these objectors are without concern what logical difficulties they may cast themselves into: they wish only to prevent men taking their comfort out of the direct assurance by the Spirit of the divinity of the Scriptures. He repudiates, in a word, the entire Romish argument: but we can scarcely infer from this, that his response to it would be that the immediate witness of the Spirit provides us with direct answers to their carping questions. It is at least equally likely from the mere fact that he speaks of these objections as cavils (I. vii. 2) and girds at the logic of the Romish controversialists as absurd, that his response would be that the testimony of the Spirit for which he was contending had no direct concernment with questions of canon and text.

The passage in the Confession of La Rochelle, on the other hand, does certainly attribute the discrimination of the canonical books in some sense—in what sense may admit of debate—to the testimony of the Spirit. In the third article of this Confession there is given a list of the canonical books.[61] The fourth article, then, runs as follows:

"We recognize these books to be canonical and the very certain rule of our faith, not so much by the common accord and consent of the Church, as by the inward witness and persuasion of the Holy Spirit, who makes us distinguish them from the other ecclesiastical books, upon which, though they may be useful, no article of faith can be founded." This article, however, was not the composition of Calvin, but was among those added by the Synod of Paris to the draft submitted by Calvin.[62]   Calvin's own article "On the Books of Holy Scripture", which was expanded by the Synod into several, reads only: "This doctrine does not derive its authority from men, nor from angels, but from God alone; we believe, too (seeing that it is a thing surpassing all human sense to discern that it is God who speaks), that He Himself gives the certitude of it to His elect, and seals it in their hearts by His Spirit."[63] In this fine statement we find the very essence of the teaching of the *Institutes* on this subject; the ideas and even the phraseology of which are reproduced.

We may learn, therefore, at most, from the Confession of La Rochelle, not that Calvin, but that some of his immediate followers attributed in some sense the discrimination of the canonical books to the witness of the Spirit.   Other evidences of this fact are not lacking.   The Belgian Confession, for example, much like that of La Rochelle, declares of the Scriptural books, just enumerated (Art. 5): "We receive all these books alone, as holy and canonical, for the regulation, foundation and establishment of our faith, and we fully believe all that they contain, not so much because the Church receives and approves them, but principally because the Spirit gives witness to them in our hearts that they are from God, and also because they are approved by themselves; for the very blind can perceive that the things come to pass which they predict." Perhaps, however, we may find a more instructive instance still in the words of one of the Protestant disputants in a conference held at Paris in 1566 between two Protestant ministers and two doctors of the Sorbonne.[64] To the inquiry, How do you know that some books are canonical and others apocryphal, the Protestant disputant (M. Lespine) answers: "By the Spirit of God which is a Spirit of discrimination, by whom all those to whom He is communicated are illuminated, so as to be made capable of judging and discerning spiritual things and of recognizing (*cognoistre*) and apprehending the truth (when it is proposed to them), by the witness and assurance which He gives to them in their hearts. And as we discriminate light and darkness by the faculty of sight which is in the eye; so, we can easily separate and recognize (*recognoistre*) truth from falsehood, and from all things in general which can be false, absurd, doubtful or indifferent, when we are invested with the Spirit of God and guided by the light which He lights in our hearts." M. Lespine had evidently read his Calvin; though there is a certain lack of crisp exactness in his language which may raise doubt whether he has necessarily reproduced him with precision. Clearly his idea is that the Spirit of God in His creative operation on the hearts of Christ's people has implanted in them—or quickened in them—a spiritual sense, which recognizes the stamp of divinity upon the books which God has given to the Church, and so separates them out from all others and thus constitutes the canon. This is to attribute the discrimination of the canonical books to the witness of the Spirit not directly but indirectly, namely, through the intermediation of the determination of the books which are of divine origin, which, then, being gathered together, constitute the canon, or

divinely given rule of our faith and life. This conception
of the movement of the mind in this matter became very
common, and was given very clear expression, for example,
by Jurieu,[65] in a context which bears as evident marks of
reminiscences of Calvin as do M. Lespine's remarks. "That
grace which produces faith in a soul", says he, "does not
begin by persuading it that a given book is canonical. This
persuasion comes only afterwards and as a consequence. It
gives to the consciousness a taste for the truth: it applies
this truth to the mind and heart; it proceeds from this subsequently that the believer believes that a given book is
canonical, because the truths which 'find' him are found in
it. In a word, we do not believe that which is contained in
a book to be divine because this book is canonical. But we
believe that a given book is canonical because we have perceived that what it contains is divine. And we have perceived this as we perceive the light when we look on the fire,
sweetness and bitterness when we eat." Whether we are to
attribute this movement of thought, however, to Calvin, is
another question.[66] There is no hint of it in his writings.

It is not even obvious that this precise movement of
thought is the conception which lay in the mind of the
authors of the additional articles in the Confession of La
Rochelle and of the similar statement in the Belgian Confession. The interpretation of these articles is particularly
interesting, as they both undoubtedly came under the eye
of Calvin and their doctrine was never disavowed by him.
It is not, however, altogether easy, because of a certain
ambiguity in the use of the term "canonical". It is on
account of the ambiguity which attends the use of this term
that in speaking of their teaching we have guardedly said
that they appear to suspend the canonicity of the Scriptural
books in some sense directly on the testimony of the Spirit.

This ambiguity may be brought sharply before us by placing in juxtaposition two sentences from Quenstedt in which the term "canonical" is employed, obviously, in two differing senses. "We deny", says he, "that the catalogue of canonical books is an article of faith, superadded to the others [articles of faith] contained in Scripture. Many have faith and may attain salvation who do not hold the number of canonical books. If the word 'canon' be understood of the *number* of the books, we concede that such a catalogue is not contained in Scripture." "These are two different questions", says he again, "whether the Gospel of Matthew is canonical, and whether it was written by Matthew. The former belongs to saving faith; the latter to historical knowledge. For if the Gospel which has come down to us under the name of Matthew had been written by Philip or Bartholomew, it would make no difference to saving faith." In the former extract the question of canonicity is removed from the category of articles of faith; in the latter it is made an integral element of saving faith. The contradiction is glaring—unless there be an undistributed middle. And this is what there really is. In the former passage, where Quenstedt is engaged in repelling the contention that there are articles of faith that must be accepted by all, which are not contained in Scripture—in defending, in a word, the Protestant doctrine of the sufficiency or perfection of Scripture—he uses the terms 'canon', 'canonical' in the purely technical sense of the extent of Scripture. In the latter passage, where he is insisting that the authority of Scripture as the Word of God hangs on its divine, not on its human, author, he uses the term 'canonical' in the sense of "divinely given". The term "canonical" was current, then, in the two senses of 'belonging to the list of authoritative Scriptures', 'entering into the body of the Scriptures', and 'God-given', 'divine'. In which of these two senses is it used in the Gallican and Belgian Confessions? If in the former, then these Confessions teach that the testimony of the Spirit is available directly for the determination of the canon: if in the latter, then they teach no such thing, but only that it is on the testimony of the Spirit that we are assured of the divine origin and character of these books.

That the Gallican Confession employs the term in the latter of these senses, seems at least possible when once attention is called to it, although regard for the last clause of the statement: "who makes us distinguish them from the other ecclesiastical books", etc., prevents the representation of this interpretation as certain. Its declaration, succeeding the catalogue of the books given in the third section, is obviously intended to affirm something that is true of them already as a definite body of books before the mind. "We recognize *these* books", it says, "to be canonical and the very certain rule of our faith". That is to say, to this body of books we ascribe the quality of canonicity and recognize their regulative character. What would seem, then, to be in question is a quality belonging to a list of books already determined and in the mind of the framer of the statement as a whole. The same may be said of the Belgian Confession. It, too, has already given a list of the canonical books, and now proceeds to affirm something that is true of "all of these books and them only". The thing affirmed is that they are "holy and canonical", where the collocation suggests that "canonical" expresses a quality which ranges with "holy". We cannot help suspecting, then, that these early confessions use the term "canonical" not quantitatively but qualitatively, not extensively but intensively; and in that sense it is the equivalent of "divine".[67] Even the inference back from them to Calvin that he may have supposed that the testimony of the Spirit is available to determine the canon becomes therefore doubtful: and no other reason exists why we should attribute this view to him. We cannot affirm that the movement of his thought was never from the divinity of Scripture, assured to us by the testimony of the Spirit, to the determination of the limits of the canon: but we have no reason to ascribe this movement of thought to him except that it was adopted by some of his successors.

On the other hand, Calvin constantly speaks as if the only thing which the testimony of the Spirit assures us of in the case of the Scriptures is the divinity of their origin and contents: and he always treats Scripture when so speaking of it as a definite entity, held before his mind as a whole.[68] In these circumstances his own practice in dealing with the question of canonicity and text, makes it sufficiently clear that he held their settlement to depend on scientific investigation, and appealed to the testimony of the Spirit only to accredit the divine origin of the concrete volume thus put into his hands. The movement of his thought was therefore along this course: first, the ascertainment, on scientific grounds, of the body of books handed down from the Apostles as the rule of faith and practice; secondly, the vindication, on the same class of grounds, of the integrity of their transmission; thirdly, the accrediting of them as divine on the testimony of the Spirit. It is not involved in this that he is to be considered to have supposed that a man must be a scholar before he can be a Christian. He supposed we become Christians not by scholarship but by the testimony of the Spirit in the heart, and he had no inclination to demand scholarship as the basis of our Christianity. It is only involved in the position we ascribe to him that he must be credited with recognizing that questions of scholarship are for scholars and questions of religion only for

Christians as such. He would have said—he does say—that he in whose heart the Spirit bears His testimony will recognize the Scriptures as divine whenever presented to his contemplation, will depend on them with sound trust and will embrace with true faith all that they propound to him. He would doubtless have said that this act of faith logically implicates the determination of the 'canon'. But he would also have said—he does in effect say—that this determination of the canon is a separable act and is to be prosecuted on its own appropriate grounds of scientific evidence. It involves indeed a fundamental misapprehension of Calvin's whole attitude to attribute to him the view that the testimony of the Spirit determines immediately such scientific questions as those of the canon and text of Scripture. The testimony of the Spirit was to him emphatically an operation of the Spirit of God on the heart, which produced distinctively a spiritual effect: it was directed to making men Christians,[69] not to making them theologians. The testimony of the Spirit was, in effect, in his view, just what we in modern times have learned to call "regeneration" considered in its noëtic effects. That "regeneration" has noëtic effects he is explicit and iterative in affirming: but that these noëtic effects of "regeneration" could supersede the necessity of scientific investigation in questions which rest for their determination on matters of fact,—Calvin would be the last to imagine. He who recognized that the conviction of the divinity of Scripture wrought by the testimony of the Spirit rests as its ground on the *indicia* of the divinity of Scripture spiritually discerned in their true weight, could not imagine that the determination of the canon of Scripture or the establishment of its text could be wholly separated from their proper basis in evidence and grounded solely in a blind testimony of the Spirit alone: which indeed in that case would be fundamentally indistinguishable from that "revelation" which he rebuked the Anabaptists for claiming to be the recipients of.

THE TESTIMONY AND THE RELIGIOUS LIFE.

When we clearly apprehend the essence of Calvin's doctrine of the testimony of the Spirit to the divinity of Scripture to be the noëtic effects of "regeneration" we shall know what estimate to place upon the criticism which is sometimes passed upon him that he has insufficiently correlated his doctrine of the testimony of the Spirit with the inner religious life of the Christian,[70] has given too separate a place to the Spirit's witness to Scripture, and thus has overestimated the formal principle of Protestantism in comparison with the material principle,[71] with the effect of giving a hard, dry and legalistic aspect to Christianity as expounded by him. With Luther, it is said, everything is made of justification and the liberty of the Christian man fills the horizon of thought; and this is because his mind is set on the "faith" out of which all good things flow and by which everything—Scripture itself—is dominated. With Calvin, on the other hand, with his primary emphasis on the authority of Scripture, accredited to us by a distinct act of the Holy Spirit, the watchword becomes obedience; and the horizon of thought is filled with a sense of obligation and legalistic anxiety as to conduct.

How Calvin could have failed to correlate sufficiently closely the testimony of the Spirit with the inner Christian life, or could have emphasized the formal principle of Protestantism at the expense of the material, when he conceived of the witness of the Spirit as just one of the effects of "regeneration", it is difficult to see. So to conceive the testimony of the Spirit is on the contrary to make the formal principle of Protestantism just an outgrowth of the material. It is only because our spirits have been renewed by the Holy Spirit that we see with convincing clearness the *indicia* of God in Scripture, that is, have the Scriptures sealed to us by the Spirit as divine. It is quite possible that Calvin may have particularly emphasized the obligations which grow out of our renewal by the Holy Spirit and the implantation in us of the Spirit of Adoption whereby we become the sons of God—obligations to comport ourselves as the sons of God and to govern ourselves by the law of God's house as given us in His Word; while Luther may have emphasized more the liberty of the Christian man who is emancipated from the law as a condition of salvation and is ushered into the freedom of life which belongs to the children of God. And it is quite possible that in this difference we may find a fundamental distinction between the two types of Protestantism—Lutheran and Reformed—by virtue of which the Reformed have always been characterized by a strong ethical tendency—in thought and in practice. But it is misleading to represent this as due to an insufficient correlation on Calvin's part of the testimony of the Spirit to the divinity of Scripture with the inner Christian life. It would be more exact to say that Calvin in this correlation thinks especially of what in our modern nomenclature we call "regeneration", while the mind of his Lutheran critics is set more upon justification and that "faith" which is connected with justification. With Calvin, at all events, the recognition of the Scriptures as divine and the hearty adoption of them as the divine rule of our faith and life is just one of the effects of the gracious operation of the Spirit of God on the heart, renewing it into spiritual life, or, what comes to the same thing, one of the gracious activities into which the newly implanted spiritual life effloresces.

Whether we should say also that it was with him the first effect of the creative operation of the Spirit on the heart, the first act of the newly renewed soul, requires some discrimination. If we mean logically first, there is a sense in which we should probably answer this question also in the affirmative. Calvin would doubtless have said that it is in the Scriptures that Christ is proposed to our faith, or, to put it more broadly, that Christ is the very substance of the special revelation documented in the Scriptures, and that the laying hold of Christ by faith presupposes therefore confidence in the revelation the substance of which He is,—which is as much as to say the embracing of the Scriptures in firm faith as a revelation from God. If the Word is the vehicle through which the knowledge of Christ is brought to the soul, it follows of itself that it is only when our minds are filled with a solid reverence for the Word, when by the light of the Spirit we are enabled and prevalently led to see Christ therein, that we can embrace Christ with a sound faith: so that it may truly be said that no man can have the least true and sound knowledge of Christ without learning from Scripture (*cf.* I. ix. 3; I. vi. 2).˙ In this sense Calvin would certainly have said that our faith in Christ presupposes faith in the Scriptures, rather than that we believe in the Scriptures for Christ's sake. But if our minds are set on chronological sequences, the response to the question which is raised is more doubtful. Faith in the revelation the substance of which is Christ and faith in Christ the substance of this revelation are logical implicates which involve one another: and we should probably be nearest to Calvin's thought if, without raising questions of chronological succession, we should recognize them as arising together in the soul. The real difference between Calvin's and the ordinary Lutheran conception at this point lies in the greater

profundity of Calvin's insight and the greater exactness of
his analysis. The Lutheran is prone to begin with faith,
which is naturally conceived at its apex, as faith in Jesus
Christ our Redeemer; and to make everything else flow
from this faith as its ultimate root. For what comes before
faith, out of which faith itself flows, he has little impulse
accurately to inquire. Calvin penetrates behind faith to the
creative action of the Holy Spirit on the heart and the new
creature which results therefrom, whose act faith is; and is
therefore compelled by an impulse derived from the matter
itself to consider the relations in which the several activities
of this new creature stand to one another and to analyse the
faith itself which holds the primacy among them (for trust
is the essence of religion, ch. ii), into its several movements.
The effect of this is that "efficacious grace"—what we call
in modern speech "regeneration"—takes the place of fundamental principle in Calvin's soteriology and he becomes preeminently the theologian of the Holy Spirit. In point of
fact it is from him accordingly that the effective study of
the work of the Holy Spirit takes its rise, and it is only in
the channels cut by him and at the hands of thinkers taught
by him that the theology of the Holy Spirit has been richly
developed.[72]

It is his profound sense of the supernatural origin of all
that is good in the manifestations of human life which
constitutes the characteristic mark of Calvin's thinking:
and it is this which lies at the bottom of and determines his
doctrine of the witness of the Holy Spirit. He did not
doubt that the act of faith by which the child of God
embraces the Scriptures as a revelation of God is his own
act and the expression of his innermost consciousness. But
neither did he doubt that this consciousness is itself the
expression of a creative act of the Spirit of God. And it

was on this account that he represented to himself the act
of faith performed as resting ultimately on "the testimony
of the Spirit". Its supernatural origin was to him the most
certain thing about it. That language very much resem-
bling his own might be employed in a naturalistic sense was,
no doubt, made startlingly plain in his own day by the teaching of Castellion. Out of his pantheising rationalism Castellion found it possible to speak almost in Calvin's words.
"It is evident", says he, "that the intention and secret counsels of God, hidden in the Scriptures, are revealed only to
believers, the humble, the pious, who fear God and have the
Spirit of God." If the wicked have sometimes spoken like
prophets, they have nevertheless not really understood what
they said, but are like magpies in a cage going through the
forms of speech without inner apprehension of its meaning.[73] But Castellion meant by this nothing more than that
sympathy is requisite to understanding. Since his day mul-
titudes more have employed Calvin's language to express
little more than this; and have even represented Calvin's
own meaning as nothing more than that the human consciousness acquires by association with God in Christ the
power of discriminating the truth of God from falsehood.
Nothing could more fundamentally subvert Calvin's whole
teaching. The very nerve of his thought is, that the confidence of the Christian in the divine origin and authority
of Scripture and the revelatory nature of its contents is of
distinctively supernatural origin, is God-wrought. The testimony of the Spirit may be delivered through the forms of
our consciousness, but it remains distinctively the testimony
of God the Holy Spirit and is not to be confused with the
testimony of our consciousness.[73a] Resting on the language
of Rom. viii. 16, from which the term 'testimony of the
Spirit' was derived, he conceived it as a co-witness along

with the witness of our spirit indeed, but on that very account distinguishable from the witness of our spirit. This particular point is nowhere discussed by him at large, but Calvin's general sense is perfectly plain. That there is a double testimony he is entirely sure—the testimony of our own spirit and that of the Holy Spirit: that these are though distinguishable yet inseparable, he is equally clear: his conception is therefore that this double testimony runs confluently together into one. This is only as much as to say afresh that the testimony of the Holy Spirit is not delivered to us in a propositional revelation, nor by the creating in us of a blind conviction, but along the lines of our own consciousness. In its essence, the act of the Spirit in delivering His testimony, terminates on our nature, or faculties, quickening them so that we feel, judge and act differently than we otherwise should. In this sense, the testimony of the Spirit coalesces with our consciousness. We cannot separate it out as a factor in our conclusions, judgments, feelings, actions, consciously experienced as coming from without. But we function differently from before: we recognize God where before we did not perceive Him; we trust and love Him where before we feared and hated Him; we firmly embrace Him in His Word where before we turned indifferently away. This change needs accounting for. We account for it by the action of the Holy Spirit on our hearts: and we call this His "testimony". But we cannot separate His action from our recognition of God, our turning in trust and love to Him and the like. For this is the very form in which the testimony of the Spirit takes effect, into which it flows, by which it is recognized. We are profoundly conscious that of ourselves we never would have seen thus, and that our seeing thus can never find its account in anything in us by nature. We are sure, therefore, that there has come upon us a revolutionary influence from without: and we are sure that this is the act of God. Calvin would certainly have cried as one of his most eloquent disciples cries to-day: "The Holy Spirit is God, and not we ourselves. What we are speaking of is a Spirit which illuminates our spirit, which purifies our spirit, which strives against our spirit, which triumphs over our spirit. And you say this Spirit is nothing but our spirit? By no means. The Holy Spirit, the Spirit of God,—this is God coming into us, not coming from us."[74] It is with equal energy that Calvin asserts the supernaturalness of the testimony of the Spirit and repels every attempt to confound it with the human consciousness through which it works. To him this testimony is just God Himself in His intimate working in the human heart, opening it to the light of the truth, that by this illumination it may see things as they really are and so recognize God in the Scriptures with the same directness and surety as men recognize sweetness in what is sweet and brightness in what is bright. Here indeed lies the very hinge of his doctrine.[75]

It has seemed desirable to enter into some detail with respect to Calvin's doctrine of the testimony of the Spirit, not only because of its intrinsic interest, but also because of its importance for understanding Calvin's doctrine of the knowledge of God and indeed his whole system of truth, and for a proper estimate of his place in the history of thought. His doctrine of the testimony of the Spirit is the keystone of his doctrine of the knowledge of God. Men endowed by nature with an ineradicable *sensus deitatis,* which is quickened into action and informed by a rich revelation of God spread upon His works and embodied in His deeds, are yet held back from attaining a sound knowledge of God by the corruption of their hearts, which dulls their

instinctive sense of God and blinds them to His revelation
in works and deeds. That His people may know Him,
therefore, God lovingly intervenes by an objective revelation of Himself in His Word, and a subjective correction
of their sin-bred dullness of apprehension of Him through
the operation of His Spirit in their hearts, which Calvin
calls the testimony of the Holy Spirit. Obviously it is
only through this testimony of the Holy Spirit that the revelation of God, whether in works or Word, is given efficacy: it is God, then, who, through His Spirit, reveals
Himself to His people, and they know Him only as taught
by Himself. But also on this very account the knowledge
they have of Him is trustworthy in its character and complete for its purpose: being God-given, it is safeguarded
to us by the dreadful sanction of deity itself. This being
made clear, Calvin has laid a foundation for the theological
structure—the scientific statement and elaboration of the
knowledge of God—than which nothing could be conceived
more firm. There remained nothing more for him to do
before proceeding at once to draw out the elements of the
knowledge of God as they lie in the revelation so assured
to us, except to elucidate the *indicia* by which the Christian
under the influence of the testimony of the Spirit is strengthened in his confidence that the Scriptures are the very Word
of God, and to repudiate the tendency to neglect these Scriptures so authenticated to us in favor of fancied continuous
revelations of the Spirit. The former he does in a chapter
(ch. viii) of considerable length and great eloquence, which
constitutes one of the fullest and most powerful expositions
of the evidence for the divine origin of the Scriptures
which have come down to us from the Reformation age.
The latter he does in a briefer chapter (ch. ix), of crisp
polemic quality, the upshot of which is to leave it strongly

impressed on the reader's mind that the whole knowledge
of God available to us, as the whole knowledge of God
needful for us, lies objectively displayed in the pages of
Scripture, which, therefore, becomes the sole source of a
sound exposition of the knowledge of God.

This strong statement is not intended, however, to imply
that the Spirit-led man can learn nothing from the more general revelation of God in His works and deeds. Calvin is so
far from denying the possibility of a "Natural Theology",
in this sense of the word, that he devotes a whole chapter
(ch. v) to vindicating the rich revelation of God made in His
works and deeds: though, of course, he does deny that any
theology worthy of the name can be derived from this
natural revelation by the "natural man", that is, by the man
the eyes of whose mind and heart are not opened by the
Spirit of God,—who is not under the influence of the testimony of the Spirit; and in this sense he denies the possibility of a "Natural Theology". What the strong statement
in question is intended to convey is that there is nothing to
be derived from natural revelation which is not also to be
found in Scripture, whether as necessary presupposition,
involved implication or clear statement; and that beside that
documented in Scripture there is no supernatural revelation
accessible to men. The work of the Spirit of God is not to
supplement the revelation made in Scripture, far less to
supersede it, but distinctively to authenticate it. It remains
true, then, that the whole matter of a sound theology lies
objectively revealed to us in the pages of Scripture: and
this is the main result to which his whole discussion tends.
But side by side with it requires to be placed as a result of
his discussion secondary only to this, this further conclusion,
directly given in his doctrine of the testimony of the
Spirit,—that only a Christian man can profitably theologize.

It is in the union of these two great principles that we find Calvin's view of the bases of a true theology. This he conceives as the product of the systematic investigation and logical elaboration of the contents of Scripture by a mind quickened to the apprehension of these contents through the inward operations of the Spirit of God. It is on this basis and in this spirit that Calvin undertakes his task as a theologian; and what he professes to give us in his *Institutes* is thus, to put it simply, just a Christian man's reading of the Scriptures of God.

The Protestantism of this conception of the task of the theologian is apparent on the face of it. It is probably, however, still worth while to point out that its Protestantism does not lie solely or chiefly in the postulate that the Scriptures are the sole authoritative source of the knowledge of God,—"formal principle" of the Reformation though that postulate be, and true, therefore, as Chillingworth's famous declaration that "the Bible and the Bible only is the religion of Protestants" would be, if only Chillingworth had kept it to this sense. It lies more fundamentally still in the postulate that these Scriptures are accredited to us as the revelation of God solely by the testimony of the Holy Spirit,— that without this testimony they lie before us inert and without effect on our hearts and minds, while with it they become not merely the power of God unto salvation, but also the vitalizing source of all our knowledge of God. There is embodied in this the true Protestant principle, superior to both the so-called formal and the so-called material principles—both of which are in point of fact but corollaries of it. For it takes the soul completely and forcibly out of the hands of the Church and from under its domination, and casts it wholly upon the grace of God. In its formulation Calvin gave to Protestantism for the first time, accordingly, logical stability and an inward sense of security. Men were no more puzzled by the polemics of Rome when they were asked, You rest on Scripture alone, you say: but on what does your Scripture rest? Calvin's development of the doctrine of the testimony of the Spirit provided them with their sufficient answer: "On the testimony of the Spirit of God in the heart." Here we see the historical importance of Calvin's formulation of this doctrine. And here we see the explanation of the two great facts which reveal its historical importance, the facts, to wit, that Calvin had no predecessors in the formulation of the doctrine, and that at once upon his formulation of it it became the common doctrine of universal Protestantism.

IV. HISTORICAL RELATIONS.

The search for anticipations of the doctrine of the testimony of the Spirit among the Fathers and Scholastics[76] reveals only such sporadic assertions of the dependence of man on the inward teaching of the Holy Spirit for the knowledge or the saving knowledge of God as could not fail in the speech of a series of Christian men who had read their Bibles. A sentence of this kind from Justin Martyr,[77] another from Chrysostom,[78] two or three from Hilary of Poitiers,[79] almost exhaust what the first age yields. It is different with Augustine. With his profound sense of dependence on God and his vital conviction of the necessity of grace for all that is good in man, in the whole circle of his activities, he could not fail to work out a general doctrine of the knowledge of God in all essentials the same as Calvin's. In point of fact, as we have already intimated, he did so. There remain, however, some very interesting and some very significant differences between the two.[80] It is interesting to note, for instance, that where

Calvin speaks of an innate *sensus deitatis* in man, as lying
at the root of all his knowledge of God, Augustine, with a
more profound ontology of this knowledge, as at least made
explicit in the statement, speaks of a continuous reflection
of a knowledge of Himself by God into the human mind.[81]
There is here, however, probably only a difference in fulness
of statement, or at most only of emphasized aspect. On the
other hand, it is highly significant that, instead of Calvin's
doctrine of the testimony of the Spirit, Augustine, in con-
formity with the stress he laid upon the "Church" and the
"means of grace" in the conference of grace, speaks of the
knowledge of God as attainable only "in the Church".[82]
Accordingly, in him also and his successors there are to be
found only such anticipations specifically of the doctrine
of the testimony of the Spirit as are afforded by the increased frequency of their references to the dependence of
man for all knowledge of God and divine things on grace
and the inward teaching of the heavenly Instructor. The
voice of men may assail our ears, says Augustine, for instance, but those remain untaught "to whom that inward
unction does not speak, whom the Holy Spirit does not inwardly teach": for "He who teaches the heart has His seat
in heaven".[83] Moses himself, yea, even if he spoke to us not
in Hebrew but in our own tongue, could convey to us only
the knowledge of what he said: of the truth of what he
said, only the Truth Himself, speaking within us, in the
secret chamber of our thought, can assure us though He
speaks neither in Hebrew nor in Greek nor in Latin, nor yet
in any tongue of the barbarians, but without organs of voice
or tongue and with no least syllabic sound.[84] Further than
this men did not get before the Reformation:[85] nor did the
first Reformers themselves get further. No doubt they
discerned the voice of the Spirit in the Scriptures, as the

Fathers did before them; and in a single sentence, written, however, after the *Institutes* of 1539 (viz., in 1555), Melanchthon notes with the Fathers that the mind is "aided in giving its assent" to divine things "by the Holy Spirit".[86] Zwingli here stands on the same plane with his brethren. He strongly repels the Romish establishment of confidence in the Scriptures on the *ipse dixit* of the Church, indeed; and asserts that those who sincerely search the Scriptures are taught by God, and even that none acquire faith in the Word except as drawn by the Father, admonished by the Spirit, taught by the unction,—as, says he, all pious men have found.[87] But such occasional remarks as this could not fail wherever the Augustinian conception of grace was vitally felt. They show only that the doctrine of the testimony of the Spirit was always implicit in that conception.[88]

The same remark applies to the first edition of Calvin's *Institutes* (1536) also, though with a difference. We cannot say, indeed, that the doctrine of the internal testimony of the Spirit to the divinity of the Scriptures is found there already in germ[89] any more than we can say the same of the Augustinian Fathers. And the criticism passed[90] on the adduction of Melanchthon's single sentence in this reference to the effect that he speaks rather "of the action of the Holy Spirit with reference to the object of faith, that is to say, to the contents of the Word of God" than "with reference to the divinity of the Scriptures themselves", is valid for Calvin's first edition. Yet it is certainly true that the general doctrine of the internal testimony of the Spirit comes much more prominently forward in even the first edition of the *Institutes* than in any preceding treatise of the sort,—that much more is made in it than in any of its predecessors of the poverty of the human spirit and the need and actuality of the prevalent influence of the

Spirit of God that man may have—whether in knowledge or act—any good thing. We shall have to go back to Augustine to find anything comparable to the conviction and insight with which even in this his earliest work Calvin urges these things. Calvin's whole thought is already dominated by the conception of the powerlessness of the human soul in its sin in all that belongs to the knowledge of God which is salvation, and its entire dependence on the sovereign operations of the Holy Spirit. In this sense it may be said that the chapters in the new *Institutes* of 1539 in which he develops this doctrine of the noëtic effects of sin and their cure by objective revelation, documented in Scripture, and subjective illumination wrought by the Holy Spirit, lay implicitly in his doctrine of man's need and its cure by the indwelling Spirit which pervades the *Institutes* of 1536. There he already teaches that the written law was required by the decay of our consciousness of the law written on the heart; that to know God and His will we have need to surpass ourselves; that it is the Spirit dwelling in us that is the source of all our right knowledge of God; and that it is due to the power of the Spirit alone "that we hear the word of the holy Gospel, that we accept it by faith, and that we abide in this faith" (p. 137). With eminent directness and simplicity he already there tells us that "our Lord first teaches and instructs us by His Word; secondarily confirms us by His sacraments; and thirdly by the light of His Holy Spirit illuminates our understandings and gives entrance into our hearts both to the Word and to the sacraments, which otherwise would only beat upon our ears and stand before our eyes, without penetrating or operating beneath them" (p. 206). There is, in other words, very rich teaching in the *Institutes* of 1536 of the entire dependence of sinful man on the Spirit of God for

every sound religious movement of the soul: but there is
no development of the precise doctrine of the testimony of
the Holy Spirit to the divinity of the Scriptures. It is not
merely that the term *testimonium Spiritus Sancti* does not
occur in this early draft, or occurs only once, and then not
in this sense:[91] it is that the thing is not explicated and
is present only as implicated in the general doctrine of grace,
which is very purely conceived.

It was left, then, to the edition of 1539 to create the
whole doctrine at, as it were, a single stroke.[92] For, as we
have already had occasion to note, Calvin's whole exposition
of the doctrine of the testimony of the Spirit to the divinity
of Scripture appears all at once in its completeness in the
second edition of the *Institutes,* the first edition which he
issued as a text-book on theology, that of 1539. This exposition was reproduced without curtailment or alteration in
all subsequent editions, and is thereby given the great en-
dorsement of Calvin's permanent approval: while the additions which are made to it in the progressive expansion
of the treatise, though large in mass, are rather devoted to
guarding it from the misapprehension as if the necessity
it asserted for the testimony of the Spirit in any way
detracted from the objective value of the *indicia* of the
divinity of Scripture, than modify the positive doctrine
expounded.

The formulation of this principle of the testimony of the
Spirit by Calvin in 1539 had an extraordinary effect both
immediate and permanent.[93] Universal Protestantism perceived in it at sight the pure expression of the Protestant
principle and the sheet-anchor of its position. The Lutherans as well as the Reformed adopted it at once and made
it the basis not only of their reasoned defence of Protestantism, but also of their structure of Christian doctrine and

of their confidence in Christian living.[94] To it they both continued to cling so long and so far as they continued faithful to the Protestant principle itself. It has given way only as the structure of Protestantism has itself given way in reaction to the Romish position, or, more widely, as the structure of Christian thought has given way in rationalizing disintegration. No doubt it has undergone at the hands of its various expounders, from time to time, more or less modification, and, in its journeyings to the ends of the earth, has suffered now and again some sea-change,— sometimes through sheer misapprehension, sometimes through sheer misrepresentation, sometimes through more or less admixture of both. A spurious revival of the doctrine was, for example, set on foot by Schleiermacher in his strong revulsion from the cold rationalism which had so long reigned in Germany to a more vital religious faith; and sentences may be quoted from his writings which, when removed out of the context of his system of thought, almost give expression to it.[95] But after all, his revival of it was rather the revival of subjectivity in religion than of the doctrine of the testimony of the Spirit as the basis of all faith: and it has borne bitter fruit in a widespread subjectivism, the mark of which is that it discards (as "external") the authority of those very Scriptures to which the testimony of the Spirit is borne. Not in such circles is the continued influence of the doctrine of the testimony of the Spirit to be sought or its continued advocacy to be found. If we would see it in its purity in the modern Church we must look for it in the hands of truer successors of Calvin— in the writings, to name only men of our own time, of William Cunningham[96] and Charles Hodge[97] and Abraham Kuyper[98] and Herman Bavinck.[99]

As we have already had occasion to note, the principle of

the testimony of the Spirit as the true basis of our confidence in the Scriptures as the Word of God was almost from the hands of Calvin himself incorporated into the Reformed Creeds. We have already pointed out the sharpness and strength of its expression in the Gallican (1557-1571) and Belgian (1501-1571) Confessions, and it finds at least the expression of suggestion in the Second Helvetic Confession (1562). It was not, however, merely into the Confessions of the Reformation age that it was incorporated. It is given an expression as clear as it is prudent, as decided as it is comprehensive, in that confession of their faith which the persecuted Waldenses issued after the massacres of 1655;[100] and it is incorporated into the Westminster Confession of Faith (1646) in perhaps the best and most balanced statement it has ever received,—the phraseology of which is obviously derived in large part from Calvin, either directly or through the intermediation of George Gillespie,[101] but the substance of which was but the expression of the firmly held faith of the whole body of the framers of that culminating Confession of the Reformed Churches.

"We recognize the divinity of these sacred books", says the Waldensian Confession (ch. iv), "not only through the testimony of the Church, but principally through the eternal and indubitable truth of the doctrine which is contained in them, through the excellence, sublimity and majesty of the pure divinity (*du tout divine*) which are apparent in them, and through the operation of the Holy Spirit which makes us receive with deference the testimony which the Church gives to them, which opens our eyes to receive the rays of the celestial light which shines in the Scriptures, and so corrects our taste that we discern this food by the divine savor which it possesses." The dependence of this fine statement on Calvin's exposition is evident; but what is most striking about it is the clarity with which it conceives and the fulness with which it expounds the exact mode of working of the testimony of the Spirit and its relation to the *indicia* of divinity in Scripture, through which, and not apart from or in opposition to which, it performs its work. So far from supposing that the witness of the Spirit is of the nature of a new and independent revelation from heaven or works only a blind faith in us, setting thus aside all evidences of the divinity of Scripture, external and internal alike, this careful statement particularly explains that our faith in the divinity of Scripture rests, under the testimony of the Spirit, on these evidences as its ground, but not on these evidences by themselves, but on them as apprehended by a Spirit-led mind and heart—the work of the Spirit consisting in so dealing with our spirit that these evidences are, under His influence, perceived and felt in their real bearing and full strength.

An even more notable statement of the whole doctrine is that incorporated into the Westminster Confession (I. 4. 5), and in a more compressed form into the Larger Catechism (Q. 4). "The authority of the Holy Scripture, for which it ought to be believed and obeyed", says the Confession, "dependeth not upon the testimony of any man or Church, but wholly upon God (who is truth itself) the author thereof; and therefore it is to be received, because it is the Word of God. We may be moved and induced by the testimony of the Church to a high and reverent esteem of the Holy Scripture; and the heavenliness of the matter, the efficacy of the doctrine, the majesty of the style, the consent of all the parts, the scope of the whole (which is to give all glory to God), the full discovery it makes of the only way of man's salvation, the many other incomparable excellencies, and the entire perfection thereof, are arguments whereby it doth abundantly evidence itself to be the Word of God; yet, notwithstanding, our full persuasion and assurance of the infallible truth and divine authority thereof, is from the inward work of the Holy Spirit, bearing witness by and with the Word in our heart." In the Larger Catechism this is reduced to the form: "The Scriptures manifest themselves to be the Word of God, by their majesty and purity; by the consent of all the parts, and the scope of the whole, which is to give all glory to God; by their light and power to convince and convert sinners, to comfort and build up believers unto salvation; but the Spirit of God bearing witness by and with the Scriptures in the heart of man, is alone able fully to persuade it that they are the very Word of God." The fundamental excellence of this remarkable statement (for the full understanding of which what is said of "faith" in chapter xiv of the Confession and Question 72 of the Catechism should be compared with it—just as Calvin referred his readers to his later discussion of 'faith' for further information on the topic of the testimony of the Spirit) is the care with which the several grounds on which we recognize the Scriptures to be from God are noted and their value appraised, and yet the supreme importance of the witness of the Spirit is safeguarded.[102] The external testimony of the Church is noted and its value pointed out: it moves and induces us to a high and reverent esteem for Scripture. The internal testimony of the characteristics of the Scriptures themselves is noted and its higher value pointed out: they "abundantly evidence" or "manifest" the Scriptures "to be the Word of God". The need and place of the testimony of the Spirit is then pointed out in the presence of this "abundant evidencing" or "manifesting": it is not to add new evidence,— which is not needed,—but to secure deeper conviction—

which is needed: and not independently of the Word with
its evidencing characteristics, but "by and with the Word"
or "the Scriptures". What this evidence of the Spirit does
is *"fully* to persuade us" that "the Scriptures are the very
Word of God",—to work in us *"full* persuasion and assurance of the infallible truth and divine authority" of the
Word of God. It is a matter of completeness of conviction,
not of grounds of conviction: and the testimony of the
Spirit works, therefore, not by adding additional grounds of
conviction, but by an inward work on the heart, enabling it
to react upon the already "abundant evidence" with a really
"full persuasion and assurance". Here we have the very
essence of Calvin's doctrine, almost in his own words, and
with even more than his own eloquence and precision of
statement.

What Calvin has given to the Reformed Churches, therefore, in his formulation of the doctrine of the Testimony of
the Spirit is a fundamental doctrine, which has been as such
expounded by the whole body of their theologians, and incorporated into the fabric of their public Confessions. Thus
it became the officially declared faith of the Reformed
Churches in France and Holland, Switzerland, Italy, Scotland and America, and continues to be the faith of their
descendants wherever the fundamental Reformed Creeds
are still professed and believed.

NOTES

CALVIN: EPIGONE OR CREATOR?

By Émile Doumergue

[1] Albrecht Ritschl, *Geschichte des Pietismus*, 1880, I. p. 76.

[2] *Ibid.*, I, p. 70. " . . . so legt er [Luther] doch diese Betrachtungen ebenso nahe . . . "

[3] *Ibid.*, I, p. 75. [4] *Ibid.*, I, pp. 74-75.

[5] *Jahrbücher für deutsche Theologie*, 1878. But Ritschl had published the first chapter of his History of Pietism in the *Zeitschrift für Kirchengeschichte*, July 1, 1877, II, pp. 1ff., and Kattenbusch quotes thence, p. 514.

[6] *Ibid.*, p. 354. [7] *Ibid.*, p. 365.

[8] Loofs, *Leitfaden der Dogmengeschichte*, 1906, p. 876. All the citations we make are found in the edition of 1893.

[9] *Ibid.*, p. 877. [10] *Ibid.*, p. 893.

[11] "*Meditatio futurae vitae, ihr Begriff und ihre herrschende Stellung im System Calvins. Ein Beitrag zum Verständniss von dessen Institutio.* 1901. *Calvins Jenseits Christentum in seinem Verhältniss zu den religiösen Schriften des Erasmus.* 1902.

[12] *Meditatio*, p. 1. [13] *Ibid.*, p. 18. [14] *Ibid.*, p. 81.

[15] *Bulletin* LVI, Sept.-Oct., 1907, pp. 475-479.

[16] *Unsere religiösen Erzieher. Eine Geschichte des Christentums in Lebensbildern*, 1908. The first volume begins with Moses and the second ends with Bismarck. It contains also a sketch of Jesus.

[17] *Ibid.*, p. 71. [18] *Ibid.*, p. 78. [19] *Ibid.*, p. 82.

[20] "Was John Calvin a Reformer or a Reactionary", in *The Hibbert Journal*, Oct. 1907, pp. 171-185.

[21] *Ibid.*, p. 171. [22] *Ibid.*, p. 184. [23] *Ibid..* p. 175.

[24] *Ibid.*, p. 182. [25] *Ibid.*, p. 176. [26] *Ibid.*, p. 171.

[27] *Ibid.*, p. 176. [28] *Ibid.*, p. 172. [29] *Ibid.*, p. 183.

[30] *Ibid.*, p. 183. [31] *Ibid..* p. 184. [32] Fr. Loofs, *Luthers Stellung zum Mittelalter und zur Neuzeit*, 1907, p. 5.

[33] Ernst Troeltsch, *Die Bedeutung des Protestantismus für die Entstehung der modernen Welt*, 1906. At the same time Troeltsch published a history of Protestantism, well developed and the result of much labor, in the collection entitled *Die Kultur der Gegenwart*, Series I, Part iv: *Die christliche Religion*, 1906, pp. 253-458.

[34] Troeltsch, p. 12.

[35] And even here the historian should make a reservation. Without doubt authentic Protestantism must be sought in the Protestantism of the 16th century and of the Reformers, and not in the Protestantism of this or that theologian of the 20th century. Yet there must be no exaggeration. In going out from Roman Catholicism, in separating itself from it, Protestantism preserved, in spite of itself, this or that trace or remnant of Catholicism, to divest itself of which completely required some time. Luther did not lay aside his monkish robe the very day of his rupture with Rome.

[36] Troeltsch, p. 14.

[37] *Ibid.*, p. 15.   [38] *Ibid.*, p. 28.   [39] *Ibid.*, pp. 16-17.

[40] *Ibid.*, p. 19.   [41] *Ibid.*, p. 19.   [42] *Ibid.*, p. 19.

[43] Loofs, *Luthers Stellung zum Mittelalter und zur Neuzeit*, pp. 11f.

[44] The accusation as to ascetism is not new. It is found among the rationalists of the 18th century, for example, in Michael Ignaz Schmidt, counsellor of the court of Joseph II and theologian, who in his *Histoire des Allemands*, speaks of the monachism of the Reformers. "The Reformers had added to their temper as Reformers a pretty dose of monastic and melancholic temper, and had taught a sad religion, that made men sad". Loofs, *Luthers Stellung*, p. 21.

[45] Troeltsch, p. 24.   [46] *Ibid.*, p. 24   [47] *Ibid.*, p. 24.

[48] *Ibid.*, p. 25.   [49] *Ibid.*, pp. 25, 26.   [50] *Ibid.*, p. 27.

[51] *Ibid.*, p. 28.   [52] *Ibid.*, pp. 22, 23.   [53] *Ibid.*, p. 33.

[54] *Ibid.*, p. 33.   [55] *Ibid.*, p. 35.   [56] *Ibid.*, pp. 36, 37.

[57] *Ibid.*, p. 37.   [58] *Ibid.*, p. 40.   [59] *Ibid.*, p. 41.

[60] *Ibid.*, p. 40.   [61] *Ibid.*, p. 41.

[62] Ritschl, *Geschichte des Pietismus*, 1880, I, p. 24. See also p. 25, where Ritschl shows the origin of the ideas of Anabaptism in the principles of Gregory, etc.

[63] "Albrecht Ritschl als Reformations-Historiker", in the *Reformirte Kirchenzeitung*, 1908, pp. 252, 253.

[64] Loofs, *Luthers Stellung*, p. 15, n. "Aber operiert nicht Tröltsch mit einem gleichen Idealbegriff von 'Renaissancebildung' und 'Täufertum'? Das Täufertum des 16. Jahrhunderts hätte wahrlich keine moderne Welt gebaut, wenn es damals zur Herrschaft gekommen wäre! Nicht nur die Ereignisse von Münster sind dafür ein Beweis. Die Stellung des gesamten Täufertums zur Askese und zum Staat ist ursprunglich viel mittelalterlicher als irgend etwas im Altprotestantismus. Was 'modern' an ihm ist, lässt schon in der mittelalterlichen Mystik sich gelegentlich nachweisen. Es ist eine Ungeheuerlichkeit, die alle Sympathie mit den Täufern nicht entschuldigen kann, dass Tröltsch mit sorglosester Abstraktion von den geschichtlich gegebenen Formen das

Täufertum im 17. Jahrhundert 'seine Apolitie aufgeben' lässt (Vortrag S. 40; vgl. Kultur S. 369f.) und doch dem von den Reformatoren geächteten Täufertum', dem Liebling des modernen Spiritualismus, die Ehre lässt, eine der beiden Hauptfaktoren für die Entstehung der modernen Welt gewesen zu sein. Wer das, was aus einzelnen Täuferischen (aber z. T. nicht nur Täuferischen) Ideen unter dem Druck eines langen Verfolgungszustandes und unter der Gunst der fortgeschrittenen Kultur Englands in Verbindung mit calvinistischen Traditionen geworden ist, 'dem Täufertum' gutschreibt, verliert wahrlich alles Recht, den Neuprotestantismus dem Altprotestantismus gegenüber zu stellen wie ein Kind, das, in fremder Familie erzogen, nur die nächsten Verwandten noch gelegentlich an die geistige Eigenart der Eltern erinnert."

[65] *Ibid.*, p. 20. This idea is developed by Troeltsch in *Kultur, etc.*, pp. 257 ff.   [66] *Ibid.*, p. 15. n.

[67] Troeltsch, pp. 60, 61.   [68] *Ibid.*, pp. 62, 63.   [69] Troeltsch, pp. 65, 66.

[70] Max Weber, "Die protestantische Ethik und der Geist des Kapitalismus", in *Archiv für sozial Wissenschaft und sozial Politik.* Vol. XX, 1904, and Vol. XXI, 1905.

[71] Weber, XX (1904), p. 19.   [72] *Ibid.*, XX (1904), p. 34.

[73] *Ibid.*, p. 36, and n. 1.   [74] *Ibid.*, p. 41.   [75] *Ibid.*, p. 43.

[76] *Ibid.*, p. 46.   [77] *Ibid.*, p. 48.   [78] *Ibid.*, p. 50.

[79] *Ibid.*, p. 26.   [80] *Ibid.*, p. 51.

[81] *Ibid.*, XXI (1905), p. 19 and n. 27; pp. 35, 76, 93, n. 52, 96, n. 55.

[82] *Ibid.*, XXI, p. 63, n. 123.   [83] *Ibid.*, XX (1904), p. 46.

[84] *Ibid.*, XX (1904), pp. 99, 100.

[85] This is not the place to discuss, fully, the ideas of heteronomy and autonomy. We are far from wishing to say that Christianity is hostile to the true autonomy of the soul and of man.

[86] *Institutio*, III, vii, 1.   [87] *Ibid.*, III, vii, 1.

[88] The Latin word, *abnegatio,* is translated by *abnegation* in 1541, and by *renouncement* in 1560.

[89] *Institutio*, III, vii, 4.   [90] *Institutio*, III, vii, 5.   [91] *Ibid.*, III, vii, 9.

[92] *Ibid.*, III, viii, 9.

[93] Sermons on Job, *Opera*, XXXIII, p. 93.

[94] Homilies on I Sam., *Opera*, XXX, p. 681.

[95] *Institutio*, III, ix, 2.   [96] *Ibid.*, III, x, 1.

[97] *Ibid.*, III, ix, 3.   [98] *Ibid.*, III, ix, 4.   [99] *Ibid.*, III, x, 1.

[100] This last phrase was added in 1559. *Institutio* III, x, 1.

[101] *Ibid.*, III, x, 2, 3.

[102] Sermon on Deuteronomy, *Opera*, XXVIII, p. 36.

[103] *Ibid.*, *Opera* XXVI, pp. 163, 164.

[104] Schulze sums up thus the eschatological character of the thought of Calvin: "The future life includes in itself the supreme good *(schliesst das höchste Gut in sich);* the presence of God and therewith happiness and salvation". *Meditatio,* p. 8.

[105] *Institutio,* III, xxv, 2.   This text is that of 1559.

[106] Schulze, *Meditatio,* p. 8.

[107] *Institutio,* III, ix, 3.   [108] *Meditatio,* p. 50.

[109] Schulze, *Meditatio,* p. 7.   [110] *Institutio,* III, iii, 14.

[111] *Ibid.,* III, iii, 20.

[112] Sermons on Daniel, *Opera* XLV, p. 459.

[113] Sermons on Deuteronomy, *Opera* XXVII, pp. 19, 20.

[114] *Institutio,* I, xv, 3.   This is the text of 1559.   It shows the sense in which Calvin's thought is developed, and rectified the earlier texts of the *Psychopannychia. Opera,* V, p. 180.

[115] Sermons on Deut., *Opera,* XXVIII, p. 101.

[116] Sermons on I Tim., *Opera,* LIII, p. 536.

[117] *Ibid.,* p. 534.   [118] *Ibid.,* p. 537.   [119] *Ibid.,* p. 533.

[120] The first sentence of the celebrated Heidelberg Catechism, which does not separate soul and body in salvation, must not be forgotten: Sect. I, Dem. I: "What is thy only comfort in life and in death? Ans. That I, with body and soul, both in life and in death, am not my own, but belong to my faithful Saviour, Jesus Christ, etc."

[121] *Institutio,* III, xxv, 7.

[122] *Ibid.,* III, xxv, 7.   [123] *Ibid.,* III, xxv, 8.   [124] *Meditatio,* p. 86.

[125] *Institutio,* III, xix, 7.   [126] *Ibid.,* III, xix, 8.

[127] Sermons on Deut., *Opera,* XXVI, p. 510.

[128] Homilies on 1 Sam., *Opera,* XXX, p. 565.

[129] Sermons on Job, *Opera,* XXXIII, pp. 39, 41.

[130] *Institutio,* III, xix, 9.

[131] Ritschl, *Geschichte des Pietismus,* I, p. 76.

[132] *Unsere religiösen Erzieher,* II, p. 82.   [133] *Institutio,* III, xix, 9.

[134] Schulze, *Meditatio,* pp. 13f.

THE REFORMATION AND NATURAL LAW.

By August Lang.

[1] Teil I, Abt. iv, 1. Hälfte, 1906, pp. 253-458; *Protestantisches Christentum und Kirche in der Neuzeit.*

[2] Böhmer, *Luther im Lichte der neueren Forschung,* Leipzig, 1906; Loofs, "Luthers Stellung zum Mittelalter und der Neuzeit", *Deutsch-evangelische Blätter,* 1907, Augustheft; Kattenbusch in *Zeitschrift für Theologie und Kirche,* 1907, Heft 1, and *Theologische Rundschau,* 1907, Heft 2; Hunzinger, *Der Glaube Luthers und das religionsgeschichtliche Christentum,* Leipzig, 1907.

[3] *Grundlinien der Kirchengeschichte,* p. 203.

[4] How extraordinarily numerous the forms are in which the theories of natural law have developed may be seen from the work of the acute professor of law at Bonn, Karl Bergbohm, *Jurisprudenz und Rechtsphilosophie,* Vol. i, *Das Naturrecht der Gegenwart,* Leipzig, 1892. Bergbohm has undertaken to study the complicated appearances, forms and operations of natural law in past and present, and with the searching broom of criticism to sweep them away from the science of jurisprudence. An example of the most extreme inconstancy in the use of the term, natural law, is afforded by the book of the philosopher, A. Trendelenburg, *Naturrecht auf dem Grunde der Ethik,* Leipzig, 1868, a work which examines by a purely philosophical method the nature of law, that is, the ethical foundation of legal enactment, both according to the principle of law and according to the legal relations derived therefrom. In spite of the fluctuating element in the conception of natural law, it remains, nevertheless, for the historian, a definite historical quantity, and of course this alone is in view in the following discussion.

[5] *Melanthonis Opera,* in *Corpus Reformatorum,* xxi, cc. 116ff.

[6] *Ibid.,* xxi, c. 117: *insita nobis a deo regula iudicandi de moribus.* A little before: *est in universum fallax humani captus iudicium propter cognatam caecitatem, ita ut etiamsi sint in animos nostros insculptae quaedam formae morum, tamen eae deprehendi vix possint.*

[7] *Ibid.,* xiii, c. 7.   [8] *Ibid.,* xxi, c. 417.   [9] *Ibid.,* xxi, c. 391.

[10] Additional passages in Tröltsch, *Vernunft und Offenbarung,* pp. 167ff.

[11] *Op. Mel.*, xi, c. 909; compare also xi, cc. 360, 639, 919; xii, c. 20.

[12] *Ibid.*, xi, c. 912; xii, cc. 21, 149.

[13] *Ibid.*, xi, c. 922; *cf.* xi, cc. 361, 631, 912, 921.

[14] *Ibid.*, xi, cc. 221, 361ff., 915; xii, c. 22.

[15] *Ibid.*, x, cc. 699f. The reasons for and against are opposed to each other without a final decision; the former are taken from natural law.

[16] *Ibid.*, ii, cc. 20-22.   [17] *Ibid.*, iii, c. 631.

[18] *Cf.* Kaltenborn, *Die Vorläufer des Hugo Grotius auf dem Gebiete des jus naturae et gentium*, 1848; Tröltsch, *Vernunft und Offenbarung*, 1891, p. 169.

[19] *Op. cit.*, pp. 173, 137.

[20] In the *Études de Théologie et d'Histoire publiées par MM. les Professeurs de la faculté de Théol. prot. de Paris en hommage à la faculté de Théologie de Montauban à l'occasion du tricentenaire de sa fondation*, Paris, 1901, pp. 285-320.

[21] "von dem Naturrecht oder dem natürlichen Gesetz."

[22] *Op. cit.*, p. 317.

[23] *Von weltlicher Obrigkeit*, Erlangen edition, 22, p. 105.

[24] *Ermahnung zum Frieden auf die 12 Artikel der Bauern*, Erlangen edition, 24², p. 290.

[25] *Grosser Sermon vom Wucher*, Weimar edition, 6, pp. 52, 60; *Von Kaufhandlung und Wucher*, Erlangen edition, 22, p. 202; *Von weltlicher Obrigkeit*, Erlangen edition, 22, p. 104.

[26] *Grosser Sermon vom Wucher*, Weimar edition, 6, p. 49.

[27] *Ermahnung zum Frieden*, Erlangen edition, 24², pp. 279, 282.

[28] *Tischreden*, herausg. von Förstemann und Bindseil, 3, 320; 4, 486; *Warnung an seine lieben Deutschen*, Erlangen edition, 25², p. 15.

[29] *Auslegung des 101 Psalms*, Erlangen edition, 39, p. 284.

[30] *Wider die himmlischen Propheten*, Erlangen edition, 29, pp. 156f.

[31] Erlangen edition, 22, pp. 63, 76, etc.; *Gal. Komment*, ii, 41.

[32] So R. Seeberg in his lecture, "Luthers Stellung zu den sittlichen und socialen Nöten seiner Zeit," in *Neue kirchliche Zeitschrift*, 1901, p. 839.

[33] Erlangen edition, 21, p. 285.

[34] Erich Brandenburg in his lecture, "Martin Luther's Anschauung vom Staate und der Gesellschaft", *Schriften des Vereins für Reformationsgeschichte*, H. 70, has placed this negative manner of regarding the state too one-sidedly in the foreground.

[35] *Von weltlicher Obrigkeit*, Erlangen edition, 22, p. 82.

[36] *Auslegung des Johannes-Evangeliums*, Erlangen edition, 50, pp. 349f.

[37] Erlangen edition, 22, p. 68; 50, p. 317.

[38] Erlangen edition, 24², p. 291; 22, p. 66.

[39] *Ein Sendbrief vom Büchlein wider die Bauern,* Erlangen edition, 24², p. 318.

[40] *Antwort von der Gegenwehr,* Erlangen edition, 64, p. 265.

[41] *Auslegung des 101. Psalms,* Erlangen edition, 39, p. 330.

[42] Erlangen edition, 22, pp. 104f.

[43] "Rechtsbrunnen."   [44] Ehrhardt, *op. cit.,* pp. 298f.

[45] *Ibid.,* pp. 290-296, 316ff.   [46] *Ibid.,* p. 318.

[47] *Ermahnung zum Frieden,* Erlangen edition, 24², p. 272.

[48] Erlangen edition, 22, pp. 59-105; with regard to the natural law, only pp. 104f.

[49] Compare the convincing exposition in Loofs' *Dogmengeschichte,* 4. Aufl., pp. 770ff.

[50] Compare with regard to this Loofs, *op. cit.,* p. 775.

[51] Rom. xiii; I Pet. ii.

[52] So, for example, *Wider die himmlischen Propheten,* Erlangen edition, 29, p. 140.

[53] Erlangen edition, 39, p. 285.   [54] "Wunderleute Gottes."

[55] On Rom. ii. 15.

[56] *Opera Calvini* in *Corpus Reformatorum,* Vol. xlix, cc. 37f.

[57] *Institutio,* I, iv, 4.

[58] *Ibid.,* II, viii, 1: *Homo per legem naturalem vix tenuiter degustat quis Deo acceptus sit cultus; certe, a recta eius ratione longissimo intervallo distat.*

[59] *Ibid.,* II, ii, 22: *Finis legis naturalis est, ut reddatur homo inexcusabilis.*

[60] *Ibid.,* IV, xx, 14: *Sunt qui recte compositam esse rempublicam negent, quae neglectis Mose politicis, communibus gentium legibus regitur. Quae sententia . . . falsa ac stolida est.*

[61] *Ibid.,* IV, xx, 16: *Dei lex, quam moralem vocamus . . . sola ipsa legum omnium et scopus et regula et terminus sit oportet.*

[62] *Ibid.,* IV, xx, 15: *Libertas certe singulis gentibus relicta est condendi quas sibi conducere providerint, leges: quae tamen ad perpetuam illam caritatis regulam [divinorum praeceptorum] exigantur, ut forma quidem varient, rationem habeant eandem.*

[63] *Opera,* xa.

[64] *Ibid.,* xa, cc. 248, 264, in both cases in a discussion of the question of taking interest, which Calvin, in distinction from Luther, within the limits of that same natural equity or of Christian brotherly love, pronounces entirely permissible.

[65] *Ibid.,* xa, cc. 236f.   [66] *Ibid.,* xa, c. 242.

[67] In the *Sermon on Deut.* xxiii, 18-20, *Opera,* xxviii, cc. 115-124.

[68] *Sermon on Tit.* ii. 15-iii. 2, *Opera,* liv, cc. 554-559.

[69] *Commentary on I Pet., Opera,* lv, cc. 244f.

[70] *Cf. Works,* iv, pp. 496f., 539f. The position of John Knox with regard to the question of natural law would require further investigation. *Cf.* Charles Martin, "De la genèse des doctrines politiques de J. K." in the *Bull. de la soc. de l'hist. du prot. franc.,* 1907, pp. 193ff.

[71] *Op. cit.,* p. 9.

[72] Gierke, *op. cit.,* pp. 144f.   [73] *Ibid.,* pp. 19, 29.

[74] *Institutio,* IV, xx, 31.   [75] IV, xx, 31.

[76] In *The Works of Rich. Hooker,* 2 vols., Oxford, 1841.

[77] *Sämmtliche Werke,* Vol. 24, pp. 238ff.

[78] *Works,* 1841, i, p. 210.   [79] *Ibid.,* i, pp. 260ff.

[80] *Ibid.,* i, pp. 270ff.   [81] *Ibid.,* i, p. 238.   [82] *Ibid.,* i, pp. 217f.

[83] *Ibid.,* i, pp. 308-314.   [84] *Ibid.,* i, p. 178.   [85] *Ibid.,* i, p. 178.

[86] *Ibid.,* i, p. 189.   [87] *Ibid.,* i, p. 217.   [88] *Ibid.,* i, pp. 178-181.

[89] *Ibid.,* i, pp. 186ff.   [90] *Ibid.,* i, pp. 191ff.

[91] *Ibid.,* i, p. 194.   [92] *Ibid.,* i, pp. 215f.   [93] *Ibid.,* i, p. 283.

[94] *De iure belli et pacis,* Prolegomena, § 30.

[95] *Cf.* Bergbohm, *op. cit.,* p. 156; Gierke, *op. cit.,* p. 235.

[96] *Op. cit.,* Lib. I, cap. iii, dist. 8. I use the *Editio nova* of 1632.

[97] *Ibid.,* I, iii, 12.   [98] *Ibid.,* I, iv, 2.   [99] *Ibid.,* I, iv, 6.   [100] *Ibid.,* I, iv, 7.

[101] *Ibid.,* Prolegomena, § 12.   [102] *Ibid.,* I, i, 10.

[103] *Ibid.,* II, i, 13.   [104] *Ibid.,* Prolegomena, § 13.   [105] *Ibid.,* I, i, 13.

[106] *Ibid.,* I, ii, 6; compare also II, i, 10.   [107] *Ibid.,* II, v, 27.

[108] Ch. Bastide, *J. Locke, ses théories politiques et leur influence en Angleterre,* Paris, 1906.

[109] *Die Revolutionskirchen Englands,* Leipzig, 1868.

[110] Bastide, *op. cit.,* pp. 42ff., 108.

[111] *Cf.* Bastide, *op. cit.,* pp. 252f.

[112] Bergbohm, *op. cit.,* pp. 151ff.; Tröltsch, *Vernunft und Offenbarung,* p. 165.

[113] *Op. Mel.,* xxi, c. 116.

[114] Dist. I, c. vii; *cf.* dist. I, c. i; dist. IX, c. xi; dist. V and VI. Bergbohm, *op. cit.,* pp. 157ff; Gierke, *Das deutsche Genossenschaftsrecht,* iii: *Die Staats- und Korporationslehre des Altertums und des Mittelalters,* Berlin, 1881, pp. 610ff.

[115] *Cf.* Bergbohm, *op. cit.,* p. 260, Anm. 37.

[116] *Summa Theologiae,* Prima secundae, qu. 90, 91, 93, 94, 95ff.

[117] *Ibid.,* qu. 91, art. 2.   [118] *Ibid.,* qu. 71, art. 6.

[119] *Ibid.,* qu. 106, art. 1.   [120] *Ibid.,* qu. 95, art. 2.

[121] *Kirchenrechtliche Abhandlungen von Stutz,* 6-8 Heft, Stuttgart, 1903, pp. 68ff., 101, 113f., 134f., 142ff., 222f., 311, 323ff., 362, 370.

[122] *Cf.* his book, *De rege et regis institutione,* Tolet., 1599.

[123] *Works,* i, p. 315. Here he calls Thomas "the greatest amongst the school divines", and cites *Sum. Theol.* i, 2, qu. 91, art. 3.

CALVIN AND COMMON GRACE.

By Herman Bavinck.

[1] Calvin, *Institutio*, II, 6, 4; III. 2, 6.

[2] III, 2, 7. [3] III, 2, 8. [4] III, 2, 14.

[5] III, 2, 16. [6] II, 6, 4. [7] III, 22, 1.

[8] III, 22, 1; 23, 2. [9] III, 21, 1. [10] III, 23, 2.

[11] II, 6, 1. [12] II, 2, 18. [13] I, 2, 1; II, 6, 1.

[14] I, 2, 2. [15] III, 2, 29. [16] III, 2, 16.

[17] III, 25, 12. [18] *Comm. on Luke*, xii. 47.

[19] *Comm. on I Cor.*, xv. 28. [20] II, 2, 18ff.

[21] II, 2, 17. [22] II, 2, 17. [23] II, 3, 3.

[24] II, 1, 4. [25] *Comm. on Romans*, vii. 19-21.

[26] I, 5, 1. [27] I, 5, 5. [28] II, 6, 1.

[29] I, 5, 3, 4. [30] I, 3, 1, 3; 5, 3; II, 2, 18.

[31] II, 2, 12. [32] II, 2, 14, 17. [33] II, 2, 12.

[34] II, 2, 12, 18. [34a] II, 2, 13. [35] II, 2, 14.

[36] II, 2, 15, 16. [37] II, 3, 4. [38] II, 2, 25.

[39] II, 3, 4. [40] II. 2, 14, 17. [41] II, 2, 17.

[42] II, 3, 5. [43] III, 7, 1. [44] I, 15, 8; II, 2, 2.

[45] III, 6, 2-4; 8, 11. [46] II, 2, 2; III, 7, 4. [47] II, 2, 1, 2, 9.

[48] II, 2, 10. [49] II, 2, 4. [50] III, 21, 1.

[51] III, 8, 2. [52] II, 2, 11; III, 7, 4. [53] III, 8, 2ff.

[54] III, 7, 4-7. [55] II, 9, 1ff.

[56] *Comm. on Isaiah*, xxiii. 12. [57] III, 7, 8-10; 8, 2ff.; 9, 1, 6.

[58] III, 9, 3. [59] III, 9, 4. [60] III, 9, 4.

[61] III, 10, 6. [62] III, 1, 10ff.

[63] III, 10, 1; *Comm. on Deut.*, i: 15; xii: 15; xxii. 5; *on Isaiah*, iii: 16; *on Lam.*, v. 5.

[64] Usury is here meant in the old sense of the taking of reasonable interest.

[65] *Comm. on Isaiah* xxiii.[12]; *on the Psalms* xv.[5]; *on I Cor.* vii.[20].

CALVIN'S DOCTRINE OF THE KNOWLEDGE OF GOD.

By Benjamin B. Warfield.

[1] Article on *Calvins Institutio, nach Form und Inhalt, in ihrer geschichtlichen Entwickelung*, printed in the *Theologische Studien und Kritiken* for 1868, p. 39. Köstlin's whole account of the origin of these sections in the edition of 1539 is worth reading (pp. 38-39).

[2] *Instit.* I. iii. 1: Quemdam inesse humanae menti, et quidem naturali instinctu, divinitatis sensum, extra controversiam ponimus; iii. 3 *ad init.:* "This indeed with all rightly judging men will always be assured, that there is engraved on the minds of men *divinitatis sensum, qui deleri numquam potest"*; iii. 3, *med.:* vigere tamen ac subinde emergere quem maxime extinctum cuperent, *deitatis sensum;* iv. 4 *ad fin.:* naturaliter insculptum esse deitatis sensum humanis cordibus; iv. 4. *fin.:* manet tamen semen illud quod revelli a radice nullo modo potest, aliquam esse divinitatem. The phraseology by which Calvin designates this "natural instinct" (*naturalis instinctus;* III. 1. *ad init*) varies from sensus divinitatis or sensus deitatis to such synonyms as: *numinis intelligentia, dei notio, dei notitia.* It is the basis on the one hand of whatever *cognitio dei* man attains to and on the other of whatever *religio* he reaches; whence it is called the *semen religionis.*

[3] That the knowledge of God is innate was the common property of the Reformed teachers. Peter Martyr, *Loci Communes*, 1576, *praef,* declares that Dei cognitio omnium animis naturaliter innata[est]. It was thrown into great prominence in the Socinian debate, as the Socinians contended that the human mind is natively a *tabula rasa* and all knowledge is acquired. But in defending the innate knowledge of God, the Reformed doctors were very careful that it should not be exaggerated. Thus Leonh. Riissen, *F. Turretini Compendium . . . auctum et illustratum* (1695), I. 5, remarks: "Some recent writers explain the natural sense of deity (*numinis*) as *an idea of God impressed on our minds.* If this idea is understood as an innate *faculty* for knowing God after some fashion, it should not be denied; but if it expresses an *actual and adequate representation of God from our birth,* it is to be entirely rejected." (Heppe, *Die Dogmatik der evangelisch-reformirten Kirche.* p. 4.)

[4] En quid sit pura germanaque religio, nempe *fides,* cum serio *Dei timore* conjuncta; ut timor et *voluntariam reverentiam* in se contineat, et secum trahat *legitimum cultum,* qualis in Lege praescribitur.

[5] The significance and relations of "the Puritan principle" of absolute

dependence on the Word of God as the source of knowledge of His will, and exclusive limitation to its prescriptions of doctrine, life, and even form of Church government and worship, are suggested by Dorner, *Hist. of Protest. Theol.*, I. 390, who criticizes it sharply from his "freer" Lutheran standpoint. But even Luther knew how, on occasion, to invoke "the Puritan principle". Writing to Bartime von Sternberg, Sept. 1, 1523, he says: "For a Christian must do nothing that God has not commanded, and there is no command as to such masses and vigils, but it is solely their own invention, which brings in money, without helping either living or dead" (*The Letters of Martin Luther, Selected and Translated* by Margaret A. Currie, p. 115).

⁶ *Cf.* P. J. Muller, *De Godsleer van Zwingli en Calvijn* (1883), p. 8: "If Zwingli follows more the *a priori,* Calvin follows the *a posteriori* method"; and E. Rabaud, *Hist. de la doctrine de l'inspiration,* etc. (1883), p. 58: "His lucid and, above everything, practical genius."

⁷ It is this distribution of Calvin's interest which leads to the impression that he lays little stress on "the theistic proofs". On the contrary, he asserts their validity most strenuously: only he does not believe that any proofs can work true faith apart from "the testimony of the Spirit", and he is more interested in their value for developing the knowledge of God than for merely establishing His existence. Hence P. J. Muller is wrong when he denies the one to affirm the other, as, *e. g.,* in his *De Godsleer van Zwingli en Calvijn* (1883), p. 11: "Neither by Zwingli nor by Calvin are proofs offered for the existence of God, although some passages in their writings seem to contain suggestions of them. The proposition, 'God exists', needed no proof either for themselves, or for their coreligionists, or even against Rome. The so-called cosmological argument has no doubt been found by some in Zwingli (Zeller, *Das theolog. Syst. Zwinglis* extracted from the *Theol. Jahrbb.* Tübingen, 1853, p. 33), and the physico-theological in Calvin (Lipsius, *Lehre der ev.-prot. Dogmatik,* ed. 2, 1879, p. 213) ; but it would not be difficult to show that we have to do in neither case with a philosophical deduction, but only with a means for attaining the complete knowledge of God." Though Calvin (also Zwingli) makes use of the theistic proofs to develop the knowledge of God, it does not follow that he (or Zwingli) did not value them as proofs of the existence of God. And we do not think Muller is successful (pp. 12 sq.) in explaining away the implication of the latter in Zwingli's use of these theistic arguments, or in Calvin's (p. 16). Schweitzer, *Glaubenslehre der ev.-ref. Kirche* (1844), I. 250, finds in Calvin's citation of Cicero's declaration that there is no nation so barbarous, no tribe so degraded, that it is not persuaded that a God exists, an appeal to the so-called *historical* argument for

the divine existence (cf. the use of it by Zwingli, Opera. III. 156) : but Calvin's real attitude to the theistic argument is rather to be sought in the implications of the notably eloquent ch. 5.

⁸ P. J. Muller, De Godsleer van Zwingli en Calvijn (1883), pp. 18 sq., does not seem to bear this in mind, although he had clearly stated it in his De Godsleer van Calvijn (1881), pp. 13-25.

⁹ Cf. F. C. Baur, Die christliche Lehre von der Dreieinigkeit, etc., III. (1843), p. 41 : "From this point of view"—he is expounding Calvin's doctrine—"the several manifestations in the history of religions are conceived not as stages in the gradually advancing evolution of the religious consciousness, but as inexcusable, sinful aberrations, as wilful perversions and defacements of the inborn idea of God."

¹⁰ Cf. J. Cramer, Nieuwe Bijdragen op het gebied van Godgeleerdheid en Wijsbegeerte, III (1881), p. 202: "By the Scripture or the Scriptures he [Calvin] understood the books of the Old and New Testaments which have been transmitted to us by the Church as canonical, as the rule of faith and life. The Apocrypha of the O. T. as they were determined by the Council of Trent, he excludes. They are to him indeed libri ecclesiastici, in many respects good and useful to be read; but they are not libri canonici 'ad fidem dogmatum faciendam' (Acta Synodi Tridentinae, cum antidoto, 1547)." In a later article, De Roomsch-Katholieke en de Oud-protestantsche Schriftbeschouwing, 1883, p. 36, Cramer declares that by the Scriptures, Calvin means "nothing else than the canon, established by the Synods of Hippo and Carthage, and transmitted by the Catholic Church, with the exception of the so-called Apocrypha of the O. T.", etc. Cf. Leipoldt, Geschichte d. N. T. Kanons, II, 1908, p. 140: "We obtain the impression that it is only for form's sake that Calvin undertakes to test whether the disputed books are canonical or not. In reality it is already a settled matter with him that they are. Calvin feels himself therefore in the matter of the N. T. canon bound to the mediæval tradition." Cf. also Otto Ritschl, Dogmengeschichte des Protestantismus, I, 1908, p. 70, to the same effect.

¹¹ Cf., e. g., J. Pannier, Le témoignage du Saint-Esprit (1893), pp. 112 sq.: "One fact strikes us at first sight: not only did Calvin not comment on the Apochryphal books, for which he wrote a very short preface, which was ever more and more abridged in the successive editions, but he did not comment on all the Canonical books. And if lack of time may explain the passing over of some of the less important historical books of the Old Testament, it was undoubtedly for a graver reason that he left to one side the three books attributed to Solomon, notably the Song of Songs. 'In the New Testament there is ordinarily mentioned only the Apocalypse, neglected by Calvin undoubtedly for

critical or theological motives analogous to those which determined the most of his contemporaries, but it is necessary to note that the two lesser epistles of John are also lacking, and that in speaking of the large epistle Calvin always expresses himself as if it were the only existing one' (Reuss, *Revue de Théologie de Strasbourg,* VI (1853), p. 229). In effect, at the very time when he was defending particularly the authority of the Scriptures against the Council of Trent, when he was dedicating to Edward VI, the King of England, his Commentaries on the 'Epistles which are accustomed to be called Canonical' (1551), he included in the Canon only the First Epistle of Peter, the First Epistle of John, James and, at the very end, the Second Epistle of Peter and Jude."—Reuss, however, in his *History of the Canon of the Holy Scriptures in the Christian Church* (1862, E. T. 1884), greatly modifies the opinion here quoted from him: "Some have believed it possible to affirm that Calvin rejected the Apocalypse because it was the only book of the N. T., except the two short Epistles of John, on which he wrote no commentary. But that conclusion is too hasty. In the *Institutes,* the Apocalypse is sometimes quoted like the other Apostolic writings, and even under John's name. If there was no commentary, it was simply that the illustrious exegete, wiser in this respect than several of his contemporaries and many of his successors, understood that his vocation called him elsewhere" (p. 318). He adds, indeed, of 2 and 3 John: "It might be said with more probability that Calvin did not acknowledge the canonicity of these two writings. He never quotes them, and he quotes the First Epistle of John in a way to exclude them: *Joannes in sua canonica, Instit.* iii. 2. 24; 3. 23 (*Opp.* ii. 415-453)." But this opinion requires revision, just as that on the Apocalypse did, as we shall see below. *Cf.* further, in the meantime, Reuss: *Hist. of the Sacred Scriptures of the N. T.,* ii. 347, and S. Berger, *La Bible au Seizième Siècle* (1879), p. 120, who expresses himself most positively: "Calvin expresses no judgment on the lesser Epistles of St. John. But we remark that he never cites them and that he mentions the First in these terms: 'As John says in his canonical.' This word excludes, in the thought of the author, the two other Epistles attributed to this Apostle."

¹³ This may have been the case with the Apocalypse, which not only Reuss, as we have seen, but Scaliger thought him wise not to have entered upon; and which he is—perhaps credibly—reported to have said in conversation he did not understand (*cf.* Leipoldt's *Geschichte des N. T. Kanons,* II, p. 48, note). But how impossible it is to imagine that this implies any doubt of the canonicity or authority of the book will be quickly evident to anyone who will note his frequent citation of

it in the same fashion with other Scripture and alongside of other Scripture (*e. g., Opp.* I. 736 = II. 500; I. 983 = II. 957; I. 1033 = II. 1063; I. 1148 = II. 521; II. 88, 357, 859. V. 191, 195, 1199, 532. VI. 176. VII. 29, 118, 333. XXXI. 650), sometimes mentioning it by name (VII. 467; I. 733 = II. 497), sometimes by the name of John (I. 715 = II. 492, VIII. 338 [along with 1 John]), sometimes by the name of both 'John' and 'the Apocalypse' (I. 506 = II. 125, VII. 116, XXX. 651, XLVIII. 122, XXIV. 43), and always with reverence and confidence as a Scriptural book. He even expressly cites it under the name of Scripture and explicitly as the dictation of the Spirit: VII. 539, "Fear not, says the Scripture (Eccles. xviii. 22). . . . Again (Rev. xxii. 11) . . . and (John xv. 2)"; I. 624, "Elsewhere also the Spirit testifies . . . " (along with Daniel and Paul). *Cf.* also such passages as II. 734, "Nor does the Apocalypse which they quote afford them any support . . . "; XLVIII. 238, "I should like to ask the Papists if they think John was so stupid that . . . etc. (Rev. xxii. 8)"; also VI. 369; V. 198.

[13] We use the simple expression "the Epistle of John"; the apparently, but only apparently, stronger and more exclusive, "the Canonical Epistle of John", which Calvin employs, although it would be misleading in our associations, is its exact synonym. Those somewhat numerous writers who have quoted the form "the *Canonical* Epistle of John" as if its use implied the denial of the *canonicity* of the other epistles of John forget that this was the ordinary designation in the West of the Catholic Epistles—"the Seven Canonical Epistles"—and that they are all currently cited by this title by Western writers. The matter has been set right by A. Lang: *Die Bekehrung Johannis Calvins* (II. 1. of Bonwetch and Seeberg's *Studien zur Geschichte der Theologie und der Kirche* (1897), pp. 26-29). On the title "Canonical Epistles" for the Catholic Epistles, see Lücke, *SK.* 1836, iii. 643-659; Bleek, *Introd. to the N. T.,* § 202 at end; Hilgenfeld, *Einleitung in d. N. T.,* p. 153; Westcott, *Epp. of St. John,* p. xxix; Salmond, Hastings *BD.* I., p. 360. In 1551, Calvin published his *Commentarii in Epistolas Canonicas*—that is that on the Catholic Epistles; also his *Commentaire sur l'Épistre Canonique de St. Jean, i. e.,* on "the Epistle of John"; also his *Commentaire sur l'Épistre Canonique de S. Jude.* Calvin does not seem ever to have happened to quote from 2 and 3 John. The reference given in the Index printed in *Opp.* xxii, viz., 3 Jno. 9, *Opp.* x, part 2, p. 81, occurs in a letter, not by Calvin but by Christof Libertetus to Farel. *Cf.* J. Leipoldt, *Geschichte des N. T. Kanons* (2nd Part, Leipzig, 1908), p. 148, note 1: "The smaller Johannine Epistles Calvin seems never to have cited. He cites 1 John in *Inst.* III. ii. 21 by the formula: dicit Johannes in sua canonica. Nevertheless it is very questionable whether inferences

can be drawn from this formula as to Calvin's attitude to 2 and 3 Jno."
He adds a reference to Lang as above.

[14] Pannier, as cited, p. 113.

[15] *Opera,* xi. 674-676: *cf.* Buisson, *Castellion* (1892), I. 198-199.
Buisson discusses the whole incident and quotes from the minutes of
the Council before which Castellion brought the matter: the point of
dispute is there briefly expressed thus: "Moss^r Calvin recognizes as
holy, and the said Bastian repudiates" the book in question.

[16] Calvin employs all these "three books attributed to Solomon" freely
as Scripture and deals with them precisely as he does with other
Scriptures. As was to be expected, he cites Proverbs most frequently,
Canticles least: but he cites them all as Solomon's and as authoritative
Scripture. "'I have washed my feet' says the believing soul in Solomon . . . " is the way he cites Canticles (*Opp.* i. 778, ii. 589, *cf.*
vii. 760). "They make a buckler of a sentence of Solomon's, which is
as contrary to them as is no other that is in the Scriptures" (vii. 130)
is the way he cites Ecclesiastes. He indeed expressly contrasts Ecclesiastes as genuine Scripture with the Apocryphal books: "As the soul
has an origin apart, it has also another preëminence, and this is what
Solomon means when he says that at death the body returns to the
earth from which it was taken and the soul returns to God who gave it
(Eccl. xii. 7). For this reason it is said in the Book of Wisdom (ii. 23)
that man is immortal, seeing that he was created in the image of God.
This is not an authentic book of Holy Scripture, but it is not improper
to avail ourselves of its testimony as of an ancient teacher (Docteur
ancien)—although the single reason ought to be enough for us that the
image of God, as it has been placed in man, can reside only in an
immortal soul, etc." (vii. 112, 1544).

[17] *Cf.* A. Bossert, *Calvin* (1906), p. 6: "Humanist himself as well as
profound theologian . . . " Charles Borgeaud, *Histoire de l'Uni-
versité de Genève* (1900), p. 21: "Before he was a theologian, Calvin
was a Humanist . . . "

[18] *Cf.* the *Preface* he prefixed to the Apocryphal Books (for the history
of which, see *Opera,* ix. 827, note): "These books which are called
Apocryphal have in all ages been discriminated from those which are
without difficulty shown to be of the Sacred Scriptures. For the
ancients, wishing to anticipate the danger that any profane books should
be mixed with those which certainly proceeded from the Holy Spirit,
made a roll of these latter which they called 'Canon'; meaning by this
word that all that was comprehended under it was the assured rule to
which we should attach ourselves. Upon the others they imposed the
name of Apocrypha; denoting that they were to be held as private

writings and not authenticated, like public documents. Accordingly the difference between the former and latter is the same as that between an instrument, passed before a notary, and sealed to be received by all, and the writing of some particular man. It is true they are not to be despised, seeing that they contain good and useful doctrine. Nevertheless it is only right that what we have been given by the Holy Spirit should have preëminence above all that has come from men." Cf., in his earliest theological treatise, the *Psychopannychia* of 1534-1542 (*Opp.* v. 182), where, after quoting Ecclus. xvii. 1 and Wisd. ii. 23 as "two sacred writers", he adds: "I would not urge the authority of these writers strongly on our adversaries, did they not oppose them to us. They may be allowed, however, some weight, if not as canonical, yet certainly as ancient, as pious, and as received by the suffrages of many. But let us omit them and let us retain . . . " etc. In the *Psychopannychia* his dealing with Baruch on the other hand is more wavering. On one occasion (p. 205) it is quoted with the formula, "sic enim loquitur propheta", and on another (p. 229), "in prophetia Baruch" corrected in 1542. In the *Institutes* of 1536 he quotes it as Scripture: "alter vero propheta scribit" (*Opp.* i. 82),—referring back to Daniel. This is already corrected in 1539 (i. 906; cf. ii. 632). In 1534-1536, then, he considered Baruch canonical: afterwards not so. His dealing with it in v. 271 (1537), vi. 560 (1545), vi. 638 (1546) is *ad hominem*.

[19] *Acta Synodi Tridentinae, cum Antidoto* (1547).

[20] *Vera ecclesiae reformandae ratio*, p. 613: quae divinitus non esse prodita, sani omnes, saltim ubi moniti fuerint judicabunt.

[21] *Acta Synodi Tridentinae, cum antidoto:* Quantum, obsecro, a Spiritus Sancti majestati aliena est haec confessio!

[22] This is translated from the French version, ed. Meyrueis, IV. 743. The Latin is the same, though somewhat more concise: nihil Petro indignum, ut vim spiritus apostolici et gratiam ubique appareat: eam prorsus repudiare mihi religio.

[23] Haec fictio indigna esset nimistro Christi, obtendere alienam personam.

[24] Ed. Meyrueis, IV. 780.   [25] *Ibid.*, IV. 362.

[26] *Ibid.*, IV. 694. Latin: mihi ad epistolam hanc recipiendam satis est, quod nihil continet Christi apostolo indignum.

[27] Cf. J. Cramer, as cited, p. 126: "It was thus, in the first place, as the result of scientific investigations that Calvin fixed the limits of the canon . . . not *a priori*, but *a posteriori*, that he came to the recognition of the canonicity of the Biblical books." But especially see the excellently conceived passage on p. 155, to the following effect: "What great importance Calvin attaches to the question whether a Biblical

book is *apostolic!* If it is not apostolic, he does not recognize it as canonical. To determine its apostolicity, he appeals not merely to the ecclesiastical tradition of its origin, but also and principally to its contents. This is what he does in the case of all the antilegomena. The touchstone for this is found in the homologoumena. That he undertakes no investigation of the apostolic origin of these latter is a matter of course. This, for him and for all his contemporaries, stood irreversibly settled. The touchstone employed by Calvin is a scientific one. The testimonium Spiritus Sancti no doubt made its influence felt. But without the help of the scientific investigation, this internal testimony would not have the power to elevate the book into a canonical book. That Calvin was treading here in the footprints of the ancient Church will be understood. The complaint sometimes brought against the Christians of the earliest centuries is unfounded, that they held all writings canonical in which they found their own dogmatics. No doubt they attached in their criticism great weight to this. But not less to the question whether the origin of the books was traceable back to the apostolical age, and their contents accorded with apostolic doctrine, as it might be learned from the indubitably apostolic writings. So far as science had been developed in their day, they employed it in the formation of the canon . . . " In a later article Cramer says: "In the determination of the compass of Scripture, Calvin, like Luther, took his start from the writings which more than the others communicated the knowledge of Christ in His kingdom and had been recognized always by the Church as genuine and trustworthy. Even if the results of his criticism were more in harmony with the ecclesiastical tradition, than was the case with those of the German reformer, he yet walked in the self-same critical pathway. He took over the canon of the Church just as little as its version and its exegesis without scrutiny" (*De Roomsch-Katholieke en de Oud-protestansche Schrift-beschouwing*, 1883, pp. 31-32). Cramer considers this critical procedure on Calvin's part inconsistent with his doctrine of the testimony of the Spirit, but (p. 38) he recognizes that we cannot speak of it as the nodding of Homer: "It is not here and there, but throughout; not in his exegetical writings alone, but in his dogmatic ones, too, that he walks in this critical path. We never find the faintest trace of hesitation."

[28] Comment on John viii. 1 (Meyrueis' ed. of the Commentaries, II. 169).

[29] Quomodo Jeremiae nomen obrepserit, me nescire fateor, nec anxie laboro; certe Jeremiae nomen errore positum esse pro Zacharia res ipsa ostendit; quia nihil tale apud Jeremiam legitur.

[30] *Opera*, III. 100. note 3.

[31] *Cf.* J. Cramer, as cited, pp. 116-117: "Calvin does not largely busy himself with textual criticism. He follows the text which was generally received in his day. It deserves notice only that he exercises a free and independent judgment and recognizes the rights of science." Cramer adduces his treatment of I Jno. v. 7 and proceeds: "He comes forward on scientific grounds against the Vulgate. The decree of Trent that this version must be followed as 'authentical', he finds silly; and reverence for it as if it had fallen down from heaven, ludicrous. 'How can anyone dispute the right to appeal to the original text? And what a bad version this is! There are scarcely three verses in any page well rendered' (*Acta Synod. Trident.*, etc., pp. 414-416)."

[32] *Institutes,* I. vii. 10. *Cf.* I. vi. 203.

[33] I. vii. 5 *ad init:* "We have received it from God's own mouth by the ministry of men.

[34] It is quite common to represent Calvin as without a theory, at least an expressed theory, of the relation of the divine and human authors of Scripture. Thus J. Cramer, as cited, p. 103, says: "How we are to understand the relation of the divine and human activities through which the Scriptures were produced is not exactly defined by Calvin. A precise theory of inspiration such as we meet with in the later dogmaticians is not found in him." Cramer is only sure that Calvin did not hold to the theory which later Protestants upheld: "It is true that Calvin gave the impulse (from which the later dogmatic view of Scripture grew up), more than any other of the Reformers. But we must not forget that here we can speak of nothing more than the impulse. We nowhere find in Calvin such a magical conception of the Bible as we find in the later dogmaticians. It is true he used the term 'dictare' and other expressions which he employs under the influence of the terminology of his day, but on the other hand . . . in how many respects does he recognize the *human* factor in the Scriptures!" (p. 142). Similarly Pannier, as cited, p. 200: "In any case Calvin has not written a single word which can be appealed to in favor of *literal* inspiration. What is divine for him, if there is anything specifically divine beyond the contents, the brightness of which is reflected upon the container, is the *sense* of each book, or at most of each phrase,—never the employment of each word. Calvin would have deplored the petty dogmatics of the *Consensus Helveticus,* which declares the vowel points of the Hebrew text inspired, and the exaggerations of the theopneusty of the nineteenth century." Yet nothing is more certain than that Calvin held both to "verbal inspiration" and to "the inerrancy of Scripture", however he may have conceived the action of God which secured these things.

[85] *Cf.* Otto Ritschl, *Dogmengeschichte des Protestantismus,* 1908, I., p. 63: "If we may still entertain doubts whether Bullinger really defended the stricter doctrine of inspiration, it certainly is found in Calvin after 1543. He may have merely taken over from Butzer the expression *Spiritus Sancti amanuenses;* but it is peculiar to him that he conceives both the books of the Old Testament inclusively as contained in the historical enumerations, and those of the New Testament, as arising out of a verbal dictation of the Holy Spirit."

[86] These phrases are brought together by J. Cramer (as cited, pp. 102-3) from the Comments on 2 Tim. iii. 16 and 2 Pet.. i. 20.

[87] *Cf.* Pannier, as cited, p. 203: "The Word of God is for him one, *verbum Dei,* and not *verba Dei.* The diversity of authors disappears before the unity of the Spirit."

[88] Ab ipsissimo Dei ore ad nos fluxuissi.

[89] E coelo fluxuissi, acsi vivae ipsae Dei voces illic exaudirentur.

[40] Hoc prius est membrum, eandem scripturae reverentiam deberi quam Deo deferimus, quia ad eo solo manavit, nec quicquam humani habet admixtum.

[41] Justa reverentia inde nascitur, quam statuimus, Deum nobiscum loqui, non homines mortales.

[42] The account of Calvin's doctrine of inspiration given by E. Rabaud, *Histoire de la doctrine de l'inspiration . . . dans les pays de langue française* (1883), pp. 52 sq., is worth comparing. Calvin's thought on this subject, he tells us, was more precise and compact than that of the other Reformers, although even his conception of inspiration was far from possessing perfectly firm contours or supplying the elements of a really systematic view (52). He was the first, nevertheless, to give the subject of Sacred Scripture a fundamental, theoretic treatment, led thereto not by the pressure of controversy, but by the logic of his systematic thought: for his doctrine of inspiration (not yet distinguished from revelation) is one of the essential bases, if not the very point of departure of his dogmatics (55). To him "the Bible is manifestly the word of God, in which he reveals himself to men", and as such "proceeds from God". "But" (pp. 56 sq.) "the action of God does not, in Calvin's view, transform the sacred authors into machines. Jewish verbalism, Scriptural materialism, may be present in germ in the ideas of the *Institutes*—and the cold intellects of certain doctors of the Protestant scholasticism of the next century developed them—but they are very remote from the thought of the Reformer. Chosen and ordained by God, the Biblical writers were subject to a higher impulse; they received a divine illumination which increased the energy of their natural faculties; they understood the Revelation better and transmitted

it more faithfully. It was scarcely requisite for this, however, that they should be passive instruments, simple secretaries, pens moved by the Holy Spirit. Appointed but intelligent organs of the divine thought, far from being subject to a dictation, in complete obedience to the immediate will of God, they acted under the impulsion of a personal faith which God communicated to them. 'Now, whether God was manifested to men by visions or oracles, what is called celestial witnesses, or ordained men as His ministers who taught their successors by tradition, it is in every case certain that He impressed on their hearts such a certitude of the doctrine, that they were persuaded and convinced that what had been revealed and preached to them proceeded from the true God: for He always ratified His word so as to secure for it a credit above all human opinion. Finally, that the truth might uninterruptedly remain continually in vigor from age to age, and be known in the world, He willed that the revelations which He had committed to the hands of the Fathers as a deposit, should be put on record: and it was with this design that He had the Law published, to which he afterwards added the Prophets as its expositors' (*Institutes,* I. vi. 2). These few lines resume in summary form the very substance of Calvin's doctrine of inspiration. We may conclude from it that he did not give himself to the elaboration of this dogma, with the tenacity and logical rigor which his clear and above all practical genius employed in the study and systematization of other points of the new doctrine. We shall seek in vain a precise declaration on the mode of revelation, on the extent and intensity of inspiration, on the relation of the book and the doctrine. None of these questions, as we have already had occasion to remark, had as yet been raised: the doctors gave themselves to what was urgent and did not undertake to prove or discuss what was not yet either under discussion or attacked. The principle which was laid down sufficed them. God had spoken—this was the faith which every consciousness of the time received without repugnance, and against which no mind raised an objection. To search out how He did it was wholly useless: to undertake to prove it, no less so" (p. 58). There is evident in this passage a desire to minimize Calvin's view of the divinity of Scripture; the use of the passage from I. vi. 2 as the basis of an exposition of his doctrine of inspiration is indicative of this—whereas it obviously is a very admirable account of how God has made known His will to men and preserved the knowledge of it through time. The double currents of desire to be true to Calvin's own exposition of his doctrine and yet to withhold his *imprimatur* from what the author believes to be an overstrained doctrine, produces some strange confusion in his further exposition.

⁴³*Cf.* J. Cramer, as cited, p. 114: "How Calvin conceives of this *dictare* by the Holy Ghost it is difficult to say. He borrowed it from the current ecclesiastical usage, which employed it of the *auctor primarius* of Scripture, as indeed also of tradition. Thus the Council of Trent uses the expression *dictante Spiritu Sancto* of the unwritten tradition inspired by the Holy Spirit." Otto Ritschl, *Dogmengeschichte des Protestantismus*, I, 1908, p. 59, argues for taking the term strictly in Calvin. It is employed, it is true, in contemporary usage in the figurative sense, of the deliverances of the natural conscience, for example; and some Reformed writers use it of the internal testimony of the Spirit. Calvin also himself speaks as if he employed it of Scripture only figuratively,—*e. g., Corpus Ref.* xxix, p. 632: verba *quodammodo* dictante Christi Spiritu. Nevertheless, on the whole Ritschl thinks he meant it in the literal sense.

⁴⁴ *Cf., e. g.,* J. Cramer, as cited, pp. 114-116, whose instances are followed in the remarks which succeed. *Cf.* also p. 125. How widespread this effort to discover in Calvin some acknowledgment of errors in Scripture has become may be seen by consulting the citations made by Dunlop Moore, *The Presbyterian and Reformed Review*, 1893, p. 60: he cites Cremer, van Oosterzee, Farrar. *Cf.* even A. H. Strong, *Syst. Theol.,* ed. 1907, vol. I, p. 217, whose list of "theological writers who admit the errancy of Scripture writers as to some matters unessential to their moral and spiritual teaching" requires drastic revision. Leipoldt (*Geschichte d. N. T. Kanons,* II, p. 169) says: "Fundamentally Calvin holds fast to the old doctrine of verbal inspiration. His sound historical sense leads him, here and there, it is true, to break through the bonds of this doctrine. In his harmony of the Gospels (*Commentarii in harmoniam ex Mat. et Lk. compositam,* 1555), *e. g.,* Calvin shows that the letters are not sacred to him; he moves much more freely here than Martin Chemnitz. But in other cases again Calvin draws strict consequences from the doctrine of verbal inspiration. He ascribes, *e. g.,* to all four Gospels precisely similar authority, although he (with Luther and Zwingli) considers John's gospel the most beautiful of them all."

⁴⁵ This is solidly shown, *e. g.,* by Dunlop Moore, as cited, pp. 61-62: also for Acts vii. 16.

⁴⁵ᵃ Despite his tendency to lower Calvin's doctrine of inspiration with respect to its effects, J. Cramer in the following passage (as cited, pp. 120-121) gives in general a very fair statement of it: "We have seen that Calvin, although he has not given us a completed theory of inspiration, yet firmly believed in the inspiration of the entirety of Scripture. It is true we do not find in him the crass expressions of the later

Reformed, as well as Lutheran, theologians. But the foundation on which they subsequently built—though somewhat onesidedly—is here. We cannot infer much from such expressions as 'from God', 'came from God', 'flowed from God'. Just as in Zwingli, these expressions were sometimes in Calvin synonyms of 'true'. Thus, at Titus ii. 12, he says he cannot understand why so many are unwilling to draw upon profane writers,—'for, since all truth is from God (*a Deo*), if anything has been said well and truly by profane men, it ought not to be rejected, for it has come from God (*a Deo est profectum*)'. More significant are such expressions as, 'nothing human is mixed with Scripture', 'we owe to them the same reverence as to God', God 'is the author of Scripture' and as such has 'dictated' (dictavit) all that the Apostles and Prophets have written, so that we must not depart from the word of God in even the smallest particular', etc. All this applies not only to the Scriptures as a whole, not merely to their fundamental ideas and chief contents, but to all the sixty-six books severally. In contra-distinction from the Apocrypha, they have been given by the Holy Spirit (*Préface mise en tête des livres apocryphes de l'Ancien Test.: Corp. Reff.* ix. 827). The book of Acts 'beyond question is the product of the Holy Spirit Himself', Mark 'wrote nothing but what the Holy Spirit gave him to write', etc. To think here merely of a providential direction by God, in the sense that God took care that His people should lack nothing of a Scriptural record of His revelation—is impossible. For, however often Calvin may have directed attention to such a 'singularis providentiae cura' (*Inst.*, V. vi. 2, *cf.* I. viii. 10; *Argument in Joh.*) with respect to Scripture, he yet saw something over and above this in the production of the sacred books. He looked upon them as the writings of God Himself, who, through an extraordinary operation of His Spirit, guarded His amanuenses from *all* error as well when they transmitted histories as when they propounded the doctrine of Christ. Thus to him Scripture (naturally in its original text) was a complete work of God, to which nothing could be added and from which nothing could be taken away."

[46] In I. vi. 14 Calvin says that the Apostle in Heb. xi. 3, 'By faith we understand that the worlds were framed by the Word of God' wishes to intimate that "the invisible divinity *was represented* indeed by such displays of His power, but that we have no eyes *to perceive it* unless they are illuminated through faith by the inner revelation of God" (Invisibilem divinitatem *representari* quidem talibus spectaculis, sed ad eam *perspiciendam* non esse nobis oculos, nisi interiore Dei revelatione per fidem illuminatur). Here he distinguishes between the external, objective representation, and the internal, subjective preparation to

perceive this representation. God is objectively revealed in His works: man in his sins is blind to this revelation: the interior operation of God is an opening of man's eyes: man then sees. The operation of God is therefore a palingenesis. This passage is already in ed. 1539 (I. 291); the last clause (nisi . . .) is not, however, reproduced in the French versions of either 1541 or 1560 (III. 60).

[47] In his response to the Augsburg Interim (*Vera Ecclesiae reformandae ratio*, 1548) he allows it to be the *proprium ecclesiae officium* to *scripturas veras a suppositis discernere;* but only that *obedienter amplectitur, quicquid Dei est,* as the sheep hear the voice of the shepherd. It is nevertheless *sacrilega impietas ecclesiae judicio submittere sacrasancta Dei oracula.* See J. Cramer, as cited, p. 104, note 3. Cramer remarks in expounding Calvin's view: "By the approbation she gives to them"—the books of Scripture—"the Church does not make them authentic, but only yields her homage to the truth of God."

[48] It would require that we should be wholly hardened (nisi ad perditam impudentiam obduruerint) that we should not perceive that the doctrine of Scripture is heavenly, that we should not have the confession wrung from us that there are manifest signs in Scripture that it is God who speaks in and through it (extorquebitur illis haec confessio, manifesta signa loquentis Dei conspici in Scriptura ex quibus pateat coelestem esse ejus doctrinam)—I. vii. 4.

[49] The exact relations of the "proofs" to the divinity of Scripture, which Calvin teaches, was sufficiently clear to be caught by his successors. It is admirably stated in the Westminster Confession of Faith, I. v. And we may add that the same conception is stated also very precisely by Quenstedt: "These motives, as well internal as external, by which we are led to the knowledge of the authority of Scripture, make the theopneusty of Sacred Scripture probable, and produce a certitude which is not merely conjectural but moral: they do not make the divinity of Scripture infallible and altogether indubitable." That is to say, they are not of the nature of *demonstration,* but nevertheless give moral certitude: the testimony of the Spirit is equivalent to demonstration,—as is the deliverance of any simply acting sense.

[50] *Cf.* Pannier, as cited, pp. 257-8: "We see that this understanding of the Scriptures, this capacity to receive the testimony of the Spirit, is not, according to Calvin, possible for all; and that, less and less . . . He continually emphasises more and more the incapacity of man to persuade another of it, without the aid of God; but he emphasises still more progressively the impossibility of obtaining this aid if God does not accord it first. 1550 (I. viii, at end): 'Those who wish to prove to unbelievers by arguments that the Scriptures are from God are

inconsiderate; for this is known *only to faith.'* 1559 (I. vii. *in fine*):
The mysteries of God are not understood, *except by those to whom it
is given* . . . It is quite certain that the witness of the Spirit does
not make itself felt except to believers, and is not *in itself* an apologetic
means with respect to unbelievers . . . The *natural* man receiveth
not spiritual things."

[51] *Cf.* Pannier, as cited, pp. 195-6: "First let us recall this,—for
Calvin this testimony of the Holy Spirit is only one act of the great
drama which is enacted in the entire soul of the religious man, and in
which the Holy Spirit holds always the principal rôle. While the later
dogmatists make the Holy Spirit, so to speak, function mechanically,
at a given moment, in the pen of the prophets or in the brain of the
readers, Calvin sees the Holy Spirit constantly active in the man
whom He wishes to sanctify, and the fact that He leads him to
recognize the divinity and the canonicity of the sacred books is only
one manifestation,—a very important one, no doubt, but only a particular one,—of His general work." It is only, of course, the Lutheran
and Rationalizing dogmatists who, constructively, subject the action of
the Spirit to the direction of man—whether by making it rest on the
application of the "means of grace" or on the action of the human will.
Calvin and his followers—the Reformed—make the act of man depend
on the free and sovereign action of the Spirit.

[52] J. Cramer, as cited, pp. 122-3, somewhat understates this, but in the
main catches Calvin's meaning: "Calvin does not, it is true, tell us in
so many words precisely what this *testimonium sp. s.* is, but it is
easy to gather it from the whole discussion. He is thinking of the Holy
Spirit, who, as the Spirit of our adoption as children, leads us to say
Amen to the Word which the Father speaks in the Holy Scriptures to
His children. He even says expressly in *Inst.* I. vii. 4: 'As if the
Spirit was not called "seal" and "earnest" just because He confers
faith on the pious.' But more plainly still, and indeed so that no doubt
can remain, we find it in Beza, the most beloved and talented pupil of
Calvin, who assuredly also in his conception of Scripture was the most
thoroughly imbued with the spirit of his teacher. In his reply to
Castellion, Beza says: 'The testimony of the Spirit of adoption does
not lie properly in this, that we believe to be true what the Scriptures
testify (for this is known also to the devils and to many of the lost),
but rather in this,—that each applies to himself the promise of salvation in Christ of which Paul speaks in Rom. viii. 15, 16.' Accordingly a
few lines further down he speaks of a 'testimony of adoption and free
justification in Christ'. In the essence of the matter Calvin will have
meant just this by his testimony of the Holy Spirit." . . . Beza's

words are in his *Ad defensiones et reprehensiones Seb. Castellionis* (*Th. Bezae Vezelii Opera*, i, Geneva, 1582, p. 503): Testimonium Spiritus adoptionis non in eo proprie positum est ut credamus verum esse quod Scriptura testatur (nam hoc ipsum quoque sciunt diaboli et reprobi multi), sed in eo potius ut quisque sibi salutis in Christo promissionem applicet, de qua re agit Paulus, Rom. viii. 15, 16. . . . That it was generally understood in the first age that this was the precise nature of the witness of the Spirit is shown by its definition in this sense not only by the Reformed, but by the Lutherans. For example, Hollaz defines thus: "The testimony of the Holy Spirit is the supernatural act (actus supernaturalis) of the Holy Spirit by means of the Word of God attentively read or heard (His own divine power having been communicated to the Scriptures) by which the heart of man is moved, opened, illuminated, turned to the obedience of faith, so that the illuminated man out of these internal spiritual movements truly perceives the Word which is propounded to him to have proceeded from God, and gives it therefore his unwavering assent." The Lutheranism of this definition resides in the clauses: "By means of the Word of God" . . . "His own divine power having been communicated to the Scriptures" . . . which make the action of the Holy Spirit to be from out of the Word, in which He dwells *intrinsicus*. But the nature of the testimony of the Spirit is purely conceived as an act of the Holy Spirit by which the heart of man is renewed to spiritual perception, in the employment of which he perceives the divine quality of Scripture.

[53] Supra humanum judicium, certo certius constituimus (non secus ac si ipsius Dei numen illic intueremur) hominum ministerio, ab ipsissimo Dei ore ad nos fluxisse (I. vii. 5).

[54] Talis ergo est persuasio quae rationes non requirat; talis notitia, cui optima ratio constet: nempe in qua securius constantiusque mens quiescit quam in ullis rationibus; talis denique sensus, qui nisi ex coelesti revelatione nasci nequeat (I. vii. 5).

[55] Köstlin, as cited, p. 412-13, esp. 413, note a, adverts to this with a reference to Dorner, *Gesch, d. protest. Theologie*, 379, who makes it characteristic of Calvin in distinction from Zwingli to draw the outer and inner Word more closely together. The justice of Dorner's view, which would seem to assign to Calvin in his doctrine of the Word as a means of grace a position somewhere between Zwingli and Luther, may well be doubted. According to Dorner, Calvin "modified the looser connection between the outward and inward Word held by Zwingli and connected the two sides more closely together." "In reference, therefore, to the principle of the Reformation", he continues, "with its

two sides, Calvin is still more than Zwingli, of one mind and spirit with the Lutheran Reformation " (E. T., 1, p. 387). Again (I. 390): "The double form of the *Verbum Dei externum* and *internum,* held by Zwingli, gives place indeed in Calvin to a more inward connecting of the two sides; the Scriptures are according to him not merely the sign of an absent thing, but have in themselves divine matter and breath, which makes itself actively felt." We do not find that Calvin and Zwingli differ in this matter appreciably [56] *Cf.* his response to Sadolet (1539), *Op.* V. 393: tuo igitur experimento disce non minus importunum esse spiritum jactare sine verbo, quam futurum sit, sine verbum ipsum obtendere.

[57] There is a certain misapprehension involved, also, in speaking of Calvin *subordinating* the *indicia* to the witness of the Spirit, as if he conceived them on the same plane, but occupying relatively lower and higher positions on this plane. The witness of the Spirit and the *indicia* move in different orbits. We find Köstlin, as cited, 413, accordingly speaking not quite to the point, when he says: "He subordinated to the power of this one, immediate, divine testimony, all those several criteria by the pious and thoughtful consideration of which our faith in the Scriptures and their contents may and should be further mediated. Even miracles, as Niedner has rightly remarked (*Philosophie- und Theologiegeschichte,* 341, note 2), take among the evidences for the divinity of the Biblical revelation, 'nothing more than a coördinate' place: we add in passing that Calvin introduces them here only in the edition of 1550, and then enlarges the section which treats of them in the edition of 1559. He does not, however, put a low estimate on such criteria; he would trust himself—as he says in an addition made in the edition of 1559 (xxx. 59)—to silence with them even stiff-necked opponents; but this certainty which faith should have, can never be attained, says he, by disputation, but can be wrought only by the testimony of the Spirit." The question between the testimony of the Spirit and the *indicia* is not a question of which gives the strongest evidence; it is a question of what each is fitted to do. The *indicia* are supreme in their sphere: they and they alone give objective evidence. But objective evidence is inoperative when the subjective condition is such that it cannot penetrate and affect the mind. All objective evidence is in this sense subordinate to the subjective change wrought by the Spirit: but considered as objective evidence it is supreme in its own sphere. The term "subordinate" is accordingly misleading here. For the rest, it is true that Calvin places the miracles by which the giving of Scripture was accompanied rather among the objective evidences of their divinity than at their apex: but this is due not to an underesti-

mation of the value of miracles as evidence, but to the very high estimate he placed on the internal criteria of divinity, by which the Scriptures evidence themselves to be divine. And above all we must not be misled into supposing that he places miracles below the testimony of the Spirit in importance. Such a comparison is outside his argument: miracles are part of the objective evidence of the divinity of Scripture; the testimony of the Spirit is the subjective preparation of the heart to receive the objective evidence in a sympathetic embrace. He would have said, of course,—he does say,—that no miracle, and no body of miracles, could or can produce "true faith": the internal creative operation of the Spirit is necessary for that. And in that sense the evidence of miracles is subordinated to the testimony of the Spirit. But this is not because of any depreciation of the evidential value of miracles; but because of the full appreciation of the deadness of the human soul in sin. The evidential value of miracles, and their place among the objective evidences of the divine origin of the Scriptures, are wholly unaffected by the doctrine of the testimony of the Spirit; and the strongest assertions of their valuelessness in the production of faith, apart from the testimony of the Spirit, do not in the least affect the estimate we put on them as objective evidences.

[68] *Cf.* Köstlin, as cited, pp. 413-14: "We find in Calvin the aforementioned several criteria set alongside of this witness of the Spirit, and indeed especially those which are internal to the Scriptures themselves, such as their elevation above all merely human products, which cannot fail to impress every reader, etc. It would certainly be desirable to trace an inner connection between this impression made by the character, by the style of speech, by the contents of Scripture, and that supreme immediate testimony of the Spirit for it. Assuredly God Himself, the Author of Scripture, works upon us also in such impressions, which we analyse in our reflecting human consideration, and in our debates strive to set before opponents; and we feel, on the other side, a need to analyse, as far as is possible for us, even the supreme witness of the Spirit, in spite of its immediacy, and to relate it with our other experiences and observations with respect to Scripture, so as to become conscious of the course by which God passes from one to the other. Calvin, however, does not enter into this; he sets the two side by side and over against one another: 'Although (Scripture) conciliates reverence to itself by its own supreme majesty, it does not seriously affect us, until it is sealed to our hearts by the Spirit' (xxix. 295; xxx. 60; ed. 3. I. 7. 5): he does not show the inner relation of one to the other. He does not do this even in the edition of 1559, where he with great eloquence speaks more fully of the power with which the

Word of the New Testament witnesses manifests its divine majesty. The witness of the Spirit comes forward with Calvin thus somewhat abruptly. By means of it the Spirit works true faith, which the Scripture, even through its internal criteria, cannot establish in divine certainty; and indeed He does not work it in the case of all those—and has no intention of working it in the case of all those—to whom the Scripture is conveyed with its criteria, but, as the section on Predestination further shows, only in the case of those who have been elected thereto from all eternity. Here we are already passing over into the relation of the Calvinistic conception of the Formal Principle or the Authority of Scripture, to its conception of the means of grace. In this matter the Lutheran doctrine stands in conflict with it. But with reference to what we have been discussing, we do not find that the Lutheran dogmaticians, when they come to occupy themselves more particularly with the *testimonium Spiritus Sancti* to the Scriptures, dealt more vitally with its relation to the operation of these criteria on the human spirit. No doubt, in Luther's own conception this was more the case: but he gave no scientific elaboration of it. "

[59] *Cf.* Köstlin, as cited, p. 417: "The certainty that the Scriptures really possess such authority, rests for us not on the authority of the Church, but just on this testimony of the Spirit. Calvin's reference here is even to the several books of Scripture: he is aware that the opponents ask how, without a decree of the Church, we are to be convinced what book should be received with reverence, what should be excluded from the canon; he himself adduces in opposition to this, even here, nothing else except the *testimonium Spiritus:* the entirety of Scripture seems to him to be equally, so to say, *en bloc,* divinely legitimated by this." So also Pannier, as cited, p. 252: "The question of canonicity never presented itself to the thought of Calvin, except in the second place as a corollary of the problem of the divinity (I. vii. 1). If the Holy Spirit attests to us that a given book is divine, He in that very act attests that it forms a part of the rule of faith, that it is canonical. Nowhere has Calvin permitted, as his successors have done, a primary place to be taken by a theological doctrine which became less capable of resisting the assaults of adversaries when isolated from the practical question. Perhaps, moreover, he did not render as exact an account as we are able to render after the lapse of two centuries, of the wholly new situation in which the Reformation found itself with respect to the canon, or of the new way in which he personally resolved the question." Accordingly, at an earlier point Pannier says: "It is true that the faculty of recognizing the Word of God under the human forms included for Calvin, and especially according to the Confession of Faith of 1559, the

faculty of determining the canonicity of the books. This is a consequence secondary but natural, and so long as they maintained the
principle, the Reformed doctors placed themselves in a false position
when they showed themselves disposed to abandon the consequences to
the criticisms of their opponents" (p. 164)). *Cf.* J. Cramer, *Nieuwe
Bijdragen*, III. 140: "But you must not think of an *immediate* witness
of the Spirit to the particular parts of the Holy Scriptures. The old
theologians did not think of that. They conceived the matter thus:
The *testimonium Spiritus Sancti* gives witness *directly* to the religio-
moral contents of Scripture only. Since, however, the religio-moral
contents must necessarily have a particular form, and the dogmatic
content is closely bound up with the historical, neither the chronological
nor the topographical element can be separated out, etc. . . . therefore the *testimonium Spiritus Sancti* gives to the total content of
Scripture witness that it is from God." This, after all, then, is not to
appeal to the *testimonium Spiritus Sancti*, directly to authenticate the
canon; but to construct a canon on the basis of a testimony of the Spirit
given solely to the divinity of Scripture, the movement of thought being
this: All Scripture given by inspiration of God is profitable; this
Scripture is given by inspiration of God; accordingly this Scripture
belongs to the category of profitable Scripture, that is to the canon.

[60] Reuss, in the 16th chapter of his *History of the Canon of the Holy
Scriptures* (E. T. 1884), expounds Calvin, with his usual learning and
persuasiveness, as basing the determination of the canon solely on the
testimony of the Spirit. But the exposition falls into two confusions:
a confusion of the authority of Scripture with its canonicity, and a
confusion of the divine with the apostolic origin of Scripture. Of
course, Calvin repelled the Romish conception that the authority of
Scripture rests on its authentication by the Church and its tradition
(p. 294), but that did not deter him from seeking by a historical investigation to discover what especial books had been committed by the
apostles to the Church as authoritative. Of course, he founded the
sure conviction of the divine origin of the Scriptures on the witness of
the Spirit of God by and with them in the heart, but that did not
prevent his appealing to history to determine what these Scriptures
which were so witnessed were in their compass. Accordingly even
Reuss has to admit that it is exceedingly difficult to carry through his
theory of Calvin's theoretical procedure consistently with Calvin's observed practice. In point of fact, the Reformers, and Calvin among them,
did not separate the Apocrypha from the O. T. on the sole basis of the
testimony of the Spirit: they appealed to the evidence of the Jewish
Church (p. 312). Nor did they determine the question of the New

Testament antilegomena on this principle: this, too, was with them "a simple question of historical criticism" (p. 316)—although Reuss here (p. 318) confuses Calvin's appeal to the internal evidence of apostolicity with appeal to "religious intuition". In a word, Reuss' exposition of Calvin's procedure in determining the canon rests on a fundamental misconception of that procedure.

[61] "All this Holy Scripture is comprised in the canonical books of the Old and New Testaments, the number (*le nombre*) of which is as follows" . . . the list ensuing.

[62] *Opp.* ix. *prolg.*, pp. lvii-lx: *cf.* Dieterlen, *Le Synode général de Paris* (1873), pp. 77, 89; Pannier, as cited, p. 127; and for a brief précis, Müller, *Bekenntnisschriften der reform. Kirche* (1903), p. xxxiii.

[63] *Opp.* ix. 741.

[64] *Actes de la dispute et conference tenue à Paris és mois de juillet et aoust 1566* (Strasbourg, 1566), printed in the *Biblioth. de la Soc. de l'Hist. du Prot. franc.* We draw from the account of it in Pannier, as cited, pp. 141 sq.

[65] *Le vray systeme de l'Eglise et la véritable analyse de la foy,* III. ii. 450. (Pannier, p. 168).

[66] As we have seen, it is attributed to Calvin by both Pannier and Cramer. Pannier (203) remarks that "if Calvin was not able to appreciate in all its purity" the new situation with regard to the canon into which the Reformation brought men, "it was even less incumbent on him to render account of the personal attitude which he himself took up with reference to it". "It is his successors only who, in adopting his conclusions (except that they apply them more *or less*), have asked themselves how they reached them, and have reconstructed the reasoning which no doubt Calvin himself had unconsciously followed." Is not this a confession that after all the view in question was not Calvin's own view? At least not consciously to himself? But Pannier would say, no doubt, either this was Calvin's view or he appealed to the testimony of the Spirit *directly* to authenticate the canon.

[67] The following is the account of the treatment of the question of the canon in these creeds, given by J. Cramer (*De Roomsch-Katholieke en de Oud-protestantsche Schrifhbeschouwing,* 1883, pp. 48 sq.) : "And on what now, does that authority rest? This question, too, is amply discussed in the Reformed Confessions, and that, as concerns the principal matter, wholly in the spirit of Calvin. Only, more value is ascribed to the testimony of the Church. No doubt the authority of the Scriptures is not made to rest on it; but it is permitted an important voice in the question of the canon. When it is said that 'all that is said in the

Holy Scriptures' is to be believed *not so much* because the Church receives them and holds them as canonical, but especially because the Holy Spirit bears witness to them in our heart that they are from God', a certain weight is attributed to the judgment of the church. This appears particularly from the way in which the canonical books are spoken of in distinction from the Apocryphal books. In enumerating the Bible books, the Belgian Confession prefixes the words: 'Against which nothing can be said' (art. IV). By this apparently is meant, that against the canonicity of these books, from a historical standpoint, with the eye on the witness of the Church, nothing can be alleged (a thing not to be said of the Apocrypha). In the same spirit the Anglican Articles, when speaking of the books of the O. and N. Testaments, says that 'Of their authority there has never been any doubt in the Church'. I will not raise the question here how that can be affirmed with the eye on the Antilegomena. It shows, however, certainly that much importance is attached to the ecclesiastical tradition. The fundamental ground, however, why the Scriptures of the O. and N. Testaments are to be held to be the Word of God is sought in the Scriptures themselves, and, assuredly, in the testimony which the Holy Spirit bears to their divinity in the hearts of believers. Like Calvin, the Confessions suppose that thus they have given an immovable foundation to the divine authority of the Scriptures, and have taken an impregnable position over against Rome, which appealed to the witness of the Catholic Church." . . . Calvin, however, allowed as much to the testimony of the Church—external evidence—as is here allowed, and the very adduction of its testimony shows that sole dependence was not placed on the testimony of the Spirit for the canonicity of a book: what it is appealed to for is the divinity of the canonical books.

[68] So even Köstlin perceives, as cited, p. 417: "The entirety of Scripture appeared to him divinely legitimated by the *testimonium Spiritus,* altogether, so to say, *en bloc.* . . . The declarations of Calvin as to the Word spoken by the prophets and apostles, which they rightly asserted to be God's Word, pass without hesitation over into declarations as to the Holy Scriptures, as such, and that in their entirety; with the proposition 'the Law and the Prophets and the Gospel have emanated from God' is interchanged the proposition 'the Scripture is from God',—and the witness of the Spirit assures us of it." So also Pannier (II. 203): ' 'Everything goes back to his considering things not in detail but *en bloc.* The word of God is for him one, *verbum Dei,* not *verba Dei.* The diversity of the authors disappears before the unity of the Spirit. The same reasoning applies to each single book as to the whole collection. All the verses hold together; and if one introduces

us to the knowledge of salvation we may conclude that the book is canonical. Given the collection, it is enough in practice, since all the parts are of a sort, to establish the value of one of them to guarantee the value of all the others. It is certain that the critical theologian and the simple believer even yet proceed somewhat differently in this matter; the simplest and surest method is that of the humble saint, and Calvin was very right not to range himself among the theologians at this point. 'The just shall live by faith.' This affirmation seemed to him a revealed truth: he concluded from it that the whole epistle to the Romans is inspired; some remarks of this kind in other passages of the Epistles, of the Gospels, and the canonicity of the New Testament is established. The same for the Old Testament. The Second Epistle of Peter and the Song of Songs. The human testimonies, internal and external criteria, useful for confirming the other parts of a book of which a passage has been recognized as inspired, are insufficient to expel from the canon a book which the witness of the Spirit has not recognized as opposed to the doctrine of salvation." We quote the whole passage to give Pannier's whole thought: but what we adduce it for is at present merely to signalize the admission it contains that Calvin dealt with the Scriptures in the matter of the testimony of the Spirit, so to speak, "in the lump"—as a whole. Pannier cites apparently as similar to Calvin's view, Gaussen, *Canon,* ii. 10: "This testimony, which every Christian has recognized when he has read his Bible with vital efficacy, may be recognized by him only in a single page; but this page is enough to spread over the book which contains it an incomparable brightness." That is, Calvin, like the simple believer, has a definite book—the Bible—in his hands and treats it as all of a piece—of course, in Calvin's case, not without reasonable grounds for treating it as all of a piece: in other words, the canon was already determined for him before he appealed to the testimony of the Spirit to attest its divinity. *Cf.* Cramer, p. 140, as quoted above. Cramer is quite right *so far,* therefore, when he says (p. 156): "Although we determine securely by means of the historical-critical method what must be carried back to the apostolical age and what accords with the apostolical doctrine, we have not yet proved the divine authority of these writings. This hangs on this,—whether the Holy Spirit gives us His witness to them. On this witness alone rests our assurance of faith, not on the force of a historical-critical demonstration." This, so far as appears, was Calvin's method.

⁶⁰ Calvin would certainly have subscribed to these words of Pannier, as cited, p. 164: The most of the Catholics "have always strangely misapprehended the illumination which, according to the Reformed, the

least of believers is capable of receiving and of applying to the reading of the Bible. It is a question, not as they suppose, of becoming theologians, but of becoming believers, of having not the plentitude of knowledge, but the certitude of faith".

[70] *Cf.* Köstlin, as cited, p. 415.—After raising the question of the relation of the witness of the Spirit to the inner experience of the Christian, and the relative priority of the two,—and remarking that in case the vital process is conceived as preceding the witness of the Spirit to the divinity of the Scriptures, it will be hard not to allow to the Christianized heart the right and duty of criticism of the Scriptures (where the fault in reasoning lies in the term *process*), Köstlin continues: "We touch here on the relation between the formal and material sides of the fundamental evangelical principle. And we think at once of the relation in which they stood to one another in Luther's representation, by which his well-known critical attitude, with respect, say, to the Epistle of James, was rendered possible. Calvin, too, now has no wish to speak of a witness of the Spirit merely with reference to the Scriptures, and is far from desiring to isolate that witness of the Spirit for the Scriptures. He comes back to it subsequently, when speaking of faith in the saving content of the Gospel, declaring that the Spirit seals the contents of the Word in our hearts (1539, xxix. 456 sq., 468 sq.; further in 1559, III. 2). He also inserted in the section on the Holy Scriptures and the witness of the Spirit to them, in 1550, an additional special sentence, in which he expressly refers to his intention to speak further on such a witness of the Spirit in a later portion of the treatise, and declares of faith in general, that there belongs to it a sealing of the divine Spirit (XXIX. 296 [1559, I. vii. 5 near end]). In any event he must have recurred to such a Spiritual testimony for the assurance of individual Christians of their personal election. But in the first instance—and this again is precisely what is characteristic for Calvin— he nevertheless treats of the doctrine of the divine origin and the divine authority of the Scriptures, and of the witness of the Spirit for them, wholly apart. The presentation proceeds with him in such a manner, that the Spirit first of all fully produces faith in this character of the Scriptures, and only then the Bible-believing Christian has to receive from the Scriptures its contents, in all its several parts, as divinely true,—though, no doubt, this reception and this faith in the several elements of the truth are by no means matters of human thought, but are rather to be performed under the progressive illumination and the progressive sealing of these contents in the heart by the Holy Spirit. Even though he, meanwhile, calls that the 'truth' of the Scriptures, which we come to feel in the power of the Spirit, he means

by this in the section before us, an absolute truth-character, which must from the start be attributed to the Scriptures as a whole, and will be experienced in and with the divinity of the Scriptures in general. So the matter already stands in the edition of 1539. . . . (XXIX. 292 sq.)." Accordingly Calvin teaches that the Scriptures in all their parts are of indefectible authority, and should be met in all their prescriptions with unlimited obedience (p. 418), because it is just God who speaks in them. Then: "With Dorner (*Geschichte der protest.-Theologie*, 380)—and even more decisively than he does it—we must remark on all this: 'The formal side of the protestant principle remains with Calvin with an over-emphasis, in comparison with the material, and with this is connected that he sees in the Holy Scriptures above all else the revelation of the will of God which he has dictated to man through the sacred writers.' And this tendency came ever more strongly forward with him in the successive revisions of the *Institutes*. His conception of the formal principle thus left no room for such a criticism as Luther employed on the several parts of the canon." Later Lutheranism, however, Köstlin concludes by saying, adopted Calvin's point of view here and even exaggerated it.

[11] "The formal side of the Protestant principle retains with Calvin the ascendency over the material; and with this is connected the fact that he sees in the Holy Scriptures chiefly the revelation of the will of God, which he has prescribed to men through the sacred writers."—Dorner, *Hist. of Protest. Theology*, I. 390. *Cf.* p. 397: "The formal principle is according to him the norm and source of dogma, whilst he does not treat faith, in the same way as Luther, as a source of knowledge for the dogmatical structure, that is to say, as the mediative principle of knowledge." Hence Dorner complains (p. 390) of the more restricted freedom which Calvin left "for the free productions of the faith of the Church in legislation and dogma", and instances his treatment of "the Apostolic Church as normative for all times, even for questions of Church constitution", and the little room he left for destructive Biblical criticism. *Cf.* what is said above of Calvin's adoption of "the Puritan principle".

[12] *Cf.* the Introduction to the English Translation of Kuyper's *The Work of the Holy Spirit*. *Cf.* what Pannier, pp. 102-4, says of Calvin's general doctrine of the work of the Spirit and the relation borne to it by his particular doctrine of the testimony of the Spirit to Scripture. "If we pass beyond the two particular chapters whose contents we have been analysing and seek in the *Institutes* from 1536 to 1560 for other passages relating to the Holy Spirit, we shall see Calvin insisting ever more and more and on all occasions,—as in the Commentaries,—upon

these diverse manifestations of the Holy Spirit, and presenting them all more or less as *testimonies*. He constantly recurs to the natural incapacity of man and the necessity of divine illumination in his mind, and especially in his heart, for the act of faith. It is from this point of view that he brings together the ideas of the Spirit and the Word of God in the definition of faith: 'It is a firm and certain knowledge of the good will of God towards us: which, being grounded in the free promise given in Jesus Christ, is revealed to our heart by the Holy Spirit.' He introduces the same ideas in his introductory remarks on the Apostles' Creed, and they lie at the basis of the explication he gives of the Third Article in all its forms, . . . *e. g.,* in the ed. of 1560: 'In sum, He is set before us as the sole fountain from which all the celestial riches flow down to us. . . . For it is by His inspiration that we are regenerated into celestial life, so as no longer to govern or guide ourselves, but to be ruled by His movement and operation; so that if there is any good in us, it is only the fruit of His grace. . . . But since faith is His prime master-piece, the most of what we read in the Scriptures of His virtue and operation relates itself to this faith, by which He brings us to the brightness of the Gospel, in a manner which justifies calling Him the King by whom the treasures of the kingdom of heaven are offered to us, and His illumination may be called the longing of our souls.' From these quotations it is made plain that the witness of the Holy Spirit which at the opening of the *Institutes* in 1539 appeared as the *means of knowledge,* was thenceforward nevertheless considered, in the progress of the work, as the *means of grace,* and that taking his start from this point of view, Calvin discovered ever more widely extending horizons, so as at the end to speak particularly of the Holy Spirit in at least four different connections, but always—even in the first—in direct and constant relation to faith, with respect to its origin, and with respect to its consequences; and by no means almost exclusively with respect to assurance of the authority of the Scriptures." The progress which Pannier supposes he traces in Calvin's doctrine of the work of the Spirit seems illusory: the general doctrine of the work of the Spirit is already pretty fully outlined in 1536. But the relating of the testimony of the Spirit to Scripture to Calvin's general doctrine of faith as the product of the Spirit is exact and important for the understanding of his teaching. From beginning to end, Calvin conceived the confidence of the Christian in Scripture, wrought by the Holy Spirit, as one of the exercises of saving faith. Calvin is ever insistent that all that is good in man comes from the Spirit—whether in the sphere of thought, feeling or act. "It is a notion of the natural man", he says on John xvi. 17 (1553: ix. 47. 33), "to despise all that the Sacred Scriptures say of the Holy Spirit, depending rather on his own reason, and to reject the celestial illumination. . . . For ourselves, feeling our penury, we know that all we have of sound knowledge comes from no other fountain. Nevertheless the words of the Lord Jesus show clearly that nothing can be known of what concerns the Holy Spirit by human sense, but He is known only by the experience of faith". "No one", says he again (*Institutes* of 1543, I. 330), "should hesitate to confess that he attains the knowledge of the mysteries of God only so far as he has been illuminated by God's grace. He that attributes more knowledge to himself is only the more blind that he does not recognize his blindness."

[73] *Opp. Calvini*, xiv. 727-737 (Pannier, as cited, p. 120).

[73a] The classical instance of this confusion is supplied by the teaching of Claude Pajon (1626-1685), who, in accordance with his general doctrine that "without any other grace than that of the Word, God changes the whole man, from his intellect to his passions", explained the "testimony of the Spirit" as nothing else than the effect of the *indicia* of divinity in Scripture on the mind. The effect of these "marks" is a divine effect, because it is wrought in prearranged circumstances prepared for this effect: *facit per alium facit per se*. The conception is essentially deistic. It is no small testimony to the cardinal place which the doctrine of "the testimony of the Spirit" held in the Reformed system of the seventeenth century that Pajon still taught it: and it is no small testimony to its current conception as just "regeneration" that Pajon too identified it with regeneration, explained, of course, in accordance with his fundamental principle that all that God works He works through means. See on the whole matter Jurieu, *Traité de la Nature et de la Grace*, 1688, pp. 25, 26, who quotes alike from Pajon and his followers.

[74] Doumergue, *Le Problème Protestant* (1892), p. 46 (Pannier, as cited, p. 192).

[75] Pannier, as cited, pp. 188 sq., is quite right in insisting on this. After quoting D. H. Meyer (*De la place et rôle de l'Apologétique dans la théologie protestante* in the *Revue de théologie et des quest. relig.*, Jan., 1893, p. 1) to the effect that "the witness of the Holy Spirit in the heart of Christians is not a subjective phenomenon: it is an objective thing and comes from God",—he continues: "Now this objective character of the witness of the Holy Spirit is precisely what appears to make it 'incomprehensible' to our modern theologians (so A. E. Martin, *La Polemique de R. Simon et J. Le Clerc*, 1880, p. 29: 'This intervention of the Holy Spirit distinct from the individual consciousness appears to us incomprehensible'). We are not speaking of those

who venture to pretend that Calvin identifies the witness of the Holy Spirit with 'the intimate feeling' of each Christian. When one takes his place by the side of Castellion he may lawfully say, For me as for him 'the inspiration of the Holy Ghost confounds itself with consciousness; these revelations made to the humble are nothing more than the intuitions of a moral and religious sense fortified by meditation' (Buisson, *Castellion*, I. 304, *cf.* 201: 'Castellion placed above the tradition of the universal Church his own sense, his own reason, or rather, let us say it all at once, for it is the foundation of the debate, his consciousness'). But when one invokes the real fathers of the real Reformation, ah, please do not take for their's the very opinions they combat. To make of the testimony of the Holy Spirit the equivalent of the testimony of the human spirit, of the individual consciousness, is to deny the real existence and the distinct rôle of the Holy Spirit, is to show that we have nothing in common with the faith expounded by Calvin so clearly, and defended through a century against the attacks of the Catholics as one of the essential bases of the Reformed theology and piety." Again, Pannier is quite right in his declaration (p. 214): "What we deny is that our reason—moral consciousness, religious consciousness, the term is of no importance—can, of itself, *make us see* the divinity of the Scriptures. It is this which *sees* it; but it is the Holy Spirit which *makes us see it.* He is not the inner eye for seeing the truth which is outside of us, but the supernatural hand which comes to open the eye of our consciosusness—an eye which is, no doubt, divine in the sense that it too was created by God, but which has been blinded by the consequences of sin."

[16] See especially P. Du Moulin, *Le Iuge des Controverses*, 1636, pp. 294 sq., and *cf.* Pannier, as cited, pp. 64-68.

[17] Diologue with Trypho 7 (*Opp.* ed. Otto, I. 32): οὐ γὰρ συνοπτὰ οὐδὲ συννοητὰ πᾶσίν ἐστιν, εἰ μή τῷ θεὸς δῷ συνιέναι, καὶ ὁ Χριστὸς αὐτοῦ: "these things cannot be perceived or understood by all, but only by the man to whom God and His Christ have given it to understand them."

[18] In Genes. V. homil. xxi (Migne, liii. 175): Διάτοι τοῦτο προσήκει ἡμᾶς ὑπὸ τῆς ἄνωθεν χάριτος ὁδηγομένους, καὶ τὴν παρὰ τοῦ ἁγίου Πνεύματος ἔλλαμψιν δεξαμένους οὕτως ἐπιέναι τὰ θεῖα λόγια: "For we must be led by the grace from above, and must receive the illumination of the Holy Spirit, to approach the divine oracles; for it is not human wisdom but the revelation of the Holy Spirit that is needed for understanding the Holy Scriptures." It will be perceived that it is more distinctly the understanding of the Scriptures than the reception of them as from God which is in question with both Justin and Chrysostom.

[19] *De Trinitate*, ii. 34: Animus humanus, nisi per fidem donum Spir-

itus hauserit, habebit quidem naturam Deum intelligendi, sed lumen scientiae non habebit; iii. 24: non enim concipiunt imperfecta perfectum, neque quod ex alio subsistit, absolute vel auctoris sui potest intelligentiam obtinere, vel propriam; v. 21: neque enim nobis ea natura est, ut se in coelestem cognitionem suis viribus efferat. A Deo discendum est quid de Deo intelligendum sit; quia non nisi se auctore cognoscitur. . . . Loquendum ergo non aliter de Deo est, quam ut ipse ad intelligentiam nostram de se locutus est. Hilary certainly teaches that for such creatures as men there can be no knowledge of God except it be God-taught: but it is not so clear that he teaches that for sinful creatures there must be a special illapse of the Spirit that such as they may know God—may perceive Him in His Word and so recognize that Word as from Him and derive a true knowledge of Him from it. It is this soteriological doctrine which is Calvin's doctrine of the Holy Spirit's testimony: not that ontological one.

[80] *Cf.* article: *Augustine's Doctrine of Knowledge and Authority,* in *The Princeton Theological Review* for July and October, 1907.

[81] *Ibid.,* p. 360 sq.   [82] *Ibid.,* p. 571 sq.

[83] *Tract. iii. in Ep. Joan. ad Parthos,* ii. 13 (Migne xxxv. 200 sq.). Again: "There is, then, I say, a Master within that teacheth: Christ teacheth; His inspiration teacheth. Where His inspiration and His unction are not, in vain do words make a noise from without."

[84] *Conff.* xi. 3 (Migne. xxxii. 811). *Cf.* vi. 5 (Migne. xxxii. 723).

[85] Pannier, *loc cit.,* says: "The whole of the testimony of the Holy Spirit is not yet here. Only once is the Holy Spirit Himself named [in these passages from Augustine] in a formal way. But Augustine has the intuition of a mysterious work wrought in the soul of the Christian, of an understanding of the Bible which comes not from man but from a power exterior and superior to him; and he sets forth the rôle which this direct correspondence between the book and the reader may play in the foundation of Christian certitude. In this, as in so many other points, Augustine was the precursor of the Reformation, and a precursor without immediate followers: for except a couple of very vague and isolated hints in Salvianus (*De Provid.,* iii. 1) and Gregory the Great (†604, Homil, in Ezek. I. x), nothing further is found on this subject through ten centuries: it comes into view again at the approach of the new age, when thought aspired to free itself from the Scholastic ruts, with Biel († 1495, *Lib. iii. Sent.* dist. 25, dub. 3) and Cajetan († 1534, *Opera.* II. i. 1)."

[86] *Loci.,* ed. 1555 (*Corpus Ref.* xxi. 605).

[87] *De vera et falsa religione:* Cum constet verbo nusquam fidem haberi quam ubi Pater traxit, Spiritus monuit, unctio docuit . . . hanc rem

solae piae mentes norunt. Neque enim ab hominum disceptatione pendet, sed in animis hominum tenacissime sedet. Experientia est, nam pii omnes eam experti sunt. *Articles of 1523* (Niemeyer, *Collectio conf. ref.*, p. 4): Art. 13: Verbo Dei quum auscultant homines pure et sinceriter verbum Dei discunt. Deinde per Spiritum Dei in Deum trahuntur et veluti transformantur. *Von Klarheit und Gewüsse des Worts Gottes* (*Opp.* I. 81): "The Scriptures came from God, not from man; . . . and the God who has shined into them will Himself give you to understand that their speech comes from God": *Cf.* the interesting biographical account of how he came to depend on the Scriptures only on p. 79.

[88] E. Rabaud, *Hist. de la doctr. de l'inspiration,* etc. (1883), pp. 32-33, 42-3, 47 sq., 50, expounds the earlier Reformers as in principle standing on the doctrine of the testimony of the Spirit. With respect to the interpretation of Scripture he remarks: "The hermeneutical principle of the witness of the Holy Spirit (if we may speak of it as a principle) is common to all the Reformers. Luther only, without being ignorant of it, makes no use of it. Besides that it responded to the polemic needs, it responded to the aspirations of the faith and of the piety of simple men, better than rational demonstrations" (p. 50, note 4). "In a general way", he remarks, pp. 32-33, "Luther considered the Bible as the sole incontestable and absolute authority. Here is the solid foundation of the edifice, the impregnable citadel in which he shut himself in order to repel all attacks. It is for him, in truth, a religious axiom, a postulate of faith, and not a dogma or a theory; it is revealed to his believing soul independently of all intellectual activity. Thus Luther, trusting in the action of the Holy Spirit, operating through the Scriptures, does not pause to prove its authority, nor to establish it dialectically: it imposes itself; a systematic treatment is not needed. More and more as circumstances demanded it, he gave reasons for his faith and his submission. Poor arguments to modern thinking, but in his times, and commended by his vibrant eloquence and powerful personality, possessing a power of persuasion very impressive. . . . It seemed idle to Luther, we may say, to enter into an argument to establish what was evident to him. He did not attempt, therefore, to prove the authority of the Bible,—he asserted it repeatedly in warm words, in passionate declarations, but rarely if ever proceeds by a formal demonstration" (p. 32-33). Raising the question of Zwingli's doctrine of the mode and extent of inspiration (p. 47), he remarks: "No more than the others does Zwingli respond to these questions, which had not yet been raised. God has spoken: the Bible contains His word: that is enough. The divinity of the Bible is once more a

fact, an axiom, so much so that he does not dream of establishing it or of defending it."

[89] So Pannier, as cited, p. 63: "Like all the other essential parts of the Reformed Dogmatics, the doctrine of the internal testimony of the Holy Spirit is found in germ in the first edition of the *Institutes,* although still without any development. It is almost possible to deny that it exists there, as has been done with predestination. Nevertheless if the doctrine is not yet scientifically formulated, it may yet be perceived to preëxist necessarily as an essential member of the complete body of doctrine which is slowly to grow up." When Pannier comes, however (pp. 72-77), to expound in detail the germs of the doctrine as they lie in the edition of 1536, it turns out that there is not only no full development of the doctrine in that edition, but also no explicit mention of it, as it is applied to the conviction which the Christian has of the divinity of Scripture; so that it preëxists in this edition only as implicit in its general doctrine of the Spirit and His work.

[90] By Pannier, p. 69.

[91] Pannier, as cited, p. 77, notes that "the words: *testimonio Spiritus Sancti* occur only a single time, at the end, and in the old sense of— 'by the divinely inspired Scriptures'." He refers to the ed. of 1536, p. 470, that is, *Opp.* I. 228: and notes that this passage was dropped in the edition of 1559 (*Opp.* IV. 796, note 5). The passage runs: "Thus Hezekiah is praised *by the testimony of the Holy Spirit*"—that is, obviously, "by the inspired Scriptures"—"for having broken up the brazen serpent which Moses had made by Divine command."

[92] Köstlin, as cited, p. 411, strongly states these facts. The whole of the discussion on the sources and norms of religious truth "is altogether lacking in the original form" of the Institutes: "Calvin worked out this section for the first time for the edition of 1539": but it is found here already thoroughly done, "in all its fundamental traits already complete and mature". He adds that the Lutheran dogmatists (as well as the Reformed) at once, however, took up the construction of Calvin and made it their own.

[93] The history of the doctrine among the Reformed is touched on by A. Schweizer, *Glaubenslehre,* I. § 32; among the old Lutherans by Klaiber, *Die Lehre der altprotestantischen Dogmatiker von dem test. Sp. Sancti* in the *Jahrbücher für d. Theologie,* 1857, pp. 1-53. Its history among French theologians is traced by Pannier, as cited, Part III, pp. 139-181, cf. 186-193: his notes on the history outside of France (pp. 181-185) are very slight. On pp. 161-163 Pannier essays to gather together, chiefly, as it appears, from the scattered citations in the Protestant controversialists of the seventeenth century (p. 162, note 2), the

hints which appear in the Romish writers, mainly Jesuits of the early seventeenth century, of recognition of the internal work of the Holy Spirit illuminating the soul. These bear more or less resemblance to the Protestant doctrine of the testimony of the Spirit. Some of the passages he cites are quite striking, but do not go beyond the common boundaries of universal Christian supernaturalism.

[94] In his brief remarks on the subject in his *Dogmengeschichte des Protestantismus*, I, 1908, p. 178 sq., Otto Ritschl seeks to discriminate between the Reformed and Lutherans in their conception of the testimony of the Spirit; but his discrimination touches rather the application than the essence of the matter.

[95] Some of them are cited, *e. g.*, by Schweizer, as cited, followed, *e. g.*, by Pannier, as cited (p. 186)—such as: "Faith is already presupposed when a peculiar authority is conceded to Scripture"—"The recognition of what is canonical comes into existence only gradually and progressively, since the sense for the truly Apostolic is a gracious gift which grows up only gradually in the Church",—"Faith cannot be established in unbelievers by the Scriptures, so that their divine authority is in the first instance proved from merely rational considerations."—There is much that is true and well said in such remarks, and they enrich the writings of Schleiermacher and his followers with a truly spiritual element. But at bottom the central position occupied is vitiated by the use of "faith" as an "undistributed middle", and the remarks of writers of this type do not so much tend to exalt the place of saving faith as to depress the authority of Scripture, by practically denying the existence or validity of *fides humana*. That attitude towards the Scriptures which gladly and heartily recognizes them as the Word of the Living God, and with all delight in them as such, seeks to subject all thought and feeling and action to their direction, certainly is, if not exactly a product of "true faith", yet (as the Westminster Confession defines it) an exercise of true faith, and a product of that inward creative operation of the Holy Spirit from which all true faith comes: that keen taste for the divine which is the outgrowth of the spiritual gift of discrimination—the "distinguishing of things that differ" which Paul gives a place among Christian graces—is assuredly a "gift of grace" which may grow more and more strong as the Christian life effloresces; and such a taste for the divine cannot be awakened in unbelievers by the natural action of the Scriptures or any rational arguments whatever, but requires for its production the work of the Spirit of God ab extra accidens. But it is a totally different question whether the peculiarity of Scripture as a divine revelation can call out no intellectual recognition in the minds of inquiring men, but must remain wholly hidden and produce no

mental reaction conformable to its nature, until true faith has already
been born in the heart: whether there are no valid tests of what is
apostolical except a spiritual sense for the truly apostolical which can
only gradually grow up in the Church; whether the unbeliever may
not be given a well-grounded intellectual conviction of the apostolic
origin, the canonical authority and the divine character of Scripture
by the presentation to him of rational evidence which, however unwill-
ingly on his part, will compel his assent. The question here is not
whether this *fides humana* is of any great use in the spiritual life: the
question is whether it is possible and actual. We may argue, if we will,
that it is not worth while to awake it—though opinions may differ
there: but how can we argue that it is a thing inherently impossible?
To say this is not merely to say that reason cannot save, which is what
Calvin said and all his followers: it is to say that salvation is intrinsically unreasonable,—which neither Calvin nor any of his true followers could for a moment allow. Sin may harden the heart so that
it will not admit, weigh or yield to evidence: but sin, which affects
only the heart subjectively, and not the process of reasoning objectively,
cannot alter the relations of evidence to conclusions. Sin does not
in the least degree affect the cogency of any rightly constructed syllo-
gism. No man, no doubt, was even reasoned into the kingdom of
heaven: it is the Holy Spirit alone who can translate us into the
kingdom of God's dear Son. But there are excellent reasons why
every man should enter the kingdom of heaven; and these reasons
are valid in the forum of every rational mind, and their validity can
and should be made manifest to all.

[96] *Theological Lectures,* etc., N. Y., 1878, pp. 317, 320 sq.

[97] *The Way of Life,* 1841; also *Systematic Theology,* as per Index.

[98] *Encyclopædie,* etc., II. 505 sq.

[99] *Gereformeerde Dogmatiek,* ed. 1, vol. I. 142-5, 420-22, 490-1.

[100] Written, no doubt, by Léger, moderator at the time of "the Table",
and preserved for us in his *Histoire générale des églises évangéliques
des vallées de Piédmont* (1669), I. 112 (*cf.* 92). See Pannier, as
cited, 133.

[101] Dr. A. F. Mitchell (*The Westminster Assembly, its History and
Standards,* the Baird Lecture for 1882, ed. 2, 1897, p. 441, note), following Prof. J. S. Candlish (*Brit. and For. Ev. Rev.,* 1877, p. 173), is "very
sure" that Gillespie has here left his mark on the Confession". The
Miscellany Questions, in the XXI of which occurs the passage from
Gillespie from which the Confession is supposed to have drawn, was a
posthumous work, published in 1649; but a number of the papers of
which it is made up have the appearance of being briefs drawn up by

Gillespie for his own satisfaction, or as preparations for speeches, or possibly even as papers handed in to committees, during the discussions of the Westminster Assembly. The language in question, however, whether in Gillespie or in the Confession, is so strongly reminiscent of Calvin, that the possibility seems to remain open that the resemblance between Gillespie and the Confession is due to their common relation to Calvin. Here is the passage in Gillespie (*Presbyterian Armoury* ed., pp. 105-106): "The Scripture is known to be indeed the word of God by the beams of divine authority it hath in itself, and by certain distinguishing characters, which do infallibly prove it to be the Word of God; such as the heavenliness of the matter; the majesty of the style; the irresistible power over the conscience; the general scope, to abase man and to exalt God; nothing driven at but God's glory and man's salvation; the extraordinary holiness of the penmen of the Holy Ghost, without respect to any particular interests of their own, or of others of their nearest relations (which is manifest by their writings); the supernatural mysteries recorded therein, which could never have entered into the reason of men; the marvellous consent of all parts and passages (though written by divers and several penmen), even where there is some appearance of difference; the fulfilling of prophecies; the miracles wrought by Christ, by the prophets and apostles; the conservation of the Scriptures against the malice of Satan and fury of persecutors;—these and the like are characters and marks which evidence the Scriptures to be the Word of God; yet all these cannot beget in the soul a full persuasion of faith that the Scriptures are the Word of God; this persuasion is from the Holy Ghost in our hearts. And it hath been the common resolution of sound Protestant writers (though now called in question by the sceptics of this age [the allusion being to "Mr. J. J. Godwin in his Hagiomastix"]) that these arguments and infallible characters in the Scripture itself, which most certainly prove it to be the Word of God, cannot produce a certainty of persuasion in our hearts, but this is done by the Spirit of God within us, according to these Scriptures, 1 Cor. ii. 10-15; 1 Thes. i. 5; 1 John ii. 27; v. 6-8, 10; John vi. 45".—Whatever may be the immediate source of the Confessional statement, Calvin is clearly the real source of Gillespie's statement.—For the essence of the matter Gillespie's discussion is notably clear and exact, particularly with reference to the relation of the indicia to the testimony of the Spirit, a matter which he strangely declares had not to his knowledge been discussed before. The clarity of his determinations here is doubtless due to the specific topic which he is in this Question investigating, viz., the validity of the argument from marks and fruits of sanctification to our

interest in Christ: a parallel question in the broader soteriological sphere
to the place of indicia in our conviction of the divinity of Scripture,
which he therefore uses illustratively for his main problem. "It may be
asked", he remarks, "and it is a question worthy to be looked into
(though I must confess I have not read it, nor heard it, handled before),
How doth the assurance by marks agree with or differ from assurance
by the testimony of the Holy Spirit? Has the soul here assurance either
way, or must there be a concurrence of both (for I suppose they are
not one and the same thing) to make up the assurance?" (105). He
proves that they are "not one and the same thing"; and then shows
solidly that for assurance there "must be a concurrence of both". "To
make no trial by marks", he says, "and to trust an inward testimony,
under the notion of the Holy Ghost's testimony, when it is without the
least evidence of any true gracious marks, this way (of its nature, and
intrinsically, or in itself) is a deluding and ensnaring of conscience"
(p. 105). That is to say, a blind confidence and conviction, without
cognizable grounds in evidence cannot be trusted. Again and very
clearly: "So that, in the business of assurance and full persuasion, the
evidences of graces and the testimony of the Spirit, are two concurrent
causes or helps, both of them necessary. Without the evidence of
graces, it is not a safe nor a well-grounded assurance" (p. 106). It
remains only to add that while arguing this out in the wider soteriological sphere, Gillespie appears to take it as a matter of course in the
accrediting of the Scriptures as divine—giving that case, in the course
of his argument, as an illustration to aid in determining his conclusion.

[102] For the meaning of the Confession's statement, supported by illus-
trative excerpts from its authors, see *The Presbyterian and Reformed
Review*, IV. 604-627; and *cf.* W. Cunningham, *Theological Lectures*,
N. Y., 1878, pp. 320 sq, and *The Presbyterian Quarterly*, Jan'y, 1894,
p. 22.